MW01608466

# TAKE THE HISTORY CHALLENGE

# TAKE THE HISTORY CHALLENGE

4,500 Questions on the History of Everything

Gavin H. Kanowitz

| ISBN: | Hardcover | 1-4010-5149-9 |
| --- | --- | --- |
| | Softcover | 1-4010-5148-0 |



Cover art work was done by Raymond Scholz.

This book was printed in the United States of America.

**To order additional copies of this book, contact:**
Xlibris Corporation
1-888-795-4274
www.Xlibris.com
Orders@Xlibris.com
14804

# CONTENTS

# DEDICATION

To my grandmother, Ruth Zinn, who always believed in me.

# ACKNOWLEDGEMENTS

A Special thanks goes to my grandfather Hymie and my father Sol for encouraging my passion for history.

Loving mention to Marion Hoffer for always being there for me as a source of strength.

Thanks as well to Vera Silk for her much valued editorial work.

## Ranking System

*Scores 14-15:* *A Historian Perfecta*
10-13: A History Guru—a specialist in this topic.
6-9: Historically Knowledgeable. Excellent score for a Historical Generalist.
2-5: You have the beginnings of a foundation. Now it's time to build.
0-1: Don't give up this is only one of many areas of history.

## 1. Ancient Egypt I

1. Which type of Pyramids were built the century before the Great Pyramids?
2. In what Egyptian location were the most famous of these pyramids built?
3. According to Egyptologists which pharaoh was responsible for building the First Great Pyramid?
4. By what other name was this pharaoh known as?
5. Who was his son?
6. Between which centuries did the Old Kingdom last?
7. Which king united Upper and Lower Egypt?
8. Who was the Egyptian God of Wisdom?
9. What people lived immediately to the South of the Egyptians?
10. What people lived immediately to the West of the Egyptians?
11. Who was the Egyptian God of Evil?
12. Who sponsored the mission that discovered 'Tut's' tomb?
13. What were the two most popular names for Egyptian pharaohs?
14. Which Egyptian god is depicted by a jackal?
15. Which Egyptian god is depicted by a falcon?

**Answers to Ancient Egypt I**

1. Step Pyramids.
2. Zosa in the 26th Century BC.
3. Cheops (or Khufu).
4. Khufu (Cheops).
5. Khafre
6. 26th to the 22nd Century BC.
7. Menes
8. Thoth
9. Nubians
10. Libyans
11. Seth
12. Ramses and Ptolemy.
13. Lord Carnarvon.
14. Anubis
15. Horus

# 2. Ancient Egypt II

1. Which Egyptian Goddess is depicted by a cow?
2. Which pharaoh introduced monotheism to Egypt?
3. Who was his Queen?
4. Who was the son God?
5. Between which centuries did the Middle Kingdom exist?
6. Name the three most prominent cities during the period of the Middle Kingdom?
7. Under which pharaoh was polytheism re-introduced into Egypt?
8. Which pharaoh was likened by later historians to an Egyptian Napoleon?
9. Who was the mother of this pharaoh?
10. Who was the Egyptian bull god?
11. Who according to mythology was creator of all the pharaohs?
12. Which people were Ramses II's greatest enemy?

13. At which battle did Ramses II record his greatest victory over this enemy?
14. Which Englishman discovered Tut's tomb?
15. What area of Egypt did the Hebrews reside in before the exodus?

**Answers to Ancient Egypt II**

1. Hathor
2. Akhenaton
3. Nephretiti
4. Ra
5. 18th to the 20th Century BC.
6. Thebes, Memphis and Luxor.
7. Tutankhamen
8. Ramses II.
9. Hatshepsut
10. Serapis
11. Ptah
12. Hittites
13. Battle of Kadesh.
14. Howard Carter.
15. Goshen

## 3. Ancient Egypt III

1. What were the names of the two store cities the Hebrews built?
2. How many pharaohs were called Ramses (to the nearest 2)?
3. What domestic animal was held up as sacred by the Ancient Egyptians?
4. Who was the God of the Nile?
5. Who was his wife?
6. During which Dynasty were the Great Pyramids built?
7. What did Ramses II three last wives have in common with respect to their burial?

8. Which European country was responsible for establishing an Egyptian Dynasty?
9. Which kingdom ruled Egypt during the 7$^{th}$ Century BC?
10. Who was the last ruler of Egypt?
11. Which people dominated Egypt between the Middle and New Kingdom?
12. How did Cleopatra VII die?
13. What disease identified from mummy investigations is thought to have caused high death rates in Ancient Egypt?
14. Who were the Hyksos?
15. To which entity was Ra united with in later Egyptian mythology?

## Answers to Ancient Egypt III

1. Pithom and Ramses.
2. 12
3. The cat.
4. Osiris
5. Isis
6. 4$^{th}$ Dynasty.
7. They were all buried in the Valley of the Queens.
8. Greece—Ptolemaic dynasty. Ptolemy was one of Alexander the Great's generals.
9. The Saite Kingdom.
10. Cleopatra VII
11. Libyans
12. She allowed herself to be bitten by an asp (a type of snake) in order to commit suicide.
13. Tuberculosis
14. An invader race who dominated Egypt during the period between the Old and Middle Kingdoms.
15. Ammon to create Ammon-Ra.

# 4. Ancient Greece I—The Early Period

1. What island was the home of the Minoan civilization?
2. Give or take a century each side, between which centuries did the Minoan Civilization exist?
3. What was its most well-known city?
4. Which British archaeologist excavated this city?
5. Who was the Minoan's most prominent king?
6. The eruption of which volcano destroyed much of the Minoan civilization?
7. What unusual (for its' times) gender power structure was inherent in Minoan civilization?
8. On which island was the Akrotiri Civilization located?
9. Which civilization succeeded the Minoans as the dominant power in the Aegean?
10. Who was the most famous queen of this civilization mentioned in 9?
11. Which archaeologist excavated the ruins of the civilization mentioned in 9, in the Northern Peloponnese?
12. Who were the Bronze Age invaders who overran Greece from the North?
13. What handicap is the bard Homer alleged to have suffered from?
14. Who is considered the first writer of Ancient Greece?
15. In what Ancient kingdom was the City of Troy located?

### Answers to Ancient Greece I—The Early Period

1. Crete—The Minoans were a proud seafaring race of possible Middle-East origin.
2. 1500-900 BC.
3. Knossus
4. Sir Arthur Evans.
5. King Minos—Father of the famed Minotaur.
6. Stromboli
7. The women were the individuals who controlled the land.

8. San Torini. I visited these ruins in 1991 and recommend those on a trip to San Torini to do the same.
9. Mycenae
10. Clytemnestra—She has a beautiful beehive tomb located in the North-East Peloponnese.
11. Heinrich Schlieman—The same man who excavated Troy.
12. The Doric Greeks.
13. Blindness—Some people argue that Homer was not one person but several different authors.
14. Hesiod
15. Thrace—A nation renowned for its sword fighters.

## 5. Ancient Greece II

1. Which people could vote in Ancient Athens?
2. Who is considered the Father of History?
3. Which important war is he known for documenting?
4. Give or take 10 years, when did the Battle of Marathon take place?
5. What was the name of the runner who ran the distance to tell the Greeks of their victory at Marathon?
6. Name two of the four buildings that sit on top of the Acropolis?
7. What were the names of the three column structures that are ever present in Greek architecture?
8. Which is the simplest of these three column structure types?
9. Which battle did the Greeks lose as a result of betrayal within their ranks?
10. To which island did the Greek leadership flee to after this defeat?
11. What was the name of the famous sea battle the Greeks defeated the Persians in?
12. Which Persian king watched this battle from the shore?
13. Who was Greece's 5th Century philosopher king?
14. Who were the two biographers of Socrates?
15. What is the origin of the word "Academy?"

**Answers to Ancient Greece II**

1. Property holding free men.
2. Herodotus
3. The Persian Wars.
4. 490 BC
5. Phidippides—Don't ask me what his time was.
6. Parthenon, Propylea, Temple of Athena at Nike, Erictheum.
7. Doric, Ionian, Corinthian.
8. Doric
9. Thermopylae
10. Aegina
11. Salamis—probably one of the greatest sea battles ever.
12. Xerxes I—History's most important person in the "X category."
13. Pericles
14. Plato and Xenophon.
15. It is derived from Plato's philosophy School: Academicus.

## 6. Ancient Greece III

1. Which philosopher ranked all biological life along a ladder?
2. Name the Seven Wonders of the Ancient World?
3. Who was the Greek God of Medicine?
4. Who was the Greek Goddess of the Harvest?
5. Who preceded the Olympians as the Chief Gods?
6. What was the name of the wars fought between Athens and Sparta?
7. How many of these wars were fought?
8. What was the most important battle of these wars?
9. Who led the Spartan forces in this battle?
10. What was the name of the historian who chronicled this war?
11. What was the name of the group that ruled Athens after their defeat?
12. Which city eventually defeated Sparta?
13. Who was the Greek Father of Comedy?

14. Which three tragedy playwrights are considered the greatest of the Greek Era?
15. Which century did the Olympic Games begin?

**Answers to Ancient Greece III**

1. Aristotle
2. Hanging Gardens of Babylon, Statue of Zeus at Olympia, Great Pyramids, Mausoleum of King Mausolus, Lighthouse of Pharos, Collosus of Rhodes, and the Temple of Diana.
3. Asclepius
4. Demeter
5. Titans
6. Peloponessian Wars.
7. Three
8. Aegospotami
9. Lysander
10. Thucididyes
11. Thirty Tyrants.
12. Thebes
13. Aristophanes
14. Aeschylus, Sophocles and Euripides.
15. 8th Century BC.

## 7. Ancient Greece IV—Myths and Ideas

1. What was the name of the Greek school that analyzed the mathematics of music?
2. How many muses were there?
3. What was Clio the muse of?
4. What was the name of the philosopher who spoke about "Indivisible Particles"?
5. What poison did Socrates drink to commit suicide?
6. What was he charged with that led to his suicide conviction?
7. Which Greek philosopher argued the Earth moved around the sun?

8. Which Greek calculated the circumference of the Earth?
9. Who sculptured the "Javelin Thrower"?
10. Which Greek town was known for its medical school?
11. Which port city was the Greek hero Jason from?
12. Who is regarded as the Father of Cynicism?
13. In which structure is this figure reported to have lived?
14. Who is regarded as the Father of Hedonism?
15. Who was the Greek God of Fire?

### Answers to Ancient Greece IV—Myths and Ideas

1. Pythagoreans
2. Nine
3. History
4. Democritus
5. Hemlock
6. Corrupting the youth.
7. Aristarchus
8. Erastothenes
9. Praxiteles
10. Epidavros
11. Argos
12. Diogenes
13. A tub
14. Epicurus
15. Hephestus

## 8. Ancient Greece V— Spotlight on Alexander the Great

1. Who was the father of Alexander the Great?
2. How did his father die?
3. What alliance did Alexander's father defeat to gain supremacy in Greece?
4. In which battle did he defeat this alliance?

5. How long did Alexander's Empire last?
6. At what age did Alexander die?
7. Which Persian king was his greatest rival?
8. What was the name of Alexander's horse?
9. Which territory did Alexander first conquer on becoming king?
10. At which battle were the Persians so badly beaten that the king had to flee for his life?
11. What did Alexander do with the captured family of the King of Persia?
12. What type of enemy did Alexander always treat harshly?
13. To what modern day country did Alexander the Great's Empire extend eastwards?
14. According to legend (although this has now been shown to be false), what did Alexander do when he discovered that he had no more worlds left to conquer?
15. Which one of these two battles were not fought and won by Alexander: Issus or Pharsalia?

**Answers to Ancient Greece V—Spotlight on Alexander the Great**

1. Philip of Macedonia.
2. He was killed by a Noble man with a grudge.
3. Delian League.
4. Chaeronea
5. 13 years.
6. 32
7. Darius III.
8. Buccephalus
9. Asia Minor.
10. Arbela
11. He ordered that they be treated as well as royalty.
12. Greeks who fought against him.
13. India
14. He wept.
15. Pharsalia—This was a battle of Roman times.

# 9. Ancient Greece VI

1. What action prevented Alexander the Great from spreading further eastwards?
2. What happened to Alexander's Empire after he died?
3. Who was Antiochus?
4. By what name is the Greek era after Alexander known as ?
5. Which island city-state was destroyed by Rome in 191 BC?
6. By what name is the Central Peloponnese region also known as?
7. Which Greek physician laid down the groundwork for anatomy?
8. What city did Archimedes live in?
9. Which Dynasty did the Greeks establish in Egypt?
10. How did Archimedes help defend his home city against Roman invaders?
11. In which book did the philosopher Ptolemy describe his Earth-centric Universe?
12. Which person was known as the lawgiver of Ancient Greece?
13. What poetess from the island of Lesbos wrote about the love of women?
14. Which philosopher claimed that you could only step into a river once?
15. Which mathematician is renowned for his work on Conic sections?

### Answers to Ancient Greece VI

1. A rebellion within the army.
2. It was split up amongst the generals.
3. The general who would control the Syrian-Israel part of the Empire.
4. Hellenic Era.
5. Rhodes
6. Arcadia
7. Galen
8. Syracuse
9. Ptolemaic

10. He used mirrors to reflect and concentrate light to burn the Roman ships.
11. The Almagest—He may have been wrong, but you have to love the name of this work.
12. Solon
13. Sappho
14. Heraclitus
15. Apollonius

## 10. Ancient Greece VII—Really Tough Questions

(Do not use the regular evaluation scale—if you get more than five of these correct consider yourself well—versed in the subject).

1. Which Greek restored democracy to Athens in 403 BC?
2. What league did Thebes lead against Sparta?
3. In 683 BC, who replaced the rule of the Hereditary Kings in Athens?
4. Which war did Sparta begin in 743 BC?
5. Which city-state was Cleomenes a member of?
6. What did he try to do?
7. What was important about the Year 430 BC in Athenian History?
8. Who did the Greeks defeat in 539 BC?
9. At what age did Spartan boys first wear clothes?
10. What was the Greek name for the Citizen's Assembly in Athens?
11. Which philosopher claimed that Man is the Measure of All Things?
12. Which Greek philosopher predicted a solar eclipse in 585 BC?
13. What does the Greek word 'kratos' mean?
14. What was a pythia?
15. Who said, "Justice is the advantage of the stronger?"

### Answers to Ancient Greece VII—Really Tough Questions

1. Pausanius
2. Arcadian League.

3. The nine Archons chosen each year from the nobles.
4. The Messenian War—ended in 716 BC.
5. Sparta
6. Re-establish the Rule of the Aristocracy in Athens. It failed—the Athenians rose up under Cleisthenes and restored democracy.
7. A plague broke out in the city.
8. Carthaginians
9. 12
10. Ecclesia
11. Protagoras
12. Thales of Miletus.
13. It means 'rule' as in Democracy—rule by the people.
14. A priestess such as the one in Delphi who would answer questions by going into a trance and shouting wildly.
15. Thrasymachus

## 11. Ancient Greece VIII

1. How did Archimedes die?
2. Who is regarded as the Father of Algebra?
3. Which Greek invented an advanced water clock?
4. Which philosopher spoke about 10 items of speech known as the categories?
5. Who wrote about the 'Simile of the Cave'?
6. Which school of philosophy was very interested in man himself and how he behaved as opposed to the universe and the big questions?
7. Who claimed that the unexamined life is not worth living?
8. Who tabulated 1080 fixed stars and compiled the first trigonometry tables?
9. Which people used the 'Linear A script?'
10. What did the Greeks call Ionia?
11. What type of vase style was prevalent in Athens c. 500 BC?
12. What was a helot?
13. Which area of Ancient Greece contained the cities of Larissa and Kosthanaia?

14. What was developed around 750 BC?
15. In which region of Greece is Athens situated?

### Answers to Ancient Greece VIII

1. He was killed by a Roman whose question he had ignored because he was so deep in thought.
2. Diophantus
3. Ctesibius
4. Aristotle. The 10 items were substance, quality, quantity, relation, place, time, position, state, action, and affection.
5. Plato
6. The Sophists.
7. Socrates
8. Hipparchus
9. Minoans
10. Asia Minor.
11. Black-Figure style—such as those depicting scenes of nude wrestlers and athletes.
12. A slave.
13. Thessaly
14. The Greek Alphabet.
15. Attica

## 12. Ancient Hebrews I

1. Who was Adam and Eve's third son?
2. Who was Methusalah's father?
3. Name eight of Joseph's eleven brothers?
4. What nationality was Laban?
5. Who are the four mothers of the Jewish people?
6. What was the name of the wealthy businessman who bought Joseph as a slave?
7. Who were Moses' father and mother?
8. Who were Joseph's two sons?

9. From which nation was Moses's wife from?
10. What fell from heaven when the Hebrews complained to God about the manna?
11. Who was the mother of Ishmael?
12. How old was Abraham when he was circumcised?
13. What was the name of the cave that Abraham purchased for his family burials?
14. Who was the only matriarchal figure not buried in this cave?
15. In which town is this cave located?

### Answers to Ancient Hebrews I

1. Seth
2. Enoch
3. Asher, Benjamin, Dan, Gad, Issacher, Judah, Levi, Naphtali, Reuben, Simon, and Zebulen.
4. Syrian
5. Sarah, Rebecca, Rachel and Leah.
6. Potiphar
7. Avram and Jochebed.
8. Ephraim and Manasseh.
9. Midianites
10. Quail—Maybe they should not have complained so quickly.
11. Hagger
12. 99
13. Cave of Machpelah.
14. Rachel
15. Hebron

## 13. Ancient Hebrews II

1. What relative of Abraham is alleged to have committed incest with his daughter?
2. Who was Abraham's father?
3. Which people was Esau the father of?

4. Why did Moses flee Egypt as a young man?
5. Who was pharaoh of Egypt at the time?
6. Name all ten plagues that effected the Egyptians?
7. Which people harassed the Hebrews on their journey to Canaan?
8. Which famous Hebrew judge was a woman?
9. Who was Gideon?
10. How did the Hebrew farmers feed the poor?
11. How many of Saul's sons were killed fighting the Philistines?
12. Who was Saul's favourite general?
13. From which City was Goliath from?
14. Who was David's favourite general?
15. Who was David's father?

**Answer to Ancient Hebrews II**

1. Lot
2. Terah
3. Edomites
4. He killed an Egyptian taskmaster who was beating up a Hebrew slave. Once he found out that the general populace knew that he, Moses, was the killer he had no choice but to flee.
5. Ramses II—although there are many who now doubt this.
6. Blood, Frogs, Pestilence, Beasts, Death of the Cattle, Boils, Hail, Locusts, Darkness, Death of the First-born.
7. Amalakites
8. Deborah
9. A Hebrew military figure who lead an army of 400 men to victory over a much larger Heathen army.
10. They left part of their fields open for the poor to harvest the crop.
11. Three including his eldest Jonathan.
12. Abner
13. Gath
14. Joab
15. Jesse

## 14. Ancient Hebrews III

1. How many Philistines did Samson kill with the jawbone of an ox?
2. How did Absalom die?
3. Who was Bathsheba's first husband?
4. Who was the most famous prophet at the time of David?
5. Why did G-d forbid David to build the First Temple?
6. From which people did David win the city of Jerusalem from?
7. Which book of verse did David write?
8. Which daughter of Saul's was David's wife?
9. Which son of Saul succeeded his father temporarily as king?
10. Who was Samuel's mentor?
11. What type of person did Saul consult before the defeat against the Philistines that would cost him his life?
12. What was the name of the main god worshipped by the Philistines?
13. How many wives is Solomon reported to have had?
14. Which queen is reputed to have tried to test Solomon's wisdom?
15. Which of Solomon's sons succeeded him as king?

### Answers to Ancient Hebrews III

1. 1000
2. He was fleeing David's troops on horseback after a failed rebellion when his hair became entangled in the branches of a tree. David's troops then executed him for treason.
3. Uriah the Hittite.
4. Nathan
5. God forbid David to build the temple as the life and times of the Hebrew King had been filled with war and bloodshed.
6. Jebusites
7. Psalms
8. Michal
9. Ishbosheth
10. Eli
11. A witch.

12. Baal
13. 1000—Poor guy.
14. Queen of Sheba.
15. Rehoboam

## 15. Ancient Hebrews IV

1. Who was the first King of Israel following the split with Judea?
2. What was the eventual fate of the Kingdom of Israel?
3. Under whose reign did the Hebrew kingdom reach its largest size?
4. Which prophet warned about the Exile in Babylon?
5. During which three festivals did the Hebrews make a pilgrimage to Jerusalem?
6. During the reign of which king was Elijah a prophet?
7. Who was this king's wife?
8. Who was Elijah's apprentice?
9. Which tribe was responsible for the religious duties in the post-exodus Israelite nation?
10. Which prophet detailed all the requirements of the Messiah?
11. Who was Ruth's mother-in-law?
12. Which famous king descended from Ruth?
13. In which year did the Jews return from Exile in Babylon?
14. Who was Samuel's mother?
15. Who were Noah's three sons?

### Answers to Ancient Hebrew IV

1. Jereboam
2. It was defeated by Assyria and its inhabitants driven into exile. Their eventual fate is one of speculation in the field of the Ten Lost Tribes.
3. Solomon
4. Jeremiah
5. Passover, Shavuot and Sukkoth.
6. King Ahab.

7. Jezebel
8. Elisha
9. The Levi.
10. Issiah
11. Naomi
12. David
13. 538 BCE.
14. Hannah
15. Ham, Shem and Japhteh.

## 16. Ancient Hebrews V

1. Who led the rebellion against the Syrian-Greeks that eventually drove the latter from the country?
2. What group of Jews did this person come from?
3. What two individuals were responsible for building the Second Temple?
4. Who was the Persian King Ahaseurus's chief wife before Esther?
5. Who was Esther's uncle?
6. What was the name of Ahaseurus's Chief Minister who was hanged at the gallows for trying to commit genocide against the Jews?
7. Who were Moses' brother and sister?
8. What was Abraham's name before it was changed?
9. What was the name of the Jewish high court?
10. Who was the Father of Tamar?
11. Which group of People destroyed the Second Temple?
12. Who was Jochanin Ben Zakai?
13. What are the two chief theories concerning the Origin of the Ethiopian Jews?
14. Which book contains the Sayings of Solomon?
15. On what Jewish holiday is the Book of Lamentations read?

### Answers to Ancient Hebrew V

1. Mathias the Maccabi and his sons of which Judah was the most renowned.
2. Hasmoneans
3. Ezra and Nehemiah.
4. Vashti
5. Mordechai
6. Haman
7. Aaron and Miriam.
8. Avram or Abram.
9. Sanhedrin
10. David
11. The Romans.
12. Leader of the Zealot Group that fought against the Romans.
13. The first claims they were the lost tribe of Dan, the second argues they were descendants of the offspring of Solomon with the Queen of Sheba.
14. Proverbs
15. Tisha B'Av.

## 17. Ancient Hebrews VI

1. Give or take a century when did the Exodus take place?
2. Which rabbi completed the Mishnah?
3. Who was King of Babylon at the time of the Exile?
4. Which Persian king allowed the Jews to return home from Babylon?
5. How old was Jesus when he was crucified?
6. What year is Jesus believed to have been born?
7. In ancient times what was the area of the West Bank known to the Jews as?
8. Where were the Dead Sea scrolls found?
9. Name Five Hebrew minor prophets?
10. Name eight of the Twelve Apostles?
11. Which writer of the Four gospels was not Jewish?

12. Who was rewarded with the head of John the Baptist?
13. What were the names of the Three Divisions of Judaism at the time of Christ?
14. What was Paul's name before it was changed?
15. What prevented the Assyrians from conquering Judea?

**Answers to Ancient Hebrews VI**

1. 1000 BC.
2. Judah Ha-Nassi.
3. Nebuchadnezzer
4. Cyrus the Great.
5. 34 years of age.
6. 4 BC.
7. Judah and Samaria.
8. Quamran, Jordan.
9. Amos, Daniel (in Hebrew scripture), Habakkuk, Haggai, Hosea, Joel, Jonah, Malachi, Micah, Nahum, Obadiah, Zechariah and Zephaniah.
10. Andrew, Bartholomew, James the Greater, James the Lesser, John, Judas Iscariot who was replaced by Matthias, Jude, Matthew, Peter, Philip, Simon the Canaanite, and Thomas.
11. Luke
12. Salome
13. Sadducees, Pharisees, Essenees.
14. Saul of Tarsus.
15. A plague amongst them.

## 18. Ancient Hebrews VII

1. Who sacrificed his only daughter because of a vow?
2. Which prophet was rebuked by his donkey for cursing G-d?
3. Who was the Father of the Civilization of Cush?
4. Who was the last King of Israel?
5. Which Amalekite leader was spared by Saul, but slain by Samuel?

6. Who was Joshua's father?
7. True or False: Hopni and Phineas were the sons of Eliezer?
8. Which patriarch was comforted by Bildad, Eliphaz and Jophar?
9. Which Babylonian King saw handwriting miraculously appear on a wall?
10. True or False: Noah was 500 years of age when he built the Ark?
11. Of 40, 50, 60 years, how long did David rule over the Israelites?
12. Which Ancient City to the Northeast of Israel had several kings named Ben-Hadad?
13. True or False: Methuselah was Noah's grandfather?
14. What is the Hebrew name for Egypt?
15. Jacob's 12 sons had a total of how many different mothers?

**Answers to Ancient Hebrews VII**

1. Jephtah
2. Balaam
3. Ham
4. Hoshea
5. Agag
6. Nun
7. False. They were the sons of Eli.
8. Job
9. Belshazzar
10. True and you thought Grandma Moses started late.
11. 40 years.
12. Damascus
13. True. Noah's father was Lamech.
14. Mizraim—Named after Mizraim who was the son of Ham and the grandson of Noah.
15. Four—Bilah, Leah, Rachel and Zilpah.

## 19. Ancient General History I

1. Between which two rivers did the Sumerian civilization develop?

2. Which famous epic takes place in the City of Urich?
3. Which Mesopotamian city is alleged to have been founded in 6000 BC?
4. In which region did the Hittites live?
5. Who is considered the founder of the Hittite Civilization?
6. What colour was invented by the Phoenicians?
7. Which sister civilization did the Phoenicians set up in Tunisia?
8. Who was the famous Phoenician King who lived during the time of Solomon?
9. What were the three most important Phoenician cities in Lebanon?
10. How did this king, mentioned in 8, assist Solomon in the building of the Temple?
11. From which region of the world were the Scythians from?
12. Which were the two famous Lydian cities?
13. True or False: The Phoenicians colonized both Spain and Cyprus?
14. Which ancient people were the predecessors of the Persians?
15. Which popular alcoholic drink was invented by the Assyrians?

**Answers to Ancient General History I**

1. Tigris and the Euphrates.
2. Epic of Gilgamesh.
3. Ur
4. Asia Minor.
5. Suppiluliumas
6. Purple
7. Carthage
8. Hiram of Tyre.
9. Tyre, Sidon and Byblos.
10. He provided the Cedar tress for the wood construction portions of the Temple.
11. Caucasus Region.
12. Sardis and Mellitus.
13. True
14. Medes
15. Beer. "I am pretty sure it was better than Budweiser."

# 20. Ancient General History II

1. Gordion was a city of which Civilization?
2. Which Assyrian King conquered the Hittites between 800-700 BC?
3. Which civilization contained the cities of Hattusas and Nesa?
4. Which civilizations, Old Kingdom, peaked between the $18^{th}$ and $17^{th}$ centuries?
5. Which occured first: The use of Cuneiform inscription by the Hittites or the First Year of the Jewish Calandar?
6. What does BCE stand for?
7. Roughly speaking when did Abraham leave Ur? Was it 2000 BC, 1900 BC or 1800 BC?
8. How many characters were there in the Ancient Egyptian Alphabet: 22, 24 or 25?
9. Which Civilization contained the City of Tanis?
10. True or False: The Phoenicians set up a colony in Gibralter?
11. Between which centuries does the earliest music date—800-700 BC, 1300-1200 BC, or 1100-1000 BC?
12. Which civilization contained the City of Pasargadae?
13. How many phases were thought to be involved in the construction of Stonehenge—3, 4, or 5?
14. Which structure were Ictinus and Callicrates the architects of?
15. What was the most important Mede City?

### Answers to Ancient General History II

1. The Phyrigian.
2. Sargon II.
3. The Hittites.
4. The Babylonians.
5. First Year of the Jewish Calendar was 3760 BC. The Hittites started using Cuneiform between 2000 and 1500 BC.
6. Before the Common Era.
7. 2000 BC or 2000 BCE.
8. 24

9. Egyptian
10. True
11. 800-700 BC.
12. Persian
13. 3 between the period 3000-1500 BC.
14. The Parthenon.
15. Media—believe it or not.

## 21. The Ancient Persians

1. Which people migrated from Southern Russia to the Near East between 2000-1800 BC?
2. From whom did the Persian kings before Christ descend from?
3. What was the name of Cyrus the Great's bodyguard?
4. How many Xerxes were Emperors of Persia?
5. What animal was at the center of the Mitras cult?
6. Which king rewrote history to wipe out all accounts of his predecessor?
7. What were the two largest cities in Persia?
8. Who was the son of Cyrus the Great?
9. Who was the most important Persian god?
10. How many Artaxerxes were Emperors of Persia?
11. What were the elite units of the Persian army called?
12. Which Empire took over Persia in 300 BC?
13. What is the origin of the word 'Magic?'
14. Who established the Sassanid Empire?
15. What was the name of the Sacred Book of the Persians?

### Answers to Ancient Persians

1. The Aryans.
2. Achaemenes—His descendants are known as the Archaemenids.
3. The Ten Thousand Immortals.
4. 2
5. The bull.

6. Darius I.
7. Shushan and Persepolis.
8. Cambyses
9. Ahura Mazda—The Persian Zeus.
10. 3
11. Invincibles
12. Seleucids
13. It derives from the Magi Cult of Ancient Persia.
14. Ardashir I.
15. Zend-Avesta.

## 22. Ancient Rome I

1. Who were the legendary founders of Ancient Rome?
2. Who were they brought up by?
3. On which river does Rome stand?
4. What Northern Italian people were Rome's original enemy?
5. Who, according to Roman legend, defended the city single handedly against these Northern Italian invaders?
6. Why did Rome and Carthage go to war in the 3rd century BC?
7. How many wars were fought between these two powers?
8. Who led the Carthaginians in the Second Punic War?
9. Who was his father?
10. What battle saw the Carthaginians win their greatest victory of the Second Punic War?
11. What battle saw the Romans win their greatest victory of the Second Punic War?
12. Which king of Pontus fought Rome between 88-66 BC?
13. Who was the victorious Roman general at the end of the Second Punic War?
14. By what other name were the Slave Rebellions known as?
15. What nationality was Spartacus?

### Answers to Ancient Rome I

1. Romulus and Remus.
2. A she-wolf.
3. The Tiber.
4. The Etruscans.
5. Horatio of the Bridge.
6. For control of sea power and trade in the Mediterranean.
7. Three
8. Hannibal
9. Hamilcar
10. Cannae
11. Zama
12. Mithridates VI
13. Scipio Africanus.
14. Servile Wars.
15. He was Thracian.

## 23. Ancient Rome II

1. What was the Ancient Roman punishment for those slaves who rebelled?
2. Who was the Roman God of Love?
3. Who was the Goddess of the Harvest?
4. Which two brothers ruled Rome jointly in the Era of the Republic?
5. Who ruled alongside Julius Caesar and Pompey in the First Triumvirate?
6. Which Roman General conquered Syria and Palestine before the Birth of Christ?
7. Which battle did the Gauls score their biggest victory over the Romans in?
8. What was the name of the sword carried by Roman soldiers?
9. What river did Julius Caesar cross despite being warned not to do so?
10. What battle did Julius Caesar record his greatest victory over Pompey?

11. Who was Pompey's son?
12. What advantage did Roman galleys have over their Greek counterparts?
13. What was the ultimate fate of Rome's first invasion of Britain?
14. Who was Julius Caesar's wife?
15. Which people was Cymbeline a chief over?

**Answers to Ancient Rome II**

1. They were crucified.
2. Cupid
3. Ceres
4. Gracchi Brothers.
5. Crassus
6. Pompey
7. Georgovia
8. Gladius
9. The Rubicon
10. Pharsalia
11. Sextus
12. They used oars instead of sails and were not therefore reliant on wind power.
13. The Fleet was wrecked by a storm and the invasion failed.
14. Calpernia
15. Britons

## 24. Ancient Rome III

1. Who was Rome's most infamous pre-Republic dictator?
2. What month and date was Julius Caesar assassinated?
3. Who was Julius Caesar's most famous mistress?
4. Who were the three leaders of the assassination plot on Julius Ceaser?
5. Into which two groups were the citizens of Rome divided into?
6. What modern country was known in Roman times as 'Helvetia?'

7. What did the Romans call London?
8. What was the name of the religious cult that was active in Britain at the time of the Roman invasion?
9. True or False: Caracturus was a Visigoth Chieftain?
10. What is the name of the most famous road that leads to Rome?
11. Who was the First Roman Emperor?
12. What was his original name?
13. In which battle were the forces of Julius Ceaser's chief assassins killed in?
14. In which battle were the forces of Mark Anthony finally defeated?
15. What unusual physical condition did the man mentioned in Question 11 suffer from?

**Answers to Ancient Rome III**

1. Sulla
2. 15$^{th}$ March—Beware the Ides of March.
3. Cleopatra VII
4. Brutus, Cassius and Casca.
5. Patricians and Plebeians.
6. Switzerland
7. Londinium
8. The Druids.
9. False. He was Briton.
10. The Appian Way.
11. Augustus
12. Octavius
13. Philippi
14. Actium. A great Sea battle pitting Anthony and Cleopatra's combined fleet against that of Augustus
15. He was colorblind.

## 25. Ancient Rome IV

1. Who was Rome's Second Emperor?

2. What island did he frequent for bathing purposes?
3. Which 'mad' Emperor succeeded this second Emperor to the Throne of Rome?
4. What does the name of this Third Emperor mean in Latin?
5. Who was the Fourth Emperor of Rome?
6. How was he related to the Third Emperor?
7. Who was Nero's mother?
8. What was the symbol of the early Christians?
9. What is Nero alleged to have done whilst Rome was burning?
10. Name one of the Three Emperors who ruled Rome in the Year of the Three Emperors?
11. What city was destroyed together with Pompei when Vesuvius erupted?
12. What people lived in the lowlands next to Northeastern Gaul?
13. What was the profession of Horace?
14. What did Agrippa do for a living?
15. Who was the most well-known of the Roman Governors of Britain?

## Answers to Ancient Rome IV

1. Tiberius—there is a city in Northern Israel named after him.
2. Isle of Capri—Rumour has it that he loved the grottos (Blue and the Green).
3. Caligula
4. From Caligitus—meaning Little Boots.
5. Claudius
6. Claudius was Caligula's uncle.
7. Agrippina the Younger—The future Emperor Nero would eventually have her killed. It is believed that Agripinna murdered Claudius.
8. The Fish—The same one very often seen on the cars of reborn Christians.
9. Fiddled—Although this is more myth than anything else—some say Nero set the fire so that Rome could burn down to the ground and he could then rebuild the city according to his own design.
10. Galba, Ortho, Vitellius—pick one.

11. Herculaneum—Interesting to note is that Vesuvius is still an active volcano.
12. Belgie—From which the name Belgium derives.
13. He was a Poet.
14. He was an Architect.
15. Marcus Agricola.

## 26. Ancient Rome V

1. Which British Queen led her people in revolt against the Romans?
2. What tribe did she lead?
3. Who was the Roman Emperor during the Masada Epic?
4. Which Jewish historian chronicled the History of Palestine at the time?
5. Which important religious building was destroyed by the Romans in Jerusalem?
6. Which Calendar did the Romans introduce into Western Civilization?
7. What two months were introduced into the Calendar by the Romans?
8. Under which Roman Emperor did Rome reach its largest size?
9. Which two philosophers are considered the Fathers of Stoicism?
10. Which Emperor wrote the 'Meditations?'
11. Who wrote the Twelve Caesars?
12. Which Emperor ordered the building of a wall between Britain and Scotland?
13. Who did he wish to keep out?
14. Who was Fabianus?
15. What was the name of the Roman soldier who was in charge of ten people?

### Answers to Ancient Rome V

1. Boadicea
2. The Iceni

3. Vespasian
4. Josephus
5. The Temple.
6. The Julian Calendar.
7. July after Julius Caesar, August after Augustus Caesar.
8. Trajan
9. Seneca and Zeno.
10. Marcus Aurelius.
11. Suetonius
12. Hadrian
13. The Picts.
14. He was a general known for his delaying tactic of retreating in battle.
15. A Decurion.

## 27. Ancient Rome VI

1. What was the title of the Roman soldier who headed a cohort?
2. Which soldier led the Second Jewish rebellion against the Romans?
3. Which Rabbi was his mentor?
4. Which philosopher was a critic of Mark Anthony?
5. Who wrote the Metamorphosis?
6. What female only cult was dedicated to purity and celibacy?
7. Under the rule of which Emperor did the Philosophy of Hedonism peak?
8. According to Isaac Asimov, what caused the Decline of the Roman Emperor?
9. In what century did the Roman Empire split?
10. What happened to the Eastern portion?
11. Which Emperor converted to Christianity on his deathbed?
12. Who was the last Western Emperor?
13. Which Edict converted the Roman Empire to Christianity?
14. Which year did the Western Empire fall?
15. Why were the Olympic Games banned?

**Answers to Ancient Rome VI**

1. A Tribune.
2. Bar-Kochba.
3. Rabbi Akiba.
4. Cicero
5. Ovid (later Franz Kafka but that is another story).
6. Vestil Virgins.
7. Diocletian—Age of the Orgy.
8. Lead in the Piping poisoned the population and caused increased sterility.
9. 4th Century AD.
10. It survived until 1453 as the Byzantine Empire. Its' Capital City, Constantinople would eventually fall to the Turks.
11. Constantine
12. Romulus Augustus (ironical that the last Emperor should have the name of Rome's founder and Rome's First Emperor).
13. Edict of Milan.
14. 476 AD.
15. It was banned by the Emperor, Theodosius, who in Christian times, saw the Olympic Games as largely a Pagan Festival.

## 28. The European Dark Ages I

1. When was Charlemagne crowned Holy Roman Emperor?
2. What is the common name for Charlemagne's Dynasty?
3. Which city was Charlemagne's capital?
4. Which of the following people were not an enemy of Charlemagne: Muslims (in Spain), Lombards, Saxons or the Vandals?
5. Who was Charlemagne's father?
6. In which battle did his ancestor Charles Martel defeat the Muslims?
7. Who was Charlemagne's successor?
8. Which treaty ended the war between his grandsons?
9. What developed at Cluny?
10. Which grandson of Charlemagne would become King of France proper?

11. Which two other grandsons were his chief rivals?
12. What was the name of the First Norse leader to set up a colony in Normandy?
13. Who was the first King of All England?
14. Into what four regions was England divided into c.850 AD?
15. Which English King set up the Royal Navy?

**Answers to European Dark Ages I**

1. 800 AD.
2. Carolingian
3. Aachen (Aix-La Chapelle).
4. Vandals
5. Pepin the Short.
6. Poitiers (Tours).
7. Louis I the Pious.
8. The Treaty of Verdun.
9. A monastery that would eventually give rise to the Clunician order.
10. Charles the Bald.
11. Lothair and Louis the German.
12. Rollo
13. Egbert
14. Northumbria, Mercia, East Anglia and Wessex.
15. Alfred the Great.

## 29. Guess Who I— Only the bravest should try these questions

1. Greek Sculptor of the Discus-thrower.
2. Roman dictator—saved the city from the Gauls during invasion in 390 BC.
3. Greek writer—Wrote the Hellenica—A history of Greece from 400 BC.
4. Roman King driven out by Senators in 509 BC.
5. He beat the Romans at Lake Trasimene.

6. Roman Statesman—Ended every speech he made with the sentence—Carthage ought to be destroyed.
7. King of Pontus 9120-63 BC)—Waged war against the Romans in Asia Minor
8. Leader of the losing side at the Battle of Alesia.
9. Who said, "Caesar never forgot anything, except an injury?"
10. It was rumoured that he was Caesar's illegitimate boy—Nevertheless he was the son of Caesar's Mistress, Servilia.
11. Cleopatra's brother who shared the throne with her.
12. Roman historian lived between 56 BC and 17 AD.
13. Wife of Augustus—Previously married to his successor as Emperor.
14. Roman General—Ended Macedonian dominance over the Greek states. He also guaranteed Greek independence.
15. Whose last words were, "Dear me, I think I am turning into a god!"

**Answers to Guess Who I**

1. Myron
2. Marcus Furius Camillus.
3. Xenophon
4. Tarquinius Superbus (aka Tarquin the Arrogant).
5. Hannibal
6. Cato the Elder.
7. Mithradates VI.
8. Vercingetorix, King of the Gauls. His forces were beaten by that of Julius Caesar's.
9. Cicero
10. Marcus Junius Brutus.
11. Ptolemy XIII.
12. Livy (Titus Livius).
13. Drusilla Livia.
14. Titus Quinctius Flamininus.
15. Emperor Vespasian.

## 30. Guess Who II— Also not for the Faint hearted

1. Spartan leader at Thermopylae.
2. 1st Century BC Scholar—codified Jewish law.
3. His name is associated with luxurious and tasteful living.
4. Wealthy man—his plans to seize power in Rome was foiled by Cicero.
5. North African leader—fought against the Roman General Gaius Marius c. 113-107 BC.
6. Writer of the Orestes and Electra.
7. Gave his name to a word used to describe a Victory at High Cost.
8. Persian King who overthrew the neighboring Kingdoms of Lydia and Media.
9. Victorious King at Battle of Milvinian Bridge.
10. Roman Emperor 193-211 AD—defeated the Parthians and the Picts and died in York, England.
11. Father of Caligula.
12. Writer of the 'Suppliants and the Seven Against Thebes.'
13. Egyptian Pharaoh who drove out the Hyksos.
14. Most famous Phrygian King.
15. Roman philosopher—author of "The True Discourse."

### Answers to Guess Who II

1. Leonidas
2. Hillel
3. Lucius Licinius Lucullus—from which the word 'Lucullan' is derived from.
4. Catiline
5. Jugurtha
6. Euripides
7. Pyrrhus—King of Epirus—from whence comes the word 'Pyrrhic' as in Pyrrhic Victory.
8. Cyrus the Great.

9. Constantine
10. Septimius Severus.
11. Germanicus Caesar.
12. Aeschylus
13. Ahmose I.
14. King Midas of the Midas Touch Fame.
15. Celsus—The True Discourse—was an attack on Christianity on ideological grounds. It suggested that the Christians were not pulling their weight in the defense of the Roman Empire.

## 31. European Dark Ages II

1. Which King ruled over the Franks between 481-511 AD?
2. Who finally overthrew the Roman Empire in the West?
3. With which power did Byzantine sign the 'Eternal Peace Treaty' in 533 AD?
4. Which people conquered Kent in 449 AD?
5. What Mediterranean Island did the Arabs conquer in 649 AD?
6. Who led the Mercians to victory over the Northumbrians in 642 AD?
7. Who completed the 'History of the Church of England' in 731?
8. Which people invaded Britain for the first time in 787 AD?
9. Who was summoned in 782 AD to head the Palace School at Aachen?
10. Who were defeated at Roncesvalles in 778 AD by the Moors and the Basques?
11. Which Russian City was founded by Rurik of Russ in 862 AD?
12. Which Council ordered the resumed worship of images in 787 AD?
13. What political entity was created in Southern Europe in 756 AD?
14. Who did Pepin the Short help save Pope Stephen III from?
15. Which Eastern European people found their first Empire in 675 AD?

**Answers to European Dark Ages II**

1. Clovis
2. Odovacar, Leader of the Goths.
3. Persia
4. The Jutes.
5. Cyprus
6. Penda
7. The Venerable Bede.
8. The Danes.
9. Alcuin of York who was summoned by Charlemagne—the school represented a revival of learning in Europe.
10. The Franks.
11. Novgorod
12. Council of Nicaea.
13. The Papal States.
14. The Lombards.
15. The Bulgars.

## 32. The Arabs I

1. Who did Mohammed marry in 624 AD?
2. From which city did Mohammed flee in 622 AD?
3. What is this action described in Question 2 also known as?
4. Where did he flee to?
5. In which year did Mohammed have his renowned vision?
6. Who was the first Caliph?
7. Against which people did Omar I engage in a holy war in 634 AD?
8. What city was captured by the Moslems in 638 AD?
9. Which battle is known as the first major Arab naval victory?
10. Which Dynasty was founded by the Caliph Muawiya in 661 AD?
11. Which Moroccan City was captured by the Muslims in 707 AD?
12. Which Country did the Moors invade in 711 AD?
13. Which City failed to yield to an Arab siege in 716 AD?
14. Which country was invaded by the Muslims between 639-642 AD?
15. The Moors consist of the Arabs and which other group?

### Answers to The Arabs I

1. Aisha
2. Mecca
3. The Hegira.
4. Medina (known then as 'Yathrib').
5. 610 AD.
6. Abu Bakr (Mohammed's father-in-law).
7. The Persians.
8. Jerusalem
9. 'The Battle of The Masts'—fought in 655 AD. The Arabs defeated the Byzantine fleet just off Alexandria.
10. The Omayyad Dynasty.
11. Tangiers
12. Spain
13. Constantinople
14. Egypt
15. Berbers of Morocco.

## 33. European Dark Ages III

1. Which country had a King called 'Charles the Simple?'
2. Which English King defeated the Danes at Ashdown?
3. Which Island did the Vikings settle in 874 AD?
4. Which country was recovered from the Arabs by the Byzantines in 880 AD?
5. Which religion did the Bulgars accept in 900 AD?
6. Which people invaded Germany in 906 AD?
7. Which Saxon King annexed Northumbria and forced the Kings of Wales, Strathclyde and the Picts to submit to him?
8. Who founded the Anglo-Saxon Chronicles—a History of England?
9. Who was the First King of Hungary?
10. What was the claim to fame of the Swedish King, Olaf Skutkonung?
11. Whose country's first ruler was Mieszko I?
12. Which Hospice was founded in Switzerland in 962?

13. Who was crowned 'Emperor' by Pope John XII, also in 962?
14. Which country was annexed to Denmark in 1000 AD?
15. Which city was besieged by the Danes in 994 AD?

**Answer to European Dark Ages III**

1. France
2. Ethelred I.
3. Iceland
4. Italy
5. The Eastern Orthodox Religion.
6. The Magyars.
7. Athelstan
8. Alfred the Great.
9. Stephen I (St. Stephen)—ruled between 998 and 1038.
10. He was the first Christian King of Sweden.
11. Poland
12. St Bernard's Hospice.
13. Otto I (the crowning represented a revival of the Roman Emperor in the West).
14. Norway
15. London—The Danes had to be bought off by the English King Ethelred II.

## 34. Early British History I

1. Who was the real King Arthur?
2. Which Century was Egbert crowned King of Wessex?
3. What was Danelaw?
4. Which Irish monk converted the Picts to Christianity?
5. Who was St. Alban?
6. What was significant about the Treaty of Wedmore?
7. What title did Edward the Elder take in 901 AD?
8. How many Saxon kings were named 'Ethelred'?
9. Which people took control of Cumberland and Westmoreland from the English in 945?

10. Who were killed on St. Brice's Day in 1002?
11. What was the nickname of Harold I?
12. Which Danish king of England died of drink in 1035?
13. Who became King of Scotland in 1040?
14. Which English King founded Westminster Abbey in 1052?
15. Who became King of the Southern portion of England in 1016, only to be assassinated in the same year?

**Answers to Early British History I**

1. He was a Roman/British chieftain who fought against the Saxon invaders of England during the early 6th Century.
2. 9th Century—802 AD to be precise.
3. Danish occupied territory in England.
4. St. Columba. He used as his base a monastery which he founded on the Island of Iona
5. A Roman Soldier who became a Christian martyr in England. He was scourged and beheaded for sheltering and changing clothes with a Christian Priest who had converted him.
6. Signed in 878 AD, the Treaty divided England into two sections: Wessex in the South, Danelaw in the North.
7. King of the Angles and Saxons.
8. Two
9. The Scots.
10. Danish settlers and mercenaries in Southern England.
11. Harold the Harefoot.
12. Hardicanute
13. Macbeth. He killed Duncan in the Battle of Elgin.
14. Edward the Confessor.
15. Edmund Ironside, the son of Ethelred II.

## 35. Early British History II

1. Who was shipwrecked in Normandy in 1064, and took a vow to support William of Normandy's claim to the throne?

2. What was William the Conqueror's claim to the English throne?
3. Who was William the Conqueror's father?
4. Who led the forces that defeated Macbeth at the Battle of Lumphanan?
5. Which powerful family dominated politics in Wessex in the early 11$^{th}$ Century?
6. What major Battle was Harold involved in prior to Hastings?
7. How did Harold die at Hastings?
8. On what day of the year in 1066 was William crowned King?
9. From a military standpoint, why was the Battle of Hastings a significant event in English History?
10. What tapestry depicts the events of the Battle of Hastings?
11. What book did William start up in England to record and document details of his kingdom?
12. What type of political and societal structure did the Normans bring to England?
13. Which son of William rebelled against him?
14. Who was William's successor as King?
15. What fortress in London did William the Conqueror build?

**Answers to Early British History II**

1. Harold (later King Harold II).
2. He claimed to have been promised it in 1051 by Edward the Confessor who was looking to build allies with the Normans.
3. Robert, Duke of Normandy, aka 'Robert the Devil.' William was his illegitimate son.
4. Malcolm Canmore, aka 'Big Head.'
5. The Godwin Family. Harold was the son of the Earl of Godwin.
6. The Battle of Stamford Bridge that took place 19 days before Hastings. Harold defeated the Norwegian King Harold Hardrada and his brother Tostig before advancing to meet William the Conqueror at Hastings.
7. He was struck by an arrow in the eye.
8. Christmas Day, 1066.
9. It represents the last time England was ever successfully invaded.

10. Bayeux Tapestry.
11. The Domesday Book.
12. Feudalism
13. His son, Robert.
14. His son, William II, aka 'William Rufus.'
15. The Tower of London.

## 36. The Arabs and the Middle East prior to 1300

1. Which Dynasty born in North Africa around 1061 would later conquer Spain?
2. Of which group was Malik Shah the conqueror of Syria and Palestine in 1075 a member of?
3. Which famous Persian poet died in 1123?
4. What was his most famous poetic work?
5. What was his most famous Mathematical work?
6. Who conquered Syria in 1174?
7. Which people began a conquest of Moorish Spain in 1145?
8. Which Dynasty ruled over Baghdad as Caliphs between 750-1258?
9. Which Shiite Dynasty ruled over Egypt and North Africa between 909 and 1171?
10. Who is hailed by Shiite Muslims as the only true successor to Mohammed?
11. Who was his wife?
12. Which Arab philosopher wrote the *Destructio Destructiones* arguing that all religion was a form of allegorical philosophy?
13. Which philosopher attempted a synthesis between Islam, Plato and Aristotle?
14. Which power did the Seljuk Muslims, under Alp Arslan, defeat in the Battle of Mazikeret in 1071?
15. Which Moroccan City was founded by Yusuf bin Tashfin in 1062?

### Answers to The Arabs and the Middle East prior to 1300

1. Almoravid Dynasty.

2. The Seljuks.
3. Omar Khayyam.
4. *The Rubaiyat* (or Quatrains).
5. The Binomial Theorem.
6. Saladin aka Salah-al-Din Yusuf ibn-Ayyub.
7. The Almohades.
8. The Abbasid Dynasty.
9. The Fatimids
10. Ali, the cousin and son-in-law of Mohammed.
11. Fatima
12. Averroes
13. Avicenna—who once said, 'Thought brings about the generality of forms."
14. The Byzantines.
15. Marrakesh

## 37. The African Kingdoms

Name the African State from the description given below (1-7):

1. East African, situated North of the Ethiopian Highlands, begins with A.
2. North African, next to Carthage, contains the cities of Caesarea and Hippo Regulus, begins with N.
3. Central African, next to Luba, begins with L
4. West African power. Its strength peaked during the period 1300-1800, begins with B.
5. Western and Central Sudan Power. Its strength peaked in 1450. By 1600, it had been overrun by Morocco, begins with S.
6. West African Kingdom. It was overrun by Mali in the 13th Century, begins with G.
7. The Pharaoh's called it, 'The land of Punt,' begins with an E.
8. Who were the dominant people in South Africa c. 1500 AD?
9. Which fabled African City of Wisdom was visited by the Florentine Merchant, Bendetto Dei, in 1470?

10. Between the $12^{th}$ and the $15^{th}$ Centuries, which city served as the chief trading center in East Africa, begins with a K?
11. Which nation was known for their fierce cavalry. The knights of this tribe wore armour and terrorized central Sudan for more than 200 years starting in the Early $16^{th}$ Century?
12. Which Central African kingdom was founded by the Bokongo Warriors in the early $15^{th}$ Century?
13. Which power converted the Nubians to Christianity?
14. Which Nigerian Tribe started forming inland city-states in 1100?
15. Why were camels introduced into the Sahara c. 500 BC?

**Answers to the African Kingdoms**

1. Axum
2. Numidia
3. Lunda
4. Benin
5. Songhai
6. Ghana
7. Ethiopia
8. The Khoisans.
9. Timbuktu
10. Kilwa
11. The Bornu.
12. Kongo
13. The Byzantines.
14. The Yoruba.
15. The Sahara became too dry for horses.

## 38. The Crusades I

1. Which pope called the First crusade?
2. Why did he call it?
3. What two orders of knights were founded in 1113 and 1118 respectively?

4. Which city fell to the crusaders in 1099?
5. Against which non-Muslim Eastern European people was a Crusade launched in 1147?
6. Which of these was not a Crusader states set up in the Mideast: The County of Tripoli, The Principality of Antioch and the County of Edessa?
7. From which country were the majority of knights who fought in the First Crusade from?
8. Which Crusader state was the first to fall to the Muslims?
9. In what region did the second Crusade led by Conrad III, the Holy Roman Emperor and Louis VIII of France, perish in 1147?
10. Which Muslim leader took Jerusalem after winning an important victory at Hattin in 1187?
11. Against which group of heretics was a crusade called by Pope Innocent III in 1208?
12. Who were the two leaders of the Third Crusade?
13. What Mediterranean Island did the Third Crusade capture in the early 1190's?
14. In addition to Muslims which religious group were often massacred by crusading parties?
15. Which type of castle is regarded as the most important innovation of Crusader Architecture?

**Answer to the Crusades I**

1. Pope Urban II at Claremont in 1095.
2. He called it in response to the Byzantine Emperor Alexius I Commenus who needed military assistance against the Seljuk Turks.
3. The Order of the Hospital of St. John (Hospitallers) and the Order of the Knights Templar respectively.
4. Jerusalem
5. The Pagan Slavs (Wends in particular).
6. They were all crusader states set up during the French crusade.
7. France
8. Edessa in 1144. It was taken by Zangi, the Muslim governor of Mosul.

9. Asia Minor (Anatolia).
10. Saladin
11. The Cathars—a sect in Southern France.
12. Richard the Lionheart of England and Philip Augustus of France.
13. Cyprus
14. The Jews.
15. The Concentric Castle.

## 39. The Crusades II

1. Which City did the Fourth Crusade take in 1204?
2. From which two countries were their important Children's Crusades?
3. Against which Baltic people was a crusade launched in 1309?
4. Which Island would serve as the last bastion of the crusader movement right up until the 18th Century?
5. Against which Middle Eastern country was the Fifth crusade directed?
6. What crusade was led by Peter the Hermit?
7. Which Holy Roman Emperor regained Jerusalem in the Sixth Crusade using Diplomacy?
8. Which Greek Island became a major base for the crusaders until its fall to the Ottoman Empire in 1522?
9. Which Germanic people were at the receiving end of a crusade led by the Teutonic knights in 1227?
10. Which French King led the Seventh Crusade?
11. What town in Northern Palestine fell to the Mamelukes in 1291?
12. What was Ruad the last of?
13. Against which North African City was the Eighth Crusade directed?
14. Which Yugoslavian City was defended in 1456 by Crusaders against the Ottoman invaders?
15. What was very often offered to those who volunteered for the Crusades?

**Answers to The Crusades II**

1. Constantinople. The crusaders formed a Latin Kingdom in the region.
2. France and Germany.
3. The Lithuanians.
4. Malta. It was home to the Knights Hospitallers.
5. Egypt between 1217-1221.
6. The People's Crusade of 1096.
7. Frederick II.
8. Rhodes
9. The Prussians.
10. Louis IX.
11. Acre
12. It was the last Christian stronghold in the Holy Land to fall to the Muslims. It was taken by the Mamelukes in 1302.
13. Tunis
14. Belgrade
15. Land

# 40. English Medieval History I

1. Which English King lost his only legitimate son in the White Ship Disaster of 1120?
2. Which Territory in France did this King win for England in 1106?
3. Who was the last Norman King of Britain?
4. Who was the First King of the Plantagenet Dynasty?
5. What was the fate of Thomas Becket?
6. What constitution reluctantly signed by Thomas Becket in 1164 defined the powers of Church and State?
7. Who was the mother of Richard the Lionheart?
8. Where was the Magna Carta signed?
9. Which Emperor kidnapped and then forced the ransom of Richard the First when the latter was returning home from the Crusades?
10. What was King John's nickname?

11. Which war followed when John tried to repudiate the Magna Carta?
12. During the reign of which English King did England lose the Territory of Guyenne to France's Louis IX?
13. What taxes bought about the Peasant Revolt in 1381?
14. Between which two years did the Hundred Years War take place?
15. Which English King was known as 'Longshanks'?

**Answers to English Medieval History I**

1. Henry I. His son was William Adelin.
2. Normandy, by defeating his brother Robert Curthose at the Battle of Tinchebrai.
3. Stephen, he was the son of Henry I's sister Adela.
4. Henry II.
5. He was murdered in Canterbury Cathedral by four knights loyal to Henry II. They were not however acting on Henry's orders.
6. The Constitution of Clarendon.
7. Eleanor of Aquitaine.
8. At Runnymede. The Magna Carta is of course the basis for the English constitution.
9. Henry VI of Germany.
10. Lackland
11. The Baron's War (1215-1217).
12. Henry III.
13. The Poll Taxes. One would have thought that Maggie Thatcher would have learnt from this.
14. 1337-1453 ie. It actually lasted for 116 years.
15. Edward I. He was the elder son of Henry III and Eleanor of Provence.

## 41. English Medieval History II

1. Who did Edward I help defeat at the Battle of Evesham in 1265?
2. Which people did Edward I expel from England?
3. Which title was Edward II the first to hold?

4. Which Wars erupted in 1295 as a result of Edward I's insistence on Full Rights of Suzerainty?
5. Which Scottish King defeated the English at the Battle of Bannockburn in 1314?
6. Who was Edward II's not so loyal wife?
7. Which forces did Edward III defeat at the Battle of Haldon Hill?
8. At which Hundred Years' War Battle was gunpowder first used?
9. Who led the Welsh independence drive c. 1400?
10. Who succeeded Edward III as King of England?
11. Who was the Father of the man mentioned in Question 10?
12. Which Dynasty succeeded the Plantagenats?
13. Who was the First King of this new house?
14. What weapon triumphed at the Battle of Agincourt in 1415?
15. How old was Henry VI when he became King of England?

**Answers to English Medieval History II**

1. Simon De Montfort.
2. The Jews.
3. Prince of Wales.
4. The Scottish Independence Wars.
5. Robert the Bruce.
6. Isabella of France. She took a lover Roger Mortimer and eventually had Edward II imprisoned in Kenilworth Castle. Edward would be murdered in Berkley Castle in 1327.
7. The Scots.
8. The Battle of Crecy in 1346.
9. Owen Glendower.
10. Richard II.
11. Edward the Black Prince. He obtained his name from the Black Armour he wore at the Battle of Crecy.
12. House of Lancaster.
13. Henry IV—the son of John the Gaunt. John was the Fourth son of Edward III.
14. The English Longbow. It proved more effective than the French crossbow. The victorious King at the Battle was Henry V.

15. One. His regent's were the Duke of Bedford in France and the Duke of Gloucester in England.

## 42. English Medieval/ Early Renaissance History

1. In which Battle did Warwick the Kingmaker die?
2. Which people who lived in the South of France were England's allies for large parts of the Hundred Years' War?
3. What seige did Joan of Arc inspire the French to break?
4. Which War broke out in England in mid 1455?
5. Who were the two sides in this war?
6. Which King was imprisoned by his uncle Richard III in the Tower of London?
7. At what Battle were the Forces of Richard III defeated?
8. What Dynasty was founded by Henry VII?
9. What economic feat did Henry VII succeed in achieving?
10. Who was Henry VIII's older brother?
11. What title did the Pope bestow on Henry VIII?
12. Which cardinal fell out of favour with Henry VIII when he failed to win a divorce for Henry from the pope? Henry was seeking to divorce Catherine of Aragon.
13. Which English statesman, an ancestor of Oliver Cromwell, finally arranged for Henry's divorce?
14. What was the name of the Act that made Henry Head of the Church of England?
15. Name all six of Henry VIII's wives?

### Answer to English Medieval/Early Renaissance History

1. The Battle of Barnet in 1471. Known also as Richard Neville he was a powerful political player in 15$^{th}$ Century England.
2. The Burgundians.
3. The Seige of Orleans.
4. The War of the Roses.

5. The House of Lancaster (Red Rose) and the House of York (White Rose).
6. Edward V. He was imprisoned with his brother never to be heard of again. It seems likely that they were murdered. In 1674, a wooden chest containing the remains of two children was found in the Tower. These were later sent to Westminster Abbey for burial.
7. The Battle of Bosworth Field in 1485.
8. The House of Tudor.
9. He balanced the budget. Unusual for any king at the time or even any politician today.
10. Arthur. He died before he could become king. Henry married his widow, Catherine of Aragon.
11. Defender of the Faith. In 1521, Henry had published a book defending the Catholic faith against the attacks by Martin Luther. Still to this day, English kings and queens carry with them that title.
12. Cardinal Thomas Wolsey. He would later be arrested on a charge of treason.
13. Thomas Cromwell.
14. The Act of Supremacy.
15. You knew this one was coming. Give yourself 1 point if you get 5 or more of these correct. They were: Catherine of Aragon, Anne Boleyn, Jane Seymour, Anne of Cleves, Catherine Howard and Catherine Parr.

## 43. British Renaissance History I

1. What was the name of the Tudor Ship that was salvaged in the 1980's?
2. Which Novel by Samuel Clemens is Edward VI featured in as a character?
3. Which French King did Henry VIII side with at the Field of the Cloth of Gold (1520)?
4. This Archbishop of Canterbury was responsible for the Book of Common Prayer (between 1549 and 1552). Who was he?

5. This opponent of Henry VIII wrote *Utopia* in 1516. He was canonized in 1935. Who was he?
6. She was Queen of England between Edward VI and Mary Tudor. Who was she?
7. What French port was lost to England during the reign of Mary Tudor?
8. Who were England's three most famous martyrs during Mary's crackdown on Protestantism?
9. What was the Title of Robert Dudley, the alleged lover of Elizabeth I?
10. Who was Elizabeth I's mother?
11. Who was brought to trial for treason following the Babington Plot in 1586 and executed at Fotheringay Castle in Northamptonshire?
12. In which year was the Spanish Armada defeated?
13. Who led the English forces in this famous battle?
14. Why could Sir Francis Drake afford to be so relaxed about the coming of the Invincible Armada? (legend has it that he was playing lawn bowls at the time)
15. Who was Mary Tudor's husband?

**Answer to English Renaissance History I**

1. The Mary Rose.
2. The Prince and the Pauper.
3. Francis I.
4. Thomas Cranmer.
5. Thomas More or St. Thomas More.
6. Lady Jane Grey. Her reign lasted nine days.
7. Calais. This was England's last piece of territory in France.
8. Hugh Latimer, Nicholas Ridley and Thomas Cranmer (give yourself 1 point if you get 2 or more out of the 3 correct).
9. Duke of Leicester.
10. Anne Boleyn.
11. Mary Queen of Scots.
12. 1588

13. Charles Howard. The leader of the Spanish force was the Duke of Medina.
14. The English Espionage Network had so thoroughly infiltrated the Spanish Court that Drake was aware of almost every move the Spanish were up to.
15. Philip II of Spain.

## 44. English Renaissance History II

1. Who was the first English printer?
2. Which ship did Francis Drake sail around the world in?
3. Who was the first Englishman to traffic in slaves from West Africa to the West Indies?
4. Who was the Secretary of State who helped Elizabeth I establish the Church of England and repeal the Catholic Legislation of Mary?
5. Which people revolted in 1597 against the English?
6. Which explorer tried to find the Northwest Passage to Cathay, but instead reached the Hudson Bay and Labrador?
7. Who were the three husbands of Mary Queen of Scots?
8. Who was imprisoned in the tower by Elizabeth I for having an affair with Bessy Throckmorton, one of the queen's maids-of-honour?
9. The fate of this famous explorer is that he was set afloat on a small boat after his crew mutinied. Who was he?
10. He lived between 1530 and 1590. He was arguably the Virgin Queen's greatest champion, uncovering numerous plots against her. Who was he?
11. Which type of pictures was Nicholas Hilliard famous for?
12. He wrote, "The Massacre of Paris, Tamberlaine, Edward II and Dr. Faustus." Who was he?
13. Who attempted to raise the City of London in 1600?
14. How many voyages did Walter Raleigh make to America?
15. Who is regarded as being primarily responsible for the conversion of the Scots to Protestantism?

**Answers to English Renaissance II**

1. William Caxton.
2. The Golden Hind.
3. Jim Hawkyns.
4. William Cecil.
5. The Irish under the leadership of Hugh O'Neill, Earl of Tyrone.
6. Martin Frobisher.
7. The Dauphin of France (later Francis II. He died leaving Mary a widow at age 18), Lord Darnley and the Earl of Bothwell. Bothwell was held responsible by many for the murder of Darnley but was never convicted of it.
8. Walter Raleigh. He would later marry Bessy on his release.
9. Henry Hudson.
10. Francis Walsingham.
11. Miniature pictures and portraits.
12. Christopher Marlowe.
13. The Earl of Essex. He failed and was beheaded in 1601.
14. Three
15. John Knox.

## 45. World History General I (1000-1400)

1. What sect was founded by Caliph al-Hakim in 1021?
2. Over which Empire did Zoë rule over between 1028 and 1050?
3. What was the most significant event of the Year 1054?
4. Which pope was deposed by the Synod of Worms in 1076?
5. What did Emperor Henry IV, and John I of England have in common, other than their obvious royalty?
6. Which Spanish City (known for its architecture) did Alphonso VI capture from the Moors in 1086?
7. What sect was founded by Hasan ibn al Sabbah (First Old Man of the Mountains) in Persia in 1090?
8. Over which city was Godfrey Bouillon elected king of in 1099?

9. Who founded the Duchy of Austria in 1156 to counter Welf power in Bavaria?
10. Which of the powers never controlled Sicily between 1091 and 1295: The Normans, Byzantines, Holy Roman Empire, Angevins, Aragonese?
11. Which kingdom was sandwiched in between Castile, Aragon and Gascony (France)?
12. What was Frederick Barbarossa's dynasty?
13. Whose powers of authority were damaged by the Investiture Contest with the Popes between 1075 and 1122?
14. From which Spanish state did Portugal break away in 1128?
15. Which Eastern people attacked Europe between 1237-1241?

## Answers to General World History I (1000-1400)

1. The Druse Sect.
2. The Byzantine Empire.
3. The Final Break between the Byzantine Church and the Roman Church. The Eastern Church was now independent.
4. Pope Gregory VII (Hildebrand of Soana).
5. They were both excommunicated.
6. Toledo
7. The Assassins.
8. Jerusalem—courtesy of the First Crusade.
9. Frederick Barbarossa.
10. The Byzantines. In 1295 Sicily would finally win independence
11. Navarre
12. The Hohenstaufen Dynasty.
13. The Holy Roman Emperors.
14. León
15. The Mongols.

## 46. World History General II (1000-1400)

1. Which building is considered the first example of Gothic architecture?
2. Which French philosopher—theologian lived between the years 1079 and 1142? He was known for his love of Héloïse and for his Nominalstic doctrines.
3. Which Empire did the Mongols attack in 1211?
4. Who was also known as Temujin?
5. What Asian order (begins with a 'D'), was founded by Djelaleddin in 1273?
6. Which European foes did the Ottomans finally defeat in 1396 at Nicopolis?
7. Which time keeping device was invented between 1270 and 1300?
8. Which country had a king c. 1200 named Sancho I?
9. Which Arab City was the Nizamayeh Academy founded in c. 1065?
10. After whom was the Ottoman state named?
11. Over which people was Ogedai a leader of?
12. Who made a name for himself in 1297 by winning the Battle of Cambuskenneth?
13. To which city did the Papal See move to during the Babylonian Captivity?
14. This great Italian Poet died in 1374. Who was he?
15. What was the purpose of the Salic Laws?

### Answers to World History General II (1000-1400)

1. The Abbey Church in St. Denis near Paris.
2. Peter Abelard.
3. The Chinese.
4. Chingis Khan (means Emperor within the Seas).
5. The Dervishes.
6. The Crusaders.
7. The mechanical clock.
8. Portugal

9. Baghdad
10. Osman I, a Turkish chieftain who ruled Sögüt.
11. The Mongols. He was Chingis Khan's second son. His death in 1241 caused a massive power struggle in the Mongol controlled lands.
12. William Wallace. He was defeated a year later at the Battle of Falkirk.
13. Avignon—from 1305 to 1377.
14. Petrach
15. Adopted in France in 1317, these laws excluded women from succession to the throne.

## 47. European History I (1400-1600)

1. Which year was Constantinople sacked in?
2. Which two sides fought the Battle of Lepanto in 1571?
3. Which pope incurred the wrath of Martin Luther by his vast project for rebuilding St. Peter's?
4. What Ottoman Sultan masterminded the Fall of Constantinople?
5. Which warlord overran the Ottoman Empire in 1402?
6. Why was the Council of Pisa called in 1409?
7. In which city in France was Joan of Arc burnt as a witch?
8. Which powerful family leader became ruler of Florence in 1434?
9. Which Ancient European city fell to the Turks in 1456?
10. What revolutionary invention occurred in 1456?
11. Which state was the most powerful in Central Europe c. 1485?
12. What important strategic foothold in southern Spain was captured by Castile from the Arabs in 1462?
13. Which Balkan state fell to the Turks in 1459?
14. From which two regions of Spain were Ferdinand the Catholic and Isabella I from respectively?
15. What wars began in 1494 by the invasion of Charles VIII?

**Answers to European History I (1400-1600)**

1. 1453
2. The Christian Holy League and the Ottoman Empire.
3. Leo X—Giovanni de Medici. An often-quoted remark of his is, "Let's enjoy the papacy!"
4. Sultan Murad II.
5. Tamerlane aka Timur the Lame.
6. To resolve the Great Schism—the two rival popes were declared deposed and a third was elected.
7. In Rouen in 1431.
8. Cosimo de Medici.
9. Athens
10. The invention of printing by moveable type courtesy of Johannes Gutenberg.
11. Hungary. It conquered Vienna in 1485.
12. Gibraltar
13. Serbia
14. Aragon and Castille.
15. The Italian Wars. These were largely a conflict between the French House of Valois and the Habsburgs. Charles invaded Italy to activate the Angevin claim to the Throne of Naples.

## 48. European History II (1400-1600)

1. What was the last Muslim enclave in Spain to fall to the Christians?
2. Who was the Mother of Charles V?
3. Who was Charles V's paternal grandfather?
4. Who was Charles V's greatest rival monarch?
5. Which two powers were united thanks to Charles' paternal and maternal lineage?
6. From which Italian City was Christopher Columbus?
7. What was the country of origin of Ferdinand Magellan?
8. How many theses of indulgences did Martin Luther pin up to the Church door at Wittenberg?

9. Fill in the missing word in this sentence: Martin Luther preached a doctrine of salvation by (..) rather than works?
10. Complete the title of this Luther Book: *A Prelude concerning the (..) Captivity of the Church.*
11. In which German city did Charles V convene the famous 1521 diet, where Luther was called to retract his teachings?
12. Protestants or Catholics—which princes were defeated at the Battle of Mühlberg in 1547?
13. Who inherited the two portions of Charles V's Empire upon his abdication in 1556?
14. Who was America named after?
15. Which two countries fought a war between 1521 and 1529 over rival claims to Italy?

**Answers to European History II (1400-1600)**

1. Granada
2. Joan (Juana) the Mad—daughter of Ferdinand of Aragon and Isabella of Castile.
3. Maximillian I.
4. Francis I of France
5. Spain and the Holy Roman Empire.
6. Genoa
7. Portugal
8. 95
9. faith
10. Babylonian
11. Worms
12. The Protestant Princes of the League of Schmalkaldic by Charles V.
13. His son, Philip II, inherited Spain. His brother, Ferdinand I, would rule in Austria.
14. The explorer Amerigo Vespucci. His name was first used in a map produced by Martin Waldseemüller in 1507.
15. France and Spain. The war ended with the signing of The Treaty of Cambrai in 1529 whereby France renounced all claims to Italy.

## 49. European History III (1400-1600)

1. Which Council was opened by Pope Paul III in 1545 to reform the Roman Catholic Church?
2. Which group would guide this council?
3. What individual introduced Christianity to Japan?
4. Which Baltic country merged with Poland in 1569, according to the Treaty of Lublin?
5. Which South American city was founded by the Portuguese in 1567?
6. Which Eastern European country was besieged by a Reign of Terror in 1564?
7. Which group in France were given Freedom of worship in 1570 by the Peace of St. Germain?
8. The provinces of which country drove out the Spanish in 1576?
9. Which Swiss religious leader wrote: *Concerning True and False Religion*?
10. Which massacre occurred in 1572?
11. Which country did Spain conquer in 1580?
12. Which civil war broke out in France in 1585?
13. Who became King of France in 1589?
14. Which European city was the Home of Calvinism?
15. What was the name of the War fought between Russia, Sweden and Denmark during the period 1557-1582 over succession to the Balkan territories?

### Answers to European History III (1400-1600)

1. The Council of Trent.
2. The Jesuits.
3. St. Francis Xavier.
4. Lithuania
5. Rio de Janeiro.
6. Russia under the rule of Ivan the Terrible.
7. The Huguenots.

8. The Netherlands.
9. Ulrich Zwingli. The book attacked monasticism and idolatry. Zwingli was killed in Zurich in an attack by citizens of anti-Protestant cantons.
10. St. Bartholomew Days Massacre—mass murder of Protestants in France.
11. Portugal
12. The War of the Three Henry's between Henri III of France, Henri of Navarre and Henri of Guise.
13. Henri IV (or Henri of Navarre) upon the murder of Henri III.
14. Geneva
15. The Livonian War.

## 50. European History IV (1400-1600)

1. Which two royal houses of Europe ended their conflict in 1559 with the signing of The Treaty of Cateau-Cambrésis ?
2. Which calendar was introduced into the Roman Catholic world in 1582?
3. Which important Edict was signed in 1598?
4. Which power defeated the Hungarians in 1596?
5. Which Dutch leader was murdered in 1584?
6. Which country controlled most of Italy c. 1560?
7. Which Italian city was controlled by the Sforzas c. 1500?
8. Who founded the Jesuits?
9. Which Italian city was sacked by Spanish and German troops in 1527?
10. Which pope commissioned Michelangelo to design the frescoes on the ceiling of the Sistine Chapel?
11. From which prominent family was Pope Alexander VI a member of?
12. Which guiding spirit of Florence, religious reformer and denouncer of Church abuse would be burned to death in 1498?
13. Which religious group led by Thomas Müntzer, was influential in Switzerland, Moravia and Holland c. 1525?

14. Which explorer rounded the Cape in 1488?
15. Who was the First European to discover the Pacific Ocean?

**Answers to European History IV (1400-1600)**

1. The Habsburgs and the Valois.
2. The Gregorian calendar—after Pope Gregory XIII.
3. The Edict of Nantes which gave the French Protestant Huguenots and the French Catholics equal political rights.
4. The Turks at the Battle of Keresztes.
5. William of Orange—aka William the Silent.
6. Spain
7. Milan
8. Ignatius Loyola in 1534.
9. Rome
10. Julius II.
11. The Borgias
12. Girolamo Savonarola.
13. The Anabaptists—they advocated adult baptism. The movement was persecuted by both the Protestants and Catholics. It was eventually stamped out although some of its followers regrouped later to form the Mennonites.
14. Bartolomeu Diaz.
15. Vasco Núñex de Balboa in 1513.

## 51. European History V (1400-1600)

1. In 1495, Milan, Venice, The Holy Roman Emperor, Pope Alexander VI, and Ferdinand V formed an alliance that forced the withdrawal of the French King Charles VIII's troops from Naples. What was this alliance called?
2. Which European explorer reached India in 1498 after rounding the Cape?
3. Which continent was divided by Pope Alexander VI's Line of Demarcation?

4. What does the word Renaissance mean?
5. Who wrote: *The Essays*?
6. Which union declared itself the Dutch Republic in 1581?
7. Who sponsored Portugal's exploration of the African coast between 1418 and 1460?
8. Who painted *The Last Judgement*?
9. Which Chinese city was settled by the Portuguese in 1557?
10. Who became Holy Roman Emperor in 1576? He would rule until 1612.
11. Which philosopher-scientist, who advocated a pantheist philosophy, was burnt at the stake in 1600 for championing Copernicus?
12. Which political figure did Niccolò Machiavelli use as his model for his book: *The Prince*?
13. Which explorer sighted Newfoundland, Cape Breton and Nova Scotia in 1497?
14. Who ruled Scotland between 1513 to 1542?
15. Which Battle established Portuguese control of the Indian Ocean in 1509?

**Answers to European History V (1400-1600)**

1. The Holy League.
2. Vasco Da Gama.
3. South America—it was divided between the Spanish and the Portuguese in 1493 based on an East-West axis.
4. Rebirth or revival.
5. Michel de Montaigne.
6. Union of Utrecht.
7. Prince Henry the Navigator.
8. Michelangelo
9. Macao
10. Rudolf II.
11. Giordano Bruno.
12. Cesare Borgia.
13. John Cabot.

14. James V.
15. Battle of Diu.

## 52. English History I 1600-1800

1. Which royal house did James I bring to power in England?
2. What was the name of the brief Parliament that was beset by disputes over money matters between James I and The House of Commons?
3. What was the name of the conspiracy led by the Robert Catesby to blow up Parliament?
4. Who attempted in May 1671 to steal the crown jewels?
5. What was James I's Scottish title?
6. Who called the Long Parliament in 1640?
7. Which Chamber was abolished by the Long Parliament in 1641?
8. Why did James I become unpopular?
9. What was the nickname of the Royalist and Parliamentary troops during the English Civil War?
10. Who led the ill-fated Royalist Cavalry at the Battle of Marston Moor?
11. In what structure did Charles I once hide to avoid detection by enemy Parliamentarian troops?
12. What percentage of England's adult male population died during the Civil Wars between 1642-1648?
13. Who did Parliament form an alliance with as a result of the Solemn League and Covenant?
14. What force was created in 1645?
15. Which English Admiral destroyed the Spanish Fleet at Santa Cruz and then died on the return journey home?

### Answers to English History I 1600-1800

1. The Stuarts.
2. The Addled Parliament.
3. The Gunpowder Plot—Guy Fawkes, the man who placed the explosives, was arrested on the 5th November 1605.

4. Thomas Blood. Disguised as a clergyman, he stole the crown, but was later captured.
5. James VI of Scotland.
6. Charles I. The Long Parliament lasted between 1640 and 1660.
7. The Star Chamber.
8. Although there were several religious issues at the time the main reason was his Policy of Favouritism, it would ultimately lead to a rebellion against James.
9. The Cavaliers and the Roundheads (or Ironsides).
10. Prince Rupert.
11. An oak tree.
12. About 10 %.
13. The Scots.
14. The New Model Army.
15. Robert Blake.

## 53. English History II (1600-1800)

1. Who led the victorious forces at the Battle of Naseby?
2. How many wars make up the English Civil War?
3. Which Protestant church did Charles I secretly promise the Scots he would set up in England?
4. In which year was Charles I executed?
5. What was the name given to the members of the English Long Parliament who were still left after Pride's purge?
6. What Battle effectively ended the English Civil Wars in 1648?
7. Who were the Covenanters?
8. Which 17th Century group championed the extension of manhood franchise to all but the poorest, religious toleration and the abolition of the monarchy and the House of Lords?
9. What was the name of the state that replaced the monarchy after the execution of Charles I?
10. What title did Oliver Cromwell hold between 1653 and 1658?
11. What religion was Cromwell?
12. Who did Cromwell defeat at Dunbar in 1650 and Worcester in 1651?

13. What parliament sat between the 4th July-12th December 1653?
14. Who was Oliver Cromwell's successor?
15. Which country did Cromwell encourage the colonization of by Protestant settlers?

**Answers to English History II (1600-1800)**

1. Thomas Fairfax.
2. Two separated by an uneasy peace between 1646 and 1648.
3. Presbyterianism
4. 1649 on the 30th of June.
5. The Rump Parliament.
6. The Battle of Preston.
7. Those who agreed with the Solemn League and Covenant and opposed the Divine Right of Kings. Covenanters also opposed the imposition of an episcopal system on the Presbyterian Church of Scotland.
8. The Levellers.
9. The Commonwealth.
10. Lord Protector.
11. He was a puritan.
12. The Scots.
13. The Barebone's Parliament.
14. His son, Richard.
15. Ireland—a factor which some say is the source of the problem in Northern Ireland today.

## 54. English History III (1600-1800)

1. What was the surname of the two Dutch father and son admirals who fought the English between 1652 and 1673?
2. How many Anglo-Dutch Wars were fought altogether up until 1784?
3. Why were these wars fought?
4. In which year was Charles II restored to the English throne?
5. Which general played a vital role in restoring Charles II to the throne? This same general would later receive the title, Duke of Albermarle, for his efforts.

6. Who was Charles II's wife?
7. Who was Charles II's most famous mistress?
8. Which acronym was given to the group of ministers who advised Charles after 1667?
9. What did Charles II promise Louis XIV of France in the Secret Treaty of Dover (1670)?
10. Who did Charles II, refuse to deny the succession of during the Exclusion Crisis of 1678-1681?
11. What act was passed in England in 1679 forbidding detention without trial?
12. Who rebelled against James II in 1685?
13. Which declaration issued by James II, extended toleration to all religions?
14. With which plot do we associate Titus Oates?
15. Which couple came to power in the Glorious Revolution of 1688?

**Answers to English History III (1600-1800)**

1. The Tromps: Father Maarten and his son Cornelis.
2. Four
3. As a result of commercial and colonial rivalry between England and the Dutch Republic (Give yourself 1 point if you have either of these answers).
4. 1660
5. General George Monck.
6. The Portuguese Princess Catherine of Braganza. They had no children.
7. Nell Gwynne. They had at least one son together—Charles Beauclerk.
8. The Cabal: After the surnames of each of the ministers: Clifford, Arlington, Buckingham, Ashley Cooper, and Lauderdale.
9. To make England Catholic.
10. His Catholic brother James—Duke of York.
11. The Act of Habeas Corpus.
12. The Duke of Monmouth.

13. The Declaration of Liberty of Conscience.
14. The Popish plot. Oates falsely claimed that there was a Catholic plot to murder Charles II.
15. William of Orange and his wife Mary, daughter of James II.

# 55. English History IV (1600-1800)

1. Which 17th Century figure was known as the Hanging Judge?
2. Which King was victor at the Battle of Boyne?
3. Who became Monarch of Great Britain and Ireland in 1702?
4. In which year did the English and Scottish parliaments unite?
5. What was the first name of the wife of the Duke of Marlborough?
6. Which European war was fought between 1701 and 1713?
7. Over which Caribbean Island was the pirate Henry Morgan made Deputy-Governor?
8. What was the real name of the pirate Blackbeard?
9. Which Scottish clan was slaughtered by the Campbells at Glencoe in 1692?
10. Who published his *Opticks* in 1704?
11. What was the Duke of Marlborough's greatest military victory of the year 1706?
12. Which stalemate battle was fought in 1709 between the French and the Allies?
13. What was James Francis Edward Stuart more commonly known as?
14. Which company failed in England in 1720 creating a 'bubble'?
15. What did France agree to recognize in Britain as a result of the Treaty of Utrecht?

### Answers to English History IV (1600-1800)

1. Judge George Jeffreys who tried the followers of the Monmouth rebellion. His court was known as the 'Bloody Assizes'.
2. William III.
3. Queen Anne.

4. 1707
5. Sarah as in Sarah Churchill. Some say that she was the power behind the throne during the reign of Queen Anne.
6. The War of the Spanish Succession.
7. Jamaica
8. Edward Teach.
9. The MacDonalds, on a pretext of disloyalty to William III.
10. Isaac Newton.
11. The Battle of Ramillies.
12. The Battle of Malplaquet.
13. The Old Pretender.
14. The South Sea Company.
15. Protestant succession.

## 56. British History I (1700-1800)

1. What was the name of the Alliance that Britain formed with Austria, France, and the Netherlands against Spain in 1718?
2. Who was the First Prime Minister of Britain?
3. What was the asiento?
4. What were Britain's two principal Mediterranean gains that they received at The Treaty of Utrecht in 1713?
5. From what royal house was George I?
6. A rebellion by which group broke out in Scotland in 1715?
7. Which war was fought between England and Spain between 1739-1741?
8. Who led the English forces at the Battle of Culloden?
9. What was the specific name of the rebellion that was bought to a halt at Culloden?
10. What was the name of the woman who helped Bonnie Prince Charlie flee to France?
11. What was the main reason why Bonnie Prince Charlie's rebellion failed?
12. Which party did Britain's first Five Prime Minister's belong to?

13. During whose term as Prime Minister was the Reform of the Calendar Act, which replaced the Julian Calendar with the more accurate Gregorian Calendar passed?
14. Why was the Office of the Prime Minister created in the first place?
15. Who was the last British king to lead his troops into battle?

**Answers to British History I (1700-1800)**

1. The Quadruple Alliance.
2. Sir Robert Walpole.
3. A contract that Britain won in 1713 to supply slaves to Spanish America.
4. Gibraltar and Minorca (give yourself 1 point if you got one of these or more).
5. The House of Hanover.
6. The Jacobites, supporters of the Old Pretender.
7. The War of Jenkin's Ear.
8. Duke of Cumberland.
9. Jacobite Forty-Five Rebellion.
10. Flora MacDonald, she disguised him as her maid.
11. He could not win English support for his cause.
12. The Whigs.
13. Henry Pelham.
14. It was created because George I had little knowledge or interest in British affairs. He could also speak no English. Robert Walpole, Britain's first Prime Minister, was actually the First Lord of the Treasury. He could not speak German and spoke to George I in Latin.
15. George II. He led the British to victory over the French at the Battle of Dettingen in 1743.

# 57. British History II (1700-1800)

1. Which product was the Bounty carrying when a mutiny broke out in 1789?
2. With which power did Britain sign The Treaty of Westminster in 1756?
3. Who did Robert Clive defeat at the Battle of Plassey in 1757?
4. Which treaty ended the 'Seven Years War'?
5. Which robber lived between 1705 and 1739?
6. How many voyages did Captain James Cook undertake?
7. Which admiral was executed in July 1757 for failing to save Minorca from the Spanish?
8. For which Caribbean Island did Spain cede Florida to England in the 18th Century?
9. Which English politician largely directed British efforts in the 'Seven Years War'?
10. What did the India Act of 1784 promote with respect to free trade?
11. Who was Prime Minister of Britain during the outbreak of the American Revolution?
12. What spoils did Britain obtain in North America at the end of the 'Seven Years War'?
13. How old was William Pitt the Younger when he became Prime Minister?
14. In which year did George III ascend to the British Throne?
15. Which party in Britain was by nature royalist in outlook?

## Answers to British History II (1700-1800)

1. Bread-fruit.
2. Prussia
3. The Nawab of Bengal.
4. Treaty of Paris.
5. The Highwayman Dick Turpin.
6. Three

7. John Byng.
8. Cuba
9. William Pitt the Elder.
10. It limited the autonomy of the English India Company.
11. Lord North. He actually tried to prevent the war, but was forced into it by the king.
12. Canada and all French Territory east of the Mississippi River.
13. 24, now how about that for overachieving.
14. 1760. He would reign for 60 years.
15. The Torys. Ironically, the word "Tory" comes from the Irish toiridhe, meaning 'a pursuer'. Toiridhe were Irish robbers who preyed on travellers. Opponents of the Torys claimed that the latter were pursuing royal favours, therefore the term itself was an insult.

## 58. European History I (1600-1700)

1. Who succeeded Henry IV as king of France?
2. Which politician dominated French politics between 1624 and 1642?
3. Between which years did the 'Thirty Years War' last?
4. Which Chief Minister of Philip IV of Spain sought to modernize his county's inefficient administration and increase its military strength between 1623 and 1643?
5. Over which country was Adolf Gustav II the King?
6. In which battle was he killed?
7. Which European region did the 'Thirty Years War' break out in?
8. Who became Holy Roman Emperor in 1619?
9. Which treaty ended the 'Thirty Years War?
10. Which European country was beset by 'the Times of Troubles' between 1604 to 1613?
11. Whose forces were besieged at La Rochelle in 1627?
12. Who led the Catholic forces to victory over the Protestants at the Battle of Dessau in 1626?
13. With which Eastern Power did Austria sign the Treaty of Zsitva-Torok in 1606?

14. What did the Dutch Explorer Wilhelm Schouten round in 1616?
15. In 1625, Christian IV entered the War against the Imperial forces. Over which country was Christian IV King?

**Answers to European History I (1600-1700)**

1. Louis XIII.
2. Cardinal Richelieu.
3. 1618-1648.
4. Duke of Olivares. He was Cardinal Richelieu's chief opponent in the 'Thirty Years War'.
5. Sweden
6. Battle of Lützen in 1632.
7. Bohemia. The Bohemians under Frederick V rebelled against the Holy Roman Empire. The Imperial forces however defeated the Bohemians at the Battle of White Mountain.
8. Ferdinand II.
9. The Treaty (Peace) of Westphalia.
10. Russia
11. The Huguenots by the forces of Cardinal Richelieu. In 1628 the Huguenots would surrender to Richelieu losing all their powers in France.
12. Albrecht Herzog von Wallenstein. He would later lose to Adolf Gustav II at Lützen in 1632.
13. Turkey
14. Cape Horn.
15. Denmark

## 59. European History II (1600-1700)

1. What did the Edict of Restitution, issued in 1629 by the Holy Roman Empire, allow for?
2. Who was the Chief Minister during the early years of Louis XIV 's reign?
3. Who was Louis XIV's mother?

4. What was Louis XIV's nickname?
5. Whom did he marry in 1660?
6. For how many years did Louis reign (to the nearest 2 years)?
7. For leading which country's revolt did João Ribeiro gain fame in 1640?
8. With which Italian city-state did Turkey fight a war with over the island of Candia (Crete) between 1644 and 1645?
9. Which revolt broke out in France between 1648 and 1649?
10. From which country did Portugal take Brazil in 1654?
11. Which two countries fought the Battle of Rocroi in 1643?
12. Which country was the scene of the First Villmergen War?
13. What internal revolt did Philip IV of Spain put down in 1652?
14. What treaty signed in 1659 confirmed French superiority over her Iberian neighbour?
15. What year was the Great Fire of London?

**Answers to European History II (1600-1700)**

1. Catholics to claim Protestant land. It was revoked in 1635 by The Treaty of Prague.
2. Cardinal Mazarin.
3. Anne of Austria.
4. The Sun King or Louis the Great.
5. The Infanta Maria Theresa daughter of Philip IV of Spain. It was through this marriage that Louis would later claim the Spanish throne for his second grandson.
6. 72 years—1643-1715.
7. Portugal's revolt against Spain. The Portuguese would eventually win independence from Spain in 1668. The Treaty of Lisbon would recognize this independence.
8. Venice. Venice would eventually surrender Crete to Turkey in 1669.
9. The revolt of the parlement faction also known as the Fronde. A second revolt would occur between 1652 and 1653—both were suppressed.
10. The Netherlands.

11. France and Spain—the French won.
12. Switzerland—it was a war between the Protestant and Catholic Cantons.
13. The Catalan Revolt.
14. Treaty of the Pyrenees.
15. 1666

## 60. European History III (1600-1700)

1. Which German leader defeated the Swedes at the Battle of Fehrbellin in 1675?
2. Over which territory did Poland and Turkey go to war with one another in 1672?
3. France's attack on the Spanish Netherlands in 1667 kick-started which war?
4. What was the name of the Alliance formed by Pope Innocent XI in 1684 to fight the Turks?
5. Together with Sweden which two countries formed the Triple Alliance against France in 1668?
6. What did Louis XIV revoke in 1685?
7. Which League was formed to fight France and thwart Louis XIV 's ambitions in 1686?
8. Which Dynasty had its' succession to the Hungarian Throne confirmed in 1687 after the Turkish defeat at the Battle of Mohács?
9. Which German region (starts with a 'P' and is not Prussia) was attacked by France in 1689?
10. Which treaty brought to an end the War between the Turks and the Poles, Austrians and Venetians in 1699?
11. Who were the victors at the Battle of Le Hogue in 1692?
12. With which Economic Policy is the French Administrator, Jean Baptiste Colbert, synonymous with?
13. The War between which two powers was brought to and by The Treaty of Nijmegen?
14. In the Netherlands, what was the stadholder?
15. In the Turkish siege of Vienna in 1683, the city was liberated by

German and a second group of troops—from which country was the second group of troops from?

**Answers to European History III 1600-1700**

1. Frederick Wilhelm (The Great Elector) of Brandenburg.
2. Ukraine. Turkey would gain the Polish Ukraine as per The Treaty of Zuravno.
3. The War of the Devolution. The Treaty of Aix-la-Chapelle ended the War. France would keep most of its conquests in Flanders.
4. The Holy League. Its' members would include Venice, Austria and Poland.
5. England and the Netherlands.
6. The Edict of Nantes. All religions except Catholicism were banned in France—50,000 Huguenots families would leave France soon afterwards.
7. The Augsburg League. The War of the Aubsburg League would last until 1697.
8. The Habsburgs.
9. Palatinate
10. The Treaty of Karlowitz. Austria won Hungary from the Turks, Venice took Morea and much of Dalmatia and the Poles gained control of the Turkish Ukraine and Podolia.
11. The English and Dutch (Augsburg forces) fleet they defeated the French.
12. Mercantilism
13. The Dutch and the French.
14. The ruler. William III of Orange became the hereditary stadholder of the Netherlands in 1672.
15. Poland

## 61. European History I (1700-1800)

1. Who did Charles II of Spain name as his successor in 1700?
2. Which two countries fought the Great Northern War?
3. Which king invaded Poland in 1701?

4. Who led the allied forces to victory over the French in the Battle of Blenheim (2 people)?
5. Who were the victorious parties in the following battles:
   a) Narva—1700 b) Oudernarde—1708 c) Poltava—1709
6. Why was the Pragmatic Sanction issued by the Holy Roman Emperor, Charles VI in 1713?
7. In terms of the Treaty of Rastatt and Baden signed in 1714 between Austria and France. Which territory did Austria gain?
8. Which religious group did the Papal Bull Unigenitus condemn?
9. Which Polish King signed The Treaty of Altranstädt in 1706?
10. Which people's revolt against the Austrians was led by Francis II Rákóczi?
11. In 1717 and 1718, Spain seized two Mediterranean islands of significance. Name one of them?
12. Who was the Chief French Minister between 1726 and 1743?
13. Which War of Succession came to an end in 1738 with the Treaty of Vienna?
14. Who succeeded Peter the Great as Tsar of Russia in 1725?
15. Which King was known as the 'Well-Beloved'?

**Answers to European History I (1700-1800)**

1. Philip of Anjou. The grandson of Louis XIV. Charles II's first choice as successor, the Prince Elector of Bavaria had died in 1699, a year after being chosen as heir.
2. Russia and Sweden. It was fought between 1700 and 1721 over supremacy in the Baltic.
3. Charles XII of Sweden.
4. The Duke of Marlborough and Prince Eugene of Savoy (the same man who in 1697 led the forces that defeated the Turks at Zenta).
5. a) Sweden (over Russia); b) The Allied forces (over the French); c) Russia (over Sweden).
   Give yourself 1 point if you got 2 or more of these correct.
6. To guarantee the succession of his daughter Maria Theresa.
7. The Spanish Netherlands.

8. The Jansenists. Although condemned the Jansenist movement continued to survive. It still manifests itself in the Netherlands in the Old Catholic Church. The Jansenists preached a doctrine of predestination, urging its followers to live an ascetic life.
9. Augustus II (aka Augustus the Strong). He is said to have fathered 300 illegitimate children and one legitimate son, who became Augustus III of Poland.
10. The Hungarian revolt. The revolt lasted from 1603-1711. In 1711, The Treaty of Szatmar was signed between Austria and Hungary.
11. Sardinia from Austria in 1717. Sicily from Savoy in 1718.
12. Cardinal Fleury.
13. War of the Polish Succession.
14. His widow, Catherine I.
15. Louis XV, the great-grandson of Louis XIV, whom he succeeded in 1715.

## 62. European History II (1700-1800)

1. Over the succession to which German kingdom, was a war fought between 1778-1779?
2. From a philosophical standpoint, what was much of the 18th Century known as?
3. Which Prussian Leader, worked to turn his kingdom into a military state? He was known as 'The Soldier King'.
4. Which Dynasty was this King a member of?
5. Which European War was waged between 1740-1748?
6. Which territory did Prussia win in this war?
7. From the times given, identify which monarch's reign corresponds to the following period:
   a) 1740-1786; b) 1762-1796; c) 1740-1780
8. How many times was Poland partitioned in the 18th Century?
9. Which city was hit by an earthquake in 1755?
10. Between which years was the 'Seven Year's War' fought?
11. Which society did Pope Clement XIV suppress in 1773?

12. Given the following battles, identify which war they took place in: a) Hohenfriedberg; b) Zorndorf; c) Quiberon Bay; d) Fontenoy
13. Who succeeded Maria Theresa as Head of the Austrian-Hungarian Empire?
14. Which level of Government did Catherine the Great reorganize in Russia in 1775?
15. Which two powers joined forces in 1756 with The Treaty of Versailles?

**Answers to European History II (1700-1800)**

1. Bavaria. It was actually a bloodless war.
2. The Age of Enlightenment.
3. Frederick Wilhelm I.
4. The Hohenzollern Dynasty.
5. War of the Austrian Succession.
6. Silesia
7. a) Frederick II 'the Great'; b) Catherine II 'the Great'; c) Maria Theresa
8. Three times—1772, 1793 and 1795. Poland would lose its independent statehood. Much of its territory would be taken over by Russia.
9. Lisbon—30,000 people died.
10. 1756-1763.
11. The Society of Jesus (aka the Jesuits).
12. a) War of the Austrian Succession. Austrian defeat.
    b) 'Seven Years War'—Prussians defeated the Russians.
    c) 'Seven Years War'—French defeat.
    d) War of the Austrian Succession. French defeated the British.
    Give yourself 1 point if you got 3 or more of these correct.
13. Her son, Joseph II.
14. Local Government.
15. France and Austria.

# 63. European History III (1700-1800)

1. Who wrote the Social Contract in 1762?
2. Who led the Peasant uprising in Russia between 1773 and 1775?
3. What was the phrase used to describe the equal division of power that existed between Austria and Prussia within the Holy Roman Empire during the reign of Frederick II 'The Great'?
4. Which French philosopher had a great influence on Frederick II 'The Great'?
5. Name one of the two gains that Russia achieved from Turkey as a result of The Treaty of Kuchuk Kainarji?
6. Who ascended to the throne in 1774?
7. The Polish Confederation of Bar was directed against which country?
8. What was abolished by Joseph II in 1781?
9. Why was the Armed Neutrality of the North formed by Russia, Denmark, Sweden and the Netherlands in 1780?
10. Which Black Sea territory was annexed by Russia in 1783?
11. What alliance did Frederick II 'The Great' form in 1785 against Austria?
12. Which two countries signed the Treaty of Jassy in 1792?
13. Name one of Louis XV's two famous mistresses?
14. Which Swedish king was assassinated in 1792 by Johan Ankarström?
15. Which people rebelled at Vinegar Hill in 1798?

### Answers to European History III (1700-1800)

1. Jean-Jacques Rousseau.
2. Emelyan Pugachev.
3. Austro-Prussian Dualism.
4. Voltaire
5. Russia gained Black Sea ports and the right to represent the Greek Orthodox Church in Turkey (this would have ramifications in the 19th Century's Crimean War).
6. Louis XVI of France.

7. Russia. It was founded in 1767.
8. Serfdom
9. To protect neutral shipping from the British.
10. The Crimea. The Russians had conquered it in 1771.
11. The League of German Princes.
12. Russia and Turkey.
13. Countess du Barry and Madame Pompadour.
14. Gustavus III.
15. The Irish—in specific the United Irishmen.

## 64. Assassinations

Which famous people were assassinated by the following killers?

1. Dr. Carl Austin Weiss.
2. Nathuran Ghodse.
3. Ramon del Rio.
4. Charles Guiteau.
5. François Ravaillac.
6. Mark David Chapman.
7. Prince Faisal ibn Masaed.

Which groups were responsible for the deaths of the following people?

8. Sir Richard Sykes.
9. Louis Carrero Blanco, Spanish Premier.
10. Aldo Moro.
11. What do the following assassination victims all have in common: Humbert I, King of Italy ; Sadi Carnot, French President; and William McKinley, US President?
12. What do the following assassination victims all have in common: Sylvanus Olympio, Togolese President; Ngo Dinh Diem, S. Vietnamese President ; and Ngarta Tombalbaye, Chad President?

Name the political leader who died in the following places in the year indicated:

13. Baghdad, 1958.
14. Hotel Ambassador, LA, 1968.
15. Léon. 1956.

**Answers to Assassinations**

1. Huey Long.
2. Mahatma Gandhi.
3. Leon Trotsky.
4. James Garfield.
5. Henry IV of France (de Navarre).
6. John Lennon.
7. King Faisal of Saudi Arabia.
8. IRA.
9. ETA.
10. Italian Red Brigade.
11. They were all killed by anarchists.
12. They were all killed in military coups.
13. King Faisal II of Iraq.
14. Robert F. Kennedy.
15. Anastasio Somoza.

## 65. The French Revolution I

1. What nationality was Jacques Necker?
2. What was the currency in France that was being used c. 1780?
3. Besides Necker name two of the three other finance ministers who worked to secure National solvency?
4. What was the 'lettre de cachet'?
5. What two wars had effectively bankrupted France by 1785?
6. Who was the editor of the *Encyclopédia*?
7. Three French philosophers from the Enlightenment are often considered to be driving forces behind the Revolution. Name two of them?
8. What did Louis XVI call on the 8th August 1788 to meet on May 1st 1789?

9. Who wrote the Pamphlet 'What is the Third Estate'?
10. Why did the First and Second Estate want Separate Estate sessions and a block vote by Estate?
11. What 'jewel' related incident had earlier in her reign tarnished the reputation of Marie Antoinette?
12. Which famous event happened on the 20th June 1789?
13. This famous astronomer was chosen on June 3rd 1789 to head the Third Estate. Who was he?
14. What disease did the Dauphin die of in 1789?
15. Which sub-class made up most of the political representatives of the Third Estate?

## Answers to French Revolution I

1. He was Swiss.
2. The livres.
3. Jacques Turgot, Charles-Alexandre de Calonne and Archbishop Etienne de Brienne.
4. A warrant issued by the king that could result in imprisonment without trial. It was usually invoked to suppress criticism of the crown.
5. The 'Seven Years War' and the American Revolution.
6. Denis Diderot. The Encyclopédia was a major work of the Enlightenment. By its very nature, it contained anti-absolutist overtones which contributed to the intellectualism of the Revolution.
7. Charles Montesquieu, Jean Jacques Rousseau and Voltaire.
8. The Estates-General. It had last been called in 1614.
9. Abbé Sieyes, he would later gain notoriety in the Revolutionary Government.
10. So the two of them together could outvote the Third Estate.
11. The Affair of the Necklace.
12. The Taking of the Tennis Court Oath. The Third Estate agreed not to disperse until a new constitution had been implemented.
13. Jean-Sylvain Bailly. He would conduct himself admirably, but would

lose popularity when he ordered the National Guard to fire on anti-royalist crowds. As an astronomer he is famed for writing the 'Histoire de l'astronomie' (1775-1787).

14. Tuberculosis
15. The Bourgeoisie.

## 66. French Revolution II

1. What did the Third Estate form on June 17, 1789?
2. Whose dismissal on the 12th of July 1789 ignited hostility on the streets of Paris?
3. What is the claim to fame of Marquis de Launay?
4. Who was in placed charge of the National Guard soon after the riots of Paris?
5. What was issued on 27 August 1789?
6. What was the 'Great Fear'?
7. To the nearest 3 million, what was the population of France at the time of the Revolution?
8. To which building did the crowd go to immediately before attacking the Bastille?
9. Which foreign regiment assisted in the defense of the Bastille?
10. What was declared dead on the 4th August 1789?
11. What was mortmain?
12. To whom was the tithe paid?
13. What event occurred on October 5-6, 1789?
14. To what Parisian Palace did Louis XIV and his family return to after the event mentioned in Question 13?
15. What profession were Vernet, Gérard, Vien, and Fragonard all members of?

### Answers to French Revolution II

1. The National Assembly. The National Assembly would create a French Constitution on July 9, 1789.
2. Jacques Necker's.

3. He was governor of the Bastille when it was stormed on the 14th July 1789. De Launay would be killed and his head placed on the end of a pike.
4. Marquis of Lafayette.
5. Declaration of the Rights of Man and Citizen—proclaiming liberty of thought, property, press and freedom from arbitrary imprisonment.
6. A fear amongst the peasantry of an aristocrat and military backlash against the people, that followed the Storming of the Bastille.
7. Twenty-five million of which 24 belonged to the Third Estate.
8. The Invalides to obtain weapons.
9. The Swiss Guards.
10. The Ancien Régime with the abolishment of privileges.
11. A condition of feudal servitude that made it possible in Ancien Régime times for a serf to sell their own property.
12. The Church.
13. The March of the Women on Versailles.
14. Tuileries
15. They were all famous artists, who were politically involved at the time.

## 67. French Revolution III

1. Why was the Guillotine invented?
2. He became a Grand Master of Freemasonary in 1771, this member of the royal family, led the opposition to the king for sometime in the 1770's and 1780's. He was once called the Father of Reform. Who was he?
3. Whose property was nationalized in November 1789?
4. Who were given the right to vote on December 24, 1789?
5. Who were the Emigres?
6. This Parisian district was the site of much Revolutionary activity. It contained the volatile Théatre Français sector. What was this district called?
7. The rise in the price of which commodity caused unrest in January 1790?

8. Which group of Jews were granted the same rights as active citizens on January 28, 1790?
9. What was the name of the new Bonds created by the National Assembly on December 19, 1789?
10. France was split up into 83 'units' in February 1790. By which more formal name were these 'units' known as?
11. Why was Paris zoned in May 1790?
12. It reduced the number of dioceses from 139 to 83, declared that Priests and bishops were to be elected and declared that the men of the cloth were civil servants. Which measure was responsible for all of the above?
13. Born in 1749, this orator and significant power broker in the National Assembly supported a constitutional monarchy on the lines of England but failed to convince, Louis XVI. He would die in 1791. Who was he?
14. For what is Claude Josephe Rouget de Lisle best remembered?
15. This Festival was celebrated in Paris in July 1790. What was it?

**Answers to French Revolution III**

1. It was seen as a more humane method of execution. The device was named after Joseph Guillotine.
2. The Duc de Orléans.
3. The Clergy's.
4. Protestants
5. Members of the privileged classes who had fled France for other parts of Europe as a result of the revolution.
6. The Cordeliers.
7. Bread
8. Sephardic Jews.
9. Assignats
10. Departments
11. To defuse the areas of unrest.
12. The Civil Constitution of the Clergy.
13. The Count of Mirabeau.

14. He wrote the words and music of the revolutionary anthem 'The Marseillaise'.
15. The Festival of the Federation.

## 68. French Revolution IV

1. This revolutionary radical was known as 'the Incorruptible'. Who was he?
2. Where was Louis XVI arrested on the 21st of June 1791?
3. From which monarch was he supposedly trying to win support to suppress the revolution?
4. What is the claim to fame of Jean-Baptiste Drouet?
5. What legend surrounds a certain physical feature of Marie Antoinette that is said to have occurred after the June 21, 1791 arrest?
6. Who were the Feuillants?
7. What came to an end on the 30th September 1791?
8. Who was Olympe de Gouges?
9. What does 'sansculottist' literally mean?
10. What device caused gridlock in the legislative assembly?
11. Before the legislative assembly was created, who did Robespierre suggest should be excluded from it?
12. What were the Brissotins later known as?
13. Which younger brother of the King played a leading role in marshaling forces hostile to the revolution abroad?
14. How many chambers did the Legislative Assembly consist of?
15. He became Assistant Public Prosecutor of the Commune in January 1792. Who was he?

### Answers to French Revolution IV

1. Maximilien Robespierre.
2. Varennes
3. King Leopold II of Austria, his brother-in-law.
4. He was the local postmaster at Ste-Menehould who recognized the royal family and notified the authorities.

5. During the four-day journey to Paris, her hair is reputed to have turned white from humiliation.
6. One of the many political clubs that were active in France at the time of the revolution.
7. The Constituent Assembly.
8. A playwright and political pamphleteer. She drafted a declaration of the rights of women.
9. Without breeches—the name was given to extreme republicans who wore simple clothing (usually in the colours of the revolution) and rejected the protocol of the ancien regime. They championed the principles of equality. The movement had much support in Paris amongst the general populace.
10. Louis XVI's overuse of his royal veto.
11. Members of the Former National Assembly. This further fermented the revolution, as it removed from government those with the most experience to run it. These individuals would reform themselves into political clubs that would often challenge the legislative assembly.
12. The Girondins. They were led by Jacques Brissot and Pierre Vergniaud.
13. Charles-Phillipe Comte d'Artois.
14. One. Even though the philosopher Montesquieu had argued for a second chamber to provide for a system of checks and balance.
15. Georges Danton.

## 69. French Revolution V

1. Which piece of clothing was the symbol of the revolution?
2. What was set up in Paris on the 10th of August 1792?
3. Which body replaced the Legislative Assembly?
4. Who headed the Commune Committee of Surveillance in September 1792?
5. Who carried out the September Massacres, which in Paris alone resulted in the death of 1400 people?

6. What was the profession of François-Christophe Kellermann?
7. What were Vendèmiaire and Termidor?
8. On what day, month and year was Louis XVI executed?
9. Under what name was the king charged for treason?
10. In which region of France were there large-scale revolts in early 1793?
11. What event finally brought down the Girondins?
12. Which Committee was formed on the 5th April 1793?
13. This journalist wrote under the pen-name le Pére Duchense. He launched a newspaper under the same name. He denounced the revolution for failing to help the poor and was executed in 1794. Who was he?
14. What did the Decree of 22nd Prairal intensify?
15. Why were Camille Desmoulins and Georges Danton executed?

**Answers to French Revolution V**

1. The bonnet rouge or red cap.
2. An Insurrectionary Commune. It challenged the legislative assembly and took control of the National Guard.
3. The National Convention.
4. Jean Paul Marat—a critical figure during the French Revolution, Marat was actually born in Boudry, Switzerland.
5. The Sans-culottes.
6. He was a general who together with Charles François Dumouriez led the French to victory over the Allies in the Battle of Valmy on the 20th September 1792.
7. Two months in the new Revolutionary Calendar, which was implemented on the 22nd September 1792. The Calendar was devised by Philippe Fabre d'Eglantine.
8. The 21st of January 1793.
9. Louis Capet—in reference to his ancestry.
10. The Vendée Region—over food shortages.
11. The defection of the General Dumouriez, who was closely associated with them. The Jacobins used this defection to discredit their rivals.

12. The Committee of Public Safety.
13. Jacques Hebert.
14. The Reign of Terror. It justified arrest on almost any pretext.
15. They incurred the wrath of Robespierre when they tried to reduce the hostilities of the reign of terror.

## 70. French Revolution VI

1. Who killed Marat?
2. Who massacred 16,000 Vendean prisoners by drowning them in the River Loire?
3. Who directed the public prosecution of Marie Antoinette?
4. Which political group was responsible for the 'White Terror'?
5. This Jacobin founder member used Napoleon to thwart a royalist coup in Paris on the 5th of June 1795. Who was he?
6. How many members made up the Directory?
7. This early Communist threatened the Directory in 1796 but failed. Who was he?
8. The 1795 Constitution provided for two legislative bodies. These were 'the Council of Ancients' and which other body?
9. Where (body part) did Robespierre injure himself when he attempted to commit suicide?
10. Which state religion was imposed in May 1794 to further support the revolution?
11. This famous revolutionary said, "What constitutes a revolution is the total destruction of things opposing it." Critical of moderation, he was a strong ally of Robespierre. Who was he?
12. Which right was restored in France in February 1795?
13. This moderate political club was set up in November 1795, but shutdown in February 1796 in a so-called suppression of the left. What was the name of the club?
14. What do Bentham, Cloots, Paine, Hamilton, Priestley, and Kosciuszko have in common?
15. This leading female revolutionary figure's last words were, "Liberty, what crimes are committed in your name." Who was she?

### Answers to French Revolution VI

1. The Girondist supporter Marie Charlotte Corday on the 13th of July 1793. Marat was sitting in a bath to relieve a skin condition which he had. Modern doctors reckon that the condition was most likely psoriatic arthritis.
2. Jean-Baptiste Carrier.
3. Antoine-Quentin—Fouquier-Tinville. She was charged on trumped-up testimony of having incestuous relations with her son, Louis XVII.
4. Royalists who massacred Jacobins after the fall of Robespierre in the West and South East of France.
5. Paul, Vicomte de Barras.
6. Five
7. François Babeuf. He would be guillotined in1797.
8. Council of Five Hundred.
9. He shot himself, injuring his jaw.
10. The Religion of the Supreme Being (aka Cult of the Supreme Being).
11. Louis Saint Just.
12. Freedom of Worship.
13. The Panthèon Club.
14. They were all made French Citizens by the National Assembly in an attempt to spread the appeal of the revolution outside France.
15. Madame Roland.

## 71. The Napoleonic Era I

1. Name three of Napoleon's four brothers?
2. What was the name of the Corsican revolutionary who rebelled against France in the 1760's?
3. Where was Napoleon's family originally from (ie. before they moved to Corsica)?
4. What military school did Napoleon attend at age nine?
5. Why did Napoleon's family flee to Marseilles?
6. In which area of the Army did Napoleon obtain his first commission?

7. In which revolutionary war battle in 1793 did Napoleon see action?
8. From which Caribbean Island were Josephine de Beaurharnais' family?
9. Why did Napoleon advance so quickly up the military ranks?
10. What was the name of the republic set up by the French in the Netherlands in 1795?
11. With which country did France sign The Treaty of Basle in 1795?
12. Whose navy mutinied at Spithead and Nore in 1797?
13. Which treaty followed the French defeat of the Austrians in 1797?
14. Which region of Italy existed as the Ligurian Republic between 1797-1805?
15. In which year was the Second Coalition set up against France?

## Answers to Napoleonic Era I

1. Joseph, Lucien, Louis and Jerome. He also had three sisters: Elisa, Pauline, and Caroline.
2. General Paoli—Napoleon's father Carlo was a lieutenant in Paoli's army.
3. Italy—of Florentine origin.
4. The Military Academy at Brienne. In 1784, at age 15, he would go to the Ecole Militaire.
5. They fled because Corsica fell into Brirish hands. The island would remain under British control until 1796.
6. Artillery, as a second lieutenant.
7. Battle of Toulon—it was the only battle of his career where Napoleon was significantly wounded.

   He was speared in the thigh by an English bayonet. Napoleon gained notoriety in this battle as he played a valuable role in breaking the English siege.
8. Martinique
9. There were many gaps in the hierarchy of the army that resulted from the Revolution's Reign of Terror. Many officers were either killed or had fled the country for political reasons.
10. The Batavian Republic. It would last until 1806.
11. Prussia

12. The British Navy.
13. The Treaty of Campo Formio.
14. Genoa
15. 1798

## 72. The Napoleonic Era II

1. Which Republic was set up by the French in Switzerland in 1798?
2. Who did Napoleon's forces defeat at Marengo in 1800?
3. Which position did Napoleon achieve in 1799?
4. What was the name of the Coup D'Etat that allowed him to reach the position mentioned in Question 3?
5. Who did Napoleon defeat at The Battle of the Pyramids?
6. Which Eastern countries fleet's took the Ionian Islands in 1798 and bombarded the Sicilian cities of Messina and Palermo shortly afterwards?
7. Why did Napoleon attack Egypt?
8. This Italian region existed for a time as the Parthenopean Republic. What was it known beforehand?
9. This man committed suicide after the failed Irish rebellion in 1798. Who was he?
10. Napoleon signed what type of agreement with Pope Pius VII in 1801 to re-establish the Roman Catholic Church in France?
11. Who was the loser in the Battles of Zurich, Trebbia and Novi?
12. Which treaty signed with Britain in 1802 ended the Revolutionary War?
13. By which other name is The Battle of the Nile (fought in 1798) known as?
14. Which Treaty ended the Holy Roman Empire?
15. Where was Napoleon crowned Emperor in 1804? Name the place and the city?

### Answers To Napoleonic Era II

1. The Helvetic Republic.

2. The Austrians.
3. First Consul (of three). He would be made First Consul for Life in 1802.
4. The Coup of the 18-19 Brumaire.
5. The Mamelukes in 1798.
6. The Russians using their Black Sea Fleet.
7. To threaten Britain's route to India.
8. Naples which existed within the Kingdom of Naples and Sicily. Sicily would gain independence from Naples in 1799.
9. Wolf Tone, the Rebellion's Leader. The French gave assistance to this rebellion.
10. A Concordat.
11. The French. They would be driven out of Italy whilst Napoleon was involved in Egypt.
12. The Treaty of Amiens.
13. The Battle of Aboukir Bay. Lord Nelson defeated the French fleet in this battle.
14. The Treaty of Lunéville signed in 1801 between France and Austria.
15. Paris in the Notre Dame Cathedral.

## 73. Napoleon Bonaparte III

1. At which city, that is also the birthplace of Albert Einstein, did France defeat Austria in 1805?
2. Which country did Napoleon make his brother Louis king of in 1806?
3. Which political unit replaced the Holy Roman Empire?
4. Which decree did Napoleon issue to usher in the economic blockade of England?
5. Who did the French defeat at The Battle of Friedland in 1807?
6. Which brother of Napoleon was made king of Spain in 1808?
7. Which war erupted in Spain in 1808 as a result of the brother mentioned in Question 6, being appointed king of Spain?
8. By which other name was the Battle of Austrelitz known as?
9. Which name was the anti-British economic front set up by Napoleon known as?

10. This indecisive battle between France and the Russian-Prussian forces was fought in 1807. Name the Battle?
11. What was the name of the treaty signed between France, Russia and Prussia on board a raft?
12. This Italian territory was annexed by Napoleon in 1809. What was it?
13. Which General led the French troops into Warsaw in 1806?
14. Who was the victorious general in the battles of Oporto and Talavera in 1809?
15. Where did the Portuguese Royal Family flee to when their country fell into French hands in 1807?

**Answers to Napoleon Bonaparte III**

1. Ulm, Germany.
2. Holland
3. The Confederation of the Rhine.
4. Berlin Decree.
5. The Russians.
6. Joseph, his eldest brother.
7. Peninsular War.
8. Battle of the Three Emperors (France, Austria and Russia).
9. The Continental System. It did not work as the British Navy was powerful enough to in turn block French or French-allied Ports. The British could also rely on their colonies for economic survival.
10. The Battle of Eylau.
11. The Treaty of Tilsit.
12. The Papal States. Pope Pius VII was taken prisoner.
13. Joachim Murat.
14. Arthur Wellesley (aka The Duke of Wellington).
15. Brazil

## 74. Napoleon Bonaparte IV

1. Who did Napoleon marry after divorcing Josephine?

2. This Northern South American country broke away from Spain in 1810. Which country was this?
3. Which country agreed to allow France free passage if France were to advance on Russia?
4. Which South-East Asian island did Britain occupy in 1811?
5. Andreas Hofer was executed in 1810. A fighter against Napoleon. What was his nationality?
6. Which general was executed in 1812 in an attempt to end the war with Russia and install Louis XVIII as king?
7. Who did Russia go to war with in 1808?
8. Which Caribbean country achieved independence from France in 1804?
9. With which country did Britain sign The Treaty of the Dardanelles in 1809?
10. He became King of Westphalia in 1807. Who was he?
11. This Congress was held in 1811. What was it called?
12. What did Napoleon suppress in 1807 to ensure his dictatorship?
13. This Order was created in 1802. What was it called?
14. He became Chief Minister of Austria in 1809. Who was he?
15. This was the year of the English Victory at the Battle of Trafalgar. What year was it?

## Answers to Napoleon Bonaparte IV

1. Marie Louisa.
2. Venezuela
3. Prussia
4. Java
5. Austrian
6. General Claude Malet.
7. Sweden
8. Haiti
9. Turkey
10. Jerome Bonaparte.
11. The Congress of Erfut.

12. Tribunate
13. Order of the Legion of Honour—Created by 'Nappy' himself.
14. Clemens Metternich.
15. 1805

## 75. Napoleon Bonaparte V

1. Who did Napoleon defeat at the Battle of Bordino?
2. Who was the losing party at The Battles of Jena and Auerstädt in 1809?
3. This Central European power fell into bankruptcy in 1811. Which power was this?
4. Who was the Duke of Reichstadt?
5. By the decree of Rambouillet, which non-European country's seized ships were ordered to be sold by the French?
6. Why did Napoleon invade Russia in 1812?
7. This Spanish city fell to the British forces in 1812. What was it?
8. To the closest 10,000 how many of Napoleon's Grand Army of 550,000 did not perish during the Russian campaign in 1812?
9. Which policy did the Russians follow that allowed them to defeat the French?
10. What was another name often associated with 'The Third Coalition'?
11. This 1813 Battle was also known as The Battle of Nations. What was it?
12. Who led the 3rd Army Corps during the Russian campaign?
13. This Russian defeated the French at Smolensk. Who was he?
14. This treaty followed The Battle of Wagram. What was it?
15. Why did Napoleon divorce Josephine?

### Answers to Napoleon Bonaparte V

1. The Russians.
2. Prussia
3. Austria
4. Napoleon's son, Napoléon François-Joseph Charles Bonaparte (aka The King of Rome).

5. The United States' ships.
6. To punish the Russians for not supporting his Continental System.
7. Madrid
8. 20,000
9. Scorched Earth Policy.
10. Grand Alliance.
11. Battle of Leipzig.
12. Marshal Ney.
13. Mikhail Kutuzov.
14. The Treaty of Schöbrunn.
15. She could not supply him with a male heir.

## 76. Napoleon Bonaparte VI

1. To which island was Napoleon exiled to in 1814?
2. What is the period from Napoleon's return from exile to his defeat in Waterloo known as?
3. Who led the Prussian forces at the Battle of Waterloo?
4. At which Battle prior to Waterloo did Napoleon defeat the Prussians?
5. Who led the Dutch forces at The Battle of Waterloo?
6. Which Western outpost did the French attack to start off The Battle of Watreloo?
7. Who were the Cuirassiers?
8. What was Napoleon's chief strategy at The Battle of Waterloo?
9. How did Wellington give his troops a significant advantage at Waterloo?
10. On what island did Napoleon die?
11. What was the name of the House on this island that he spent his last years?
12. A school of thought argues that Napoleon was poisoned with this chemical. What was the chemical?
13. Complete this Bonaparte quote, "Courage is like love, it must have hope to . . . ."
14. This was Napoleon's most common nickname. What was it?
15. Which country did Napoleon try to flee to after his defeat at Waterloo?

### Answers to Napoleon VI

1. The Island of Elba.
2. The Hundred Days.
3. Field-Marshal Blucher.
4. The Battle of Ligny (Blucher was almost killed in this battle).
5. Prince of Orange.
6. Hougoumont Farm (at the end of a battle, a barn on this farm was set alight killing both the French and British wounded who had been placed there.)
7. The French Cavalry.
8. To break the Anglo-Dutch line before the Prussians could arrive to strengthen it.
9. He placed them on a hill which had a 'reverse slope'. They were thus protected from the French. There was also a wooded area nearby, which could shelter his troops. Wellington had actually mapped out the area in 1814. Did he have some vision of the future? Nobody knows.
10. St. Helena in the South Atlantic.
11. Longwood House.
12. Arsenic—produced chemically under certain damp conditions by the green wallpaper of the house.
13. " . . . . nourish it".
14. The Little Corporal.
15. The United States—his route however was blocked by the British who he eventually surrendered to.

## 77. Guess Who—20th Century Figures

From the clues provided—pick the individual

1. Prime Minister of Israel 1963-1969.
2. Albania King deposed by Mussolini's forces.
3. Founder of the Protestant Unionist Party.
4. Speaker of the House before Newt Gingrich.

5. Politician and Visionary who took the helm of Singapore politics in 1959.
6. U.S. Financier and Philanthropist. He bought the near bankrupt Occidental Petroleum in 1961 and turned it into a major player in the Oil industry.
7. A social reformer and tireless worker on behalf of the poor. She formed Hull House in Chicago. She was later awarded the Nobel Peace Prize in 1931.
8. Ecuadorian President who was removed in 1997 because of mental instability.
9. Spanish cellist. Did wonders with the music of Bach.
10. American Actor and Director—founder of the Globe Trust—a project to rebuild Shakespeare's Globe Theatre.
11. German Grand Admiral. Encouraged building of submarines and capitol warships in the 1930s. He was dismissed in 1943 after disagreeing with Hitler.
12. Founder of McDonalds.
13. French Fashion designer known for her chemise dress and the collarless cardigan jacket.
14. He was the Liberal Leader and Prime Minister until he was ousted by Lloyd George in 1916.
15. This American took Olympic Gold in Archery in 1976.

## Answers to Guess Who 20th Century Figures

1. Levi Eshkol.
2. King Zog I.
3. Rev. Ian Paisley.
4. Tom Foley.
5. Lee Kwan Yew.
6. Armand Hammer.
7. Jane Addams.
8. Abdala Bucaram.
9. Pablo Casals.
10. Sam Wanamaker.

11. Erich Raeder.
12. Ray Kroc.
13. Coco Chanel.
14. Herbert Asquith.
15. Darrell Pace.

## 78. Playwrights

Given the play—identify the Playwright.

1. The Go-Between.
2. The Old Neighborhood.
3. The Phoenix on the Roof.
4. Hakon Jarl.
5. Doctor's Dilemma.
6. Day's Journey Into Night.
7. California Suite.
8. The Playboy of the Western World.
9. Et Dukkehjem.
10. Le Misanthrope.
11. Titus Andronicus.
12. Lady Windermere's Fan.
13. The Night of the Iguana.
14. The Children's Hour.
15. The Threepenny Opera.

### Answers to Playwrights

1. Harold Pinter.
2. David Mamet.
3. Eimar Ultan O'Duffy.
4. Adam Oehlenschläger.
5. George Bernard Shaw.
6. Eugene O'Neill.
7. Neil Simon.

8. John Synge.
9. Henrik Ibsen.
10. Molière (real name: Jean Baptiste Poquelin).
11. William Shakespeare.
12. Oscar Wilde.
13. Tennessee Williams.
14. Lilian Hellman.
15. Bertolt Brecht.

## 79. History of Chemistry I

1. Who is regarded as the Father of the Periodic Table?
2. In 1746, Andreas Margraf re-discovered a metal. What was this metal?
3. Who invented the reverse centigrade scale?
4. The Ancient Greeks said that the Four Elements were Earth, Air, Water and Fire. In 390 BC, Plato added a fifth element to this list. What was it?
5. Which element was discovered on the sun before it was discovered on Earth?
6. Which American has his name associated with the concept of 'Free Energy'?
7. Which noble gas was identified in 1894?
8. This French chemist isolated Fluorine. He also spent considerable time trying to convert graphite into diamonds. Who was he?
9. What is a REDOX reaction?
10. The name of these two scientists underline the definition of acids and bases. Who are they?
11. This Scientist showed that air was composed of two parts, an active part (oxygen) and an inactive part (nitrogen). Who was he?
12. This substance was the first organic chemical to be synthesized from an inorganic source. What was it?
13. In 1898, Pierre and Marie Curie separated two radioactive elements. What were they?
14. What chemical group lies alongside the nobel gases in the periodic table?

15. In 1898—a busy year in Chemistry, James Dewar produced the liquid form of a common gas. What was this gas?

### Answers to History of Chemistry I

1. Dmitri Mendeleyev.
2. zinc
3. Anders Celsius in 1742.
4. ether
5. helium
6. Josiah Gibbs, who besides being a pioneer in thermodynamics and phase changes, was also heavily involved in vector algebra.
7. argon
8. Ferdinand Moissan.
9. A reaction involving both reduction (gain of electrons) and oxidation (loss of electrons).
10. Johannes Bronsted and Thomas Lowry. Their definition states that an acid is a proton donor and a base is a proton acceptor.
11. Antoine Lavoisier.
13. urea
13. radium and polonium.
14. The halogens.
15. hydrogen

## 80. History of Chemistry II

1. This English Chemist has a law associated with partial pressures. Who was he?
2. This Chemist unraveled the ring structure of the Benzene molecule from a dream he had of snakes eating each other's tails. Who was he?
3. This father and son combination were jointly awarded the Nobel prize for their work in X-Ray diffraction. Who were they?
4. In 1913, Frederick Soddy coined a common term used to describe an element with several forms having different mass number. What was this term?

5. This 1914 Nobel Prize Winner and his team determined the atomic weight of 60 or so elements. He was well-known for his high level of accuracy. Who was he?
6. A political active leftist in politics, this 18th Century Chemist heated mercuric oxide in 1774 to produce a gas that would be later called 'oxygen'. Who was he?
7. Credit him with the discovery of neon (new), krypton (hidden) and xenon (strange) noble gases. Who was he?
8. What letter completes the following sequence: s, p, d . . . . ?
9. He determined protein's secondary Alpha Helix structure. Who was this American?
10. In 1866, Charles Hall developed a process to produce this useful metal. The method made use of a technique known as electrolytic action. What was this metal?
11. Who said "Equal volumes of all gases at the same temperature and pressure contain an equal number of molecules?"
12. What chicle based substance was developed by Thomas Adams in 1870?
13. This French Chemist, discovered a law outlining which of two reactions in equilibrium would be favoured under changing temperature and pressure conditions. Who was he?
14. The first synthetic dye, this substance was developed by William Perkin in 1856. What was it?
15. He is the father of the Frozen Food industry. Who is he?

## Answers to History of Chemistry II

1. John Dalton, who also described colour blindness (Daltonism) using observations taken from himself and his family, worked on the force of steam, the elasticity of vapours and the expansion of gases. In addition he developed an atomic theory to explain the laws of chemical combination and the conservation of mass.
2. August Kekule.
3. The Braggs (William the father and Lawrence the son). The prize was awarded for Physics, but X-Ray Diffraction has proved to be a valuable tool in chemistry.

4. An isotope.
5. Theodore Richards.
6. Joseph Priestley. Priestley can also be considered as the Father of the Fizzy Drink Industry. He found that gas produced from fermentation (carbon dioxide) created a pleasant drink called seltzer. Flavored seltzer is known now days as soda pop.
7. William Ramsay.
8. The letter 'f'. These letters describe the shape of an electron orbital around the nucleus.
9. Linus Pauling. He received a Nobel Prize in Chemistry in 1954 for his work, as well as a Nobel Peace Prize (1962) because of his opposition to Nuclear weapons, however in every day life he is more commonly associated as a champion of high Vitamin C dosage intake as a method of fighting the common cold or the flu.
10. aluminum
11. Amedeo Avogadro in 1811.
12. Chewing gum. It should however be noted that an earlier spruce based type of gum had been developed by John Curtis in 1848.
13. Henri le Chatelier.
14. aniline
15. Clarence Birdseye.

## 81. History of Chemistry III

1. Which Belgian-American is considered the Father of Plastics?
2. What active ingredient that goes into heavy water was isolated by Harold Urey?
3. This German-Swedish Chemist discovered several acids including uric acid, lactic acid, citric acid and tartaric acid. He also investigated the poisonous gases: hydrogen fluoride, hydrogen cyanide and hydrogen sulfide. The discovery of Chlorine must be credited to him as well. Who was he?
4. Who is regarded as the Father of Organic Chemistry?
5. What process involves the conversion of molten pig iron into steel by blowing air into it in a tilted converter?

6. This Frenchman derived a law to describe gas volume in a chemical reaction. In addition, he was also involved in the discovery of the element Boron. Who was he?
7. This element with an Atomic Number of 3 was discovered by Johan Arfvedson in 1817. What is it?
8. Used in photography, this chemical was also discovered in 1817?
9. This economically important element which falls in the same group as Carbon was discovered in 1824 by Jons Berzelius. What is it?
10. In 1823, Michael Faraday succeeded in liquefying this element that is in the same group as Fluorine and Iodine. What element is this?
11. This German proposed the modern view of catalysis as a surface phenomenon. He is considered the Father of Physical Chemistry. A Nobel Prize Winner in 1909, he did a great deal of work on Electrolytic Dissociation. Who was he?
12. Speaking of electrolytic dissociation, which Swedish Chemist was the first to establish the theory behind it?
13. What branch of Chemistry, associated with such a device as the Hydrogen fuel cell, is a direct offshoot of electrolytic dissociation?
14. This substance which consists of three atoms of oxygen was identified by Christian Schonbein in 1839. What is it?
15. This substance was invented by William Carothers in 1935. What was it?

**Answers to History of Chemistry III**

1. Leo Baekeland. He developed Bakelite, the first synthetic phenolic resin.
2. Deuterium
3. Carl Scheele.
4. Friederich Wohler.
5. The Bessemer process named after the Englishman, Henry Bessemer.
6. Joseph Gay-Lussac.
7. lithium
8. cadmium

9. silicon. Berzelius was the first to also identify cerium, selenium and thorium.
10. chlorine
11. Friederich Ostwald.
12. Svante Arrhenius.
13. Electrochemistry
14. ozone
15. nylon

## 82. Conspiracy Theory

1. What was the name given to a CIA project that used drugs to produce assassins that could be activated on demand?
2. What U.S. Government project is alleged to have brought numerous Nazi war criminals to America, many of whom it is claimed, acted as covert agents for the CIA?
3. Who did the CIA try to assassinate with an exploding cigar?
4. Which company, it is claimed, bought many railroad systems in the US only to shut them down?
5. What Secret Society was George Bush a member of during his Yale University years?
6. What two American brothers had an office in Berlin from which they conducted business with Hitler until well into the Second World War?
7. Which figure is seen as the evil mastermind behind the Hemp conspiracy?
8. What do conspiracy theorists argue that Sirhan Sirhan and James Earl Ray were not?
9. Why, according to conspiracy theory, was there an assassination attempt on George Wallace?
10. Who is supposed to be buried under Giants stadium?
11. Why was it so controversial that Allen Dulles was a member of the Warren Commission?
12. What did Dwight Eisenhower warn against before leaving office?
13. Who wrote *The Chariots of the Gods*?

14. Who gave his name to phenomena that are dismissed by Science because they are inconvenient to the prevailing philosophy of thought?
15. This name is often used to describe a secret organization or society who are controlling events from behind the scene and who work to control the human mind?

### Answers to Conspiracy Theory

1. MK Ultra.
2. Project Paper Clip.
3. Fidel Castro.
4. General Motors (GM).
5. The Skull and Bones Society.
6. The Dulles Brothers (Allen—a later head of the CIA and John Foster—Secretary of State under Eisenhower).
7. Randolph Hearst. It is claimed that he forced the Hemp industry to shutdown by driving to make it illegal in order to encourage people to use paper. Hearst owned numerous paper mills.
8. Lone Assassins. (The former is 'officially' recognized as the killer of Robert Kennedy, the latter of Martin Luther King).
9. It was masterminded by the 'right' to swing the vote in favor of Richard Nixon. An event that effected the critical 1968 election.
10. Jimmy Hoffa.
11. Allen Dulles had been dismissed earlier by John F. Kennedy as CIA Director for the failure of the Bay of Pigs Mission. Having Dulles on the Warren Commission, which investigated the death of Kennedy, was to many not only a conflict of interest, but a dangerous stumbling block to the elucidation of the truth. The right wing Dulles, who obviously was no fan of Kennedy, may have drastically affected the outcome of the Commission's ruling.
12. The growing Power in the U.S. of the Military Industrial Complex.
13. Erich von Daniken.
14. Charles Fort—What is described are Fortean phenomena such as Frogs raining from heaven or Unidentified Flying Objects.
15. Illuminati

# 83. U.S. Senators

Unravel the following cryptic clues concerning recent U.S. Senators and their home states.

1. This former actor is a Tennessee Senator.
2. Kentucky Senator. First name Wendell.
3. Conn—CD—Who is he?
4. William Cohen's old state.
5. The Microsoft Senator.
6. J.J. from V.
7. S.C.'s junior Senator.
8. State of Bob Graham.
9. KJH
10. He beat Alfonse D'Amoto to get into the Senate.
11. This state has a Senator whose last name is the same as a recent former chancellor of Germany.
12. State of Bryd and Rockerfeller.
13. Ted Steven's turf.
14. Opponent Dianne Feinstein beat to get into the Senate.
15. Both Senators here are Daniel K.

### Answers to U.S. Senators

1. Fred Thompson.
2. Wendell Ford.
3. Charles Dodd of Connecticut.
4. Maine.
5. Slade Gorton.
6. Jim Jeffords from Vermont.
7. Ernest Hollings.
8. Florida
9. Kay Jay Hutchinson, Texan Senator.
10. Charles Schumer.
11. Wisconsin—the Senator is Herb Kohl.

12. West Virginia.
13. Alaska
14. John Seymour.
15. Hawaii—Senators are Daniel K. Inouye and Daniel K. Akaka.

## 84. History of Evolution

1. This 16th Century German scholar is regarded as the Father of Geology. Who was he?
2. In to what two groups did John Ray divide all flowering plants?
3. Robert Hooke noticed these vital units of life, when viewing a slice of cork. What are they?
4. His most famous work was the Historie Naturelle, in which he described in 44 volumes everything known about the natural world. He also angered the church by suggesting that the planet was older than 6000 years. Who was he?
5. This Astronomer-Geophysicist brought together some of the missing pieces of evolutionary thought through his Theories of Plate Tectonics and Continental Drift?
6. This Philosopher-Economist contributed greatly to evolutionary thought by his studies on over-population. Who was he?
7. His rigorous defense of the Origin of the Species earned him the title 'Darwin's Bulldog'. Who was he?
8. What famous statement about Ontogeny was made by Ernst Haeckel?
9. This early evolutionist spoke about how species pass on acquired traits. Name the individual?
10. What was Charles Darwin's most single significant contribution to evolutionary thought?
11. This branch of evolutionary analysis is credited to Ernst Mayr. What is it?
12. In what area of evolutionary theory did Sewell Wright and Ronald Fisher both add to?
13. From what career did Darwin drop out of when he left the University of Edinburgh?

14. What was the first name of Charles Darwin's famous scientist grandfather?
15. What type of fossil is Mary Anning credited with discovering?

**Answer to the History of Evolution**

1. Georgius Agricola (or Georg Bauer). His greatest work was *De Re Metallica.*
2. Monocots and Dicots.
3. Plant cells.
4. Comte de Buffon.
5. Alfred Wegener.
6. Thomas Malthus.
7. Thomas Huxley.
8. Ontogeny recapitulates Phylogeny ie. during its embryonic development an organism passes through different stages of its evolutionary history. This is now thought to be a false theory.
9. Jean Baptiste-Lamarck.
10. The concept of Natural Selection.
11. Systematics (The study of Phylogeny and Classification).
12. Population genetics.
13. Medicine
14. Erasmus as in 'Erasmus' Darwin.
15. An ichthyosaur fossil.

## 85. General Sports History I

1. How many major golf titles has Jack Nicklaus won?
2. In which sport would you find the Thomas and Uber Cups?
3. Which three countries have won all of Rugby's World Cups?
4. In which sport is the Brier Cup contested?
5. In which country was the sport of Polo invented?
6. At which race track is the Italian F1 Grand Prix routinely held?
7. In which sport did Ivan Mauger make a name for himself?
8. In the triathalon, which event sometimes replaces the swimming segment?

9. In which sport is Tommi Makkinen a top competitor?
10. Which Champion golfer was known for dressing in black?
11. Which sport can claim Victor Barna as a Champion?
12. In which sport can you win with an Ipon?
13. Where is the Grand National run?
14. What was the nationality of the legendary cricketer Gary Sobers?
15. What is the length of the Le Mans endurance race?

**Answers to General Sports History I**

1. 18
2. Badminton
3. New Zealand (1987), Australia (1991 and 1999), and South Africa (1995).
4. Curling
5. India
6. Monza
7. Speedway
8. Canoeing
9. Rally Driving.
10. Gary Player.
11. Table Tennis.
12. Judo
13. Aintree in England.
14. He came from Barbados.
15. Twenty-four hours.

## 86. Poetry

Name the Poet/Poetess of the following works.

1. Sonnets from the Portuguese
2. Kubla Khan
3. The Colossus
4. Idylls of the King
5. North of Boston

6. Elegy written in a Country Churchyard
7. Don Juan
8. Les Illuminations
9. Os Lusiades
10. Celtic Twilight
11. The Excursion
12. Evangeline
13. Songs of Innocence
14. Divine Comedy
15. Le Grand Testament

**Answers to Poetry**

1. Elizabeth Barrett Browning.
2. Samuel Taylor Coleridge.
3. Sylvia Plath.
4. Alfred Tennyson.
5. Robert Frost.
6. Thomas Gray.
7. Lord George Byron.
8. Arthur Rimbaud.
9. Luis de Camões—The Greatest Portuguese Poet.
10. William Butler Yeats.
11. William Wordsworth.
12. Henry Wadsworth Longfellow.
13. William Blake.
14. Dante Aligheri—he was apparently inspired by a girl he never met—Beatrice Portinori.
15. François Villon.

## 87. Philosophical Concepts

Which Philosopher is most associated with the following concepts?

1. The Principle of the Best and Monads.

2. The Geometry of Philosophy.
3. "Conflict leading to the emergence of a classless society."
4. Knowledge is Power.
5. "Truth like morality is a relative affair."
6. The élan vital.
7. Deconstructionism
8. "Individuals can sin, but the true church, as an institution of God cannot."
9. "Entities are not to be multiplied without necessity."
10. The Dasein.
11. "Existence precedes Essence."
12. "Economic Freedom is the obvious & simple system of natural liberty."
13. "The chair exists because I am perceiving it so."
14. Sociology—The Science of society
15. The Essence of Experience

## Answers to Philosophical Concepts

1. Gottfried Leibniz.
2. Baruch Spinoza.
3. Karl Marx.
4. Francis Bacon.
5. Friedrich Nietzche.
6. Henri Bergson.
7. Jacques Derrida.
8. St. Augustine.
9. William of Occam (Qualified the 'Keep it Simple' rule of philosophy).
10. Martin Heidegger.
11. Jean-Paul Sartre.
12. Adam Smith.
13. George Berkley.
14. Auguste Comte.
15. Edmund Husserl.

# 88. Scandinavian History

1. Which people were the first inhabitants of Finland?
2. Which Swedish King conquered Finland in 1157, made it part of Sweden and converted the people to Christianity?
3. Which country was 'christianized' by Saint Ansgar and Harald Bluetooth during the 10th Century?
4. What massacre occurred in Sweden in 1520?
5. Who is regarded as the Father of the 'Modern Swedish State'?
6. What church doctrine was adopted in Sweden in the 1500's?
7. Which queen united Denmark, Sweden and Norway in 1397?
8. Which country was united with Denmark from 1380-1944?
9. Which set of islands won home rule from Denmark in 1948?
10. Which region became a territory of Denmark in 1953?
11. Why was property confiscated from the Swedish Catholic Church in the 16th Century?
12. Which Ancient Roman writer referred to Sweden in his famous work Germania?
13. What is the name of the Danish parliament?
14. Which country was ruled by Charles XIV between 1814 and 1844?
15. Which two parties dominate Norwegian politics?

### Answers to Scandinavian History

1. The Lapps or Sami people.
2. Eric IX.
3. Denmark
4. The Stockholm Bloodbath. Sweden was conquered by the Danes led by Christian II. He then went ahead and put many leading Swedes to death.
5. Gustavus Vasa.
6. Lutheranism
7. Queen Margrethe.
8. Iceland
9. The Faroe Islands.

10. Greenland
11. To pay for war debts.
12. Tacitus
13. The Folketing.
14. Sweden. He was Marshal Jean Bernadotte of France.
15. The Conservative and Labour Parties.

## 89. Pre-Human history

1. Place these five Periods in order starting with the oldest: Cretaceous, Silurian, Jurassic, Permian, and Devonian?
2. Into which two periods is the Carboniferous age traditionally broken down?
3. Beginning with an 'R', this advanced primate lived between 14 to 8 million years ago. What was it?
4. Which famous skull was shown to be a hoax in the 1950s?
5. Which famous Madagascar native animal is classified as a prosimian?
6. How many millions of years ago did the dinosaurs disappear?
7. If Protozoans are single-celled creatures, what name is given to multi-celled creatures?
8. Early reptiles were divided into the theocodonts (from which Dinosaurs evolved) and what other group (from which Mammals evolved)?
9. Where in Tanzania were the world's oldest footprints of man discovered?
10. What was roughly the brain-size of Australopithecus: 500cc, 800cc, or 1000cc?
11. Which species was known as 'Handy Man'?
12. Which species is thought to have been the first to make use of fire?
13. What is the name given to the great extinction 225 million years ago that lasted for 85 million years and is thought to have killed off two-thirds of all marine life, three-quarters of all amphibians, and four-fifths of all reptiles?
14. It is thought that the echinoderms and another group of which

humanity is part of diverged from one another just over 500 million years ago. What is this other group?

15. Which era are we living in presently?

**Answers to Pre-Human History**

1. Silurian, Devonian, Permian, Jurassic, Cretaceous.
2. Mississippian and Pennsylvanian.
3. Ramapithecus
4. The Piltdown skull.
5. The Lemur.
6. Sixty-five million years ago.
7. Metazoans
8. Therapsids
9. The Olduvai Gorge.
10. 500cc (no larger than that of a modern ape).
11. Homo Habilis.
12. Homo Erectus (Upright Man).
13. The Permian-Triassic Catastrophe.
14. The Chordates or Chordata ie. animals with a rod-like structure that supports the body.
15. Cenozoic

## 90. Early History of Man

1. Which period came to an end in 10,000 BC?
2. Which discovery of note was found in Willendorf, Austria?
3. Which continent gave birth to the Clovis Civilization?
4. Which two theories describe the origin of Modern Man?
5. What is the claim to fame of Altamira, Spain?
6. Which continent contains the 'Dyukhtai tradition'?
7. To the closest 10,000 years, what is the age of the oldest fossils of modern man?
8. Which age lasted between 2700-1900 BC?
9. Which animal was domesticated around 8000 BC?
10. What is the claim to fame of Bluefish, Alaska?

11. Which cereal was first cultivated in Asia in 8000 BC?
12. The Jomon Pottery tradition is associated with which country?
13. In which Southern European country did the Neanderthals finally go extinct?
14. To the closest 100 cc's, what is the average brain capacity of modern man?
15. Place these three cultural periods of modern European man in order, starting with the earliest: Gravettian, Magdalenian, and Aurignacian?

### Answers to the Early History of Man

1. The Ice Age.
2. A female figure with exaggerated sexual characteristics known as the Venus of Willendorf. It is thought to be a product of the Gravettian culture.
3. North America.
4. The Out of Africa Theory and The Parallel Evolution Theory.
5. It has cave paintings thought to originate some 14,000 years ago.
6. Asia, in particular, Northeast Asia.
7. Ninety-thousand years. The fossils were found in Qafzeh, Israel.
8. The Neolithic Age (of the Stone Age).
9. Goats
10. It is thought to be the first site of settlement by modern man in North America.
11. Rice along the Yangtze River.
12. Japan
13. Spain
14. 1400 cc. Neanderthal man had a brain capacity of 1500 cc.
15. Aurignacian, Gravettian, and Magdalenian.

## 91. Aviation History

1. These two brothers were the first to fly in a balloon?
2. Henri Giffard is most associated with this, a certain aeronautical vehicle. What is it?

3. What was the name of the first plane to achieve heavier-than-air machine flight?
4. How did Lt. Thomas E. Selfridge gain fame in 1908?
5. Who made the first airplane flight in Europe?
6. Who built and flew the first multi-engine aircraft?
7. What did Auguste Picard and Charles Knipfer succeed in achieving in a balloon in 1931?
8. How did one become a member of the Caterpillar club
9. Who navigated the first flight over the North Pole?
10. Who was the first person to fly around the world solo?
11. Who flew alone on a 15-hour flight between Harbour Grace, Newfoundland to Ireland in 1933?
12. Which airline first initiated passenger transatlantic airline service?
13. What was important about the *Gossamer Condor*?
14. Which airplane holds the speed record over a straight course and a closed circuit?
15. What type of transatlantic flight first took place in July 1952?

**Answers to Aviation History**

1. The Montgolfier brothers, Jacques and Joseph in 1783.
2. The First dirigible. A steam powered balloon that was inflated with coal gas and allowed him to reach a speed of 6.7 mph over Paris in 1852.
3. The Wright Brothers Flyer in 1903 at Kitty Hawk N.C. Flight time was 59 seconds.
4. Selfridge was the first airplane fatality. He and Orville Wright were up at 75 feet, when their propeller hit a bracing wire and broke. The plane spun out of control and Selfridge was killed and Wright was injured.
5. The Brazilian Alberto Santos-Dumont in 1906.
6. Igor Sikorsky whilst still in his native Russia. The year was 1913.
7. The first flight into the stratosphere.
8. In the early days of aviation, one became a member when one's life was saved by a parachute.

9. Richard Byrd in 1926. Byrd also headed the first team to fly over the South Pole.
10. Wiley Post in 1933. It took him 7 days, 18 hours, and 49.5 minutes.
11. Amelia Earhart,
12. BOAC
13. It was the first human-powered aircraft. It was designed by American Paul MacCready in 1977.
14. The Lockheed SR-71A. Both records were achieved in July 1976 at Beale AFB, California.
15. The first transatlantic flight using a helicopter.

## 92. Legal History

1. Which civilization is associated with Urukagina's Code?
2. In which country did the Laws of Manu play an important role?
3. Which Byzantine Emperor is associated with the Corpus Juris Civilis?
4. Which civilization is associated with the Book of Punishments?
5. Which European country had the first law school?
6. Which state's slave code became the model for the other American slave states?
7. Which country came out with a Bill of Rights in 1689?
8. In what respect did the Napoleonic Code differ most from English Common law?
9. Which Eastern country had a Seventeen Article Constitution?
10. Surname of the Englishman who in 1765 set about writing all of English common-law into four readable volumes?
11. Which Swiss City is associated with copyright law?
12. During which trial was it said, "The true test is not the existence of the (superior) order, but whether moral choice (in executing it) was in fact possible."
13. In the U.S., what does the 'EEOC' stand for?
14. What does Ceteris paribus mean?
15. This 1935 American Federal statute recognized employee rights to collective bargaining. What was the statute called?

**Answers to Legal History**

1. The Mesopotamians. This code indicated that the king was appointed by God and that citizens were allowed to know why they were punished.
2. India. It forms the basis of the caste system.
3. Justinian. Elements from this law can still be found in the laws of several Western countries.
4. China. It limited the types of punishments for certain crimes.
5. Italy in the city of Bologna.
6. South Carolina's.
7. England
8. The Code Napoleon is written, not judge made law.
9. Japan
10. Blackstone
11. Berne, signed in 1886 in Berne, the Convention for the Protection of Literary and Artistic works. It now includes most of the world's major trading powers.
12. The Nuremberg War Crimes Trials.
13. Equal Employment Opportunity Commission. It was created by Executive Order 10952 during the Kennedy era. This executive order was the first document to make use of the phrase 'affirmative action'.
14. All things being equal or unchanged.
15. The Wagner Act.

## 93. The Slave Trade

1. What ship was seized off of Long Island in 1839?
2. On which island was a slave rebellion brutally suppressed in 1831?
3. Which 1795 treaty between Spain and the U.S. would further augment the slave trade?
4. Which crown colony was set-up by Britain in 1808 as a home for freed slaves?

5. Which 1815 court case ruling hindered Britain's suppression of the slave trade?
6. What did the U.S. decline from participating in 1837?
7. Which painting by Turner created much revulsion against the slave trade in 1839?
8. Which American state banned slavery in 1777?
9. What did the American Colonization society espouse?
10. Which country abolished slavery in its' colonies in 1794?
11. Which abolitionist editor was murdered by an anti-abolitionist mob in Alton, Illinois in 1837?
12. Which American state received the first African slaves in 1619?
13. Which abolitionist was hired by the Massachusetts Anti-Slavery Society as a full-time lecturer in 1841?
14. Which was the last country in the Americas to abolish slavery?
15. In 1819, what did U.S. Law equate slave trading to?

## Answers to The Slave Trade

1. The Amistad.
2. Jamaica
3. Pickney's Treaty. It increased commerce between the U.S. and Spain.
4. Sierre Leone. Capital Freetown.
5. The Le Louis Case Ruling which indicated that British naval ships could not search foreign ships.
6. To participate with Britain and France in 1837 to create an international patrol to prevent Atlantic slave trading
7. The Slave Ship (aka Slavers Throwing Overboard the Dead and Dying—Typhoon Coming on).
8. Vermont
9. The return of slaves to Africa. The colony of Cape Mesurado (later Liberia) was set up in 1821 for this purpose.
10. France
11. Elijah Lovejoy.

12. Virginia. Ironically Virginia would have the largest abolitionist movement of all Southern states up until the Civil War.
13. Frederick Douglass.
14. Brazil in 1888.
15. Piracy—both were punishable by death.

## 94. History of Mathematics

Which Mathematician is most associated with the following accomplishments:

1. The Proof of Fermat's Last Theorem.
2. The invention of Logarithms.
3. The infinite and the theories of sets.
4. Publication of the Mécanique céleste.
5. The zeta function and the distribution of prime numbers.
6. Known as the founder of theory of functions of a complex variable.
7. Co-inventor of the Calculus with Isaac Newton.

Name the Mathematician from the clues given:

8. A genius in Group Theory. He was killed in a duel in 1832.
9. This German Polymath is associated with the Normal Distribution Curve and a Theory of Elliptic and Complex Functions.
10. A child from the poverty of India. He died in 1920 and did work in the fields of elliptic integrals, partitions and analytical number theory.
11. Together with his contemporary Blaise Pascal, he helped establish Probability Theory. Much of his work was communicated in letters. He was also active in the field of differential calculus and number theory.
12. 18th Century Swiss Mathematician. Totally blind in his later life, he used his effective memory to carry out complex calculations in his mind. His notation for '*e*' and '*pi*' have been used ever since. His most famous work was *Introductio in analysin infinitorum* (1748). He wrote later works on Integral and Differential Calculus.

13. Wrote *Fundamenta nova* in 1829. This German Mathematician was known for his work on Elliptic Functions. He also was involved in the fields of differential equations, number theory and determinants.
14. French Mathematician. His ideas have influenced topology, triangulation and homology. He wrote about chaos mathematics in an 1889 paper. He created the Theory of Automorphic Functions and was well-known in the fields of Physics, Mechanics and Astronomy.
15. This German Mathematician listed 23 problems, which he felt were important to Mathematics at the International Congress of 1900. Some of these problems have been solved whilst others still remain elusive. He died in 1943, having critically examined the basis of Geometry. He made numerous contributions to other areas of Mathematics, including the Theory of Invariants and Algebraic Geometry.

## Answers to History of Mathematics

1. Andrew Wiley.
2. John Napier.
3. Georg Cantor.
4. Pierre Laplace. He worked on the Gravitational Attraction of Spheroids. He formulated the Fundamental Differential Equation in Physics, which is named after him.
5. Bernhard Riemann.
6. Augustin Cauchy. He was also a leading figure in the development of Group Theory.
7. Gottfried Leibniz.
8. Evariste Galois.
9. Carl Gauss.
10. Srinivasa Ramanujan.
11. Pierre de Fermat.
12. Leonhard Euler.
13. Carl Jacobi.

14. Henri Poincaré.
15. David Hilbert.

## 95. History of Physics I

1. Who coined the term the 'Big Bang'?
2. In which field of Physics would you find the names of the following individuals: Weber, Gauss, and Tesla?
3. Which American was the Great Champion of Direct Current?
4. In Newton's Law of Gravitation, what is the relationship between the force of gravity and the distance between objects?
5. Who discovered the neutron?
6. For what work did Albert Einstein win his Nobel Prize in Physics?
7. Which Scottish Mathematician devised equations for Electromagnetic Radiation?
8. Which Scientist first determined the size of the Universal Gravitation Constant?
9. In which field would you speak of Balmer and Lyman Lines?
10. Who was the first to compare the reflection of light with that of sound waves?
11. Who, in witnessing a supernova, argued that the heavens are not changeless?
12. Which nearby galaxy was described by the Astronomer Al Razi?
13. Which optics invention did Roger Bacon focus on?
14. Newton's First Law of Motion defines a certain property of matter. What is it?
15. What type of particle accelerator was invented by Ernest Lawrence in 1929?

### Answers to History of Physics I

1. Fred Hoyle.
2. Electromagnetism
3. Thomas Edison.
4. The force of gravity varies inversely with respect to the square of the distance between the objects.

5. James Chadwick.
6. The Photoelectric Effect.
7. James Clerk Maxwell.
8. Henry Cavendish.
9. Spectroscopy
10. Leonardo Da Vinci.
11. Tycho Brahe.
12. The Andromeda Galaxy.
13. The Magnifying Lens.
14. Inertia—resistance to acceleration.
15. The cyclotron.

## 96. History of Physics II

1. Which one of these three phenomena cannot be attributed to 'Thales of Miletus': Prediction of an eclipse, defining of water as a base element, and the definition of the sun as a hot glowing rock?
2. Which of Heraclitus, Zeno, or Anaximander defined fire as a primary substance?
3. Who published, *A Corpuscular Theory of Light and Colour* in 1704?
4. Name the Italian Philosopher who in 1671 calculated accurately the distance to Mars?
5. Although more known in the world of Cartography, he argued in 1546 about the magnetic poles of Earth. Who was he?
6. How did Aristrachus of Samos determine the distance of the moon from Earth, as well as the size of the moon?
7. Which type of telescope did Galileo Galilei invent?
8. Which civilization described sunspots c. 170 BC?
9. Which English Scientist is regarded as the Father of Empiricism?
10. Which Danish Scientist discovered the Magnetic Field of an Electric Current?
11. Who invented the Electric Dynamo?
12. What is the most commonly talked about type of singularity?
13. Which Law of Physics argues that Load X load arm = Effort X Effort Arm?

14. Which Law of Physics argues that Force is proportional to the rate of change of momentum and the change of momentum is in the direction of the force?
15. True or False: Albert Einstein wrote about Brownian Motion?

**Answers to History of Physics II**

1. The definition of the sun as a hot glowing rock. This was the work of Anaxgoras. The same guy who said that the Sun, Moon, and Earth are all made of the same material.
2. Heraclitus. Zeno is noted for the paradoxes of discrete or continuous space and time. Anaximander argued that the Earth has a curved surface.
3. Isaac Newton. He was partially correct. Modern theory now argues that light has both a particle and wave nature.
4. Giovanni Cassini. Cassini also theorized that Saturn's rings were made up of small objects and that the rings are separated.
5. Gerardus Mercator—of the Mercator Projection fame.
6. He observed the Earth's shadow during a lunar eclipse.
7. The Refracting Telescope.
8. The Chinese.
9. Roger Bacon.
10. Hans Oersted.
11. Michael Faraday.
12. A Black Hole.
13. The Law of the Lever.
14. Newton's Second Law of motion which in formulaic terms translates to Force = Mass X Acceleration
15. True

## 97. History of Physics III

1. Of Democritus, Aristotle or Plato, who said that space is continuous and always filled with matter?
2. From which civilization was the Scientist who used a pinhole camera to prove that light travels in straight line?

3. Which substance was used by the Chinese in the first century for compasses?
4. In 1668, John Wallis spoke about the conservation of this entity, which is the product of mass and velocity. What is this entity?
5. Who invented the Mercury Barometer?
6. Which Frenchman invented a Mechanical Calculator in 1648?
7. Who said, "The distance of a falling object increases as the square of time?"
8. Which concept does Robert Hooke's famed law of 1676 deal with?
9. Which optical phenomenon did Isaac Newton use a prism to demonstrate?
10. What is the opposite of a vector?
11. Who, together with Michael Faraday, is regarded as 'The Father of Electromagnetic Induction'?
12. With which field of Physics do we associate Max Born?
13. Which law deals with the electrostatic force between two charged particles?
14. Which two entities were united by Hermann Minkowski?
15. In Albert Einstein's Special Theory of Relativity, what happens to mass as the speed of light is approached?

**Answers to History of Physics III**

1. Aristotle
2. He was an Arab. The Scientist was Ali Al-hazen.
3. Loadstone
4. Momentum
5. Evangelista Torricelli.
6. Blaise Pascal.
7. Galileo Galilei.
8. The Law of Elastics and Springs.
9. The Dispersion of Light.
10. A scalar. It has magnitude but no direction. A vector has both magnitude and direction.
11. Joseph Henry.
12. Quantum Mechanics.

13. Coulomb's Law.
14. Space and time in a geometrical sense.
15. It tends toward infinity.

## 98. History of Physics IV

1. Which substance did Gabriel Farenheit's 1709 thermometer make use of to indicate temperature?
2. Whose planetary laws were verified by Godfried Wendilin in 1626, with respect to the moons of Jupiter?
3. Name the Dutchman who is considered 'The Father of the Optical Telescope'?
4. From a famous scientific family, he helped develop the Kinetic Theory of Gas. Who was he?
5. Which of these concepts cannot be attributed to Gottfried Leibniz: The rejection of absolute time and space, first concepts of action, wave explanation of the refraction of light, and differential calculus?
6. What did William Cullen say about evaporation in 1756 with respect to heat?
7. During the 18th Century, Jean d'Alembert studied that property of a liquid that resists flow. Which property did he study?
8. Who was the first to notice that animals have electricity?
9. Which two entities did Mikhail Lomonosov identify the conservation of?
10. What is a Leyden jar used for?
11. This Englishman described the transmission of heat through a vacuum in 1798. He is more renowned however for his work on a miner's safety lamp. Who was he?
12. The Unit of Potential Difference is named after him. Who was he?
13. In which country was the metric system developed?
14. He gave his name to numbers used to describe galaxies. He also catalogued nebulae, in 1781. Who was he?
15. His law is defined by the equation: R=V/I. Who was he?

### Answers to History of Physics IV

1. Alcohol. His 1714 thermometer used mercury.
2. Johannes Kepler's Laws.
3. Hans Lippershey.
4. Daniel Bernoulli. His uncle was Jean Bernoulli, a giant in calculus. His father, Jean, was a pioneer in both Chemistry and differential equations.
5. The wave explanation of the refraction of light. This was the work of Ignace Pardies and later Leonard Euler.
6. That it causes cooling.
7. Viscosity
8. Luigi Galvani in 1771.
9. Mass and Energy.
10. The storage of electric charge.
11. Humphrey Davy.
12. Alessandro Volta. He invented the Chemical Battery.
13. In France around 1790.
14. Charles Messier.
15. Georg Ohm. The equation is of course Ohm's Law.

## 99. History of Physics V

1. He developed the Absolute Temperature Scale. Who was he?
2. This Swedish Scientist, who measured Hydrogen spectral lines, gave his name to a unit of wavelength. What is that unit?
3. He spoke about the Heat Death of the Universe. His initials were HVH. Who was he?
4. He identified Alpha and Beta radiation. Who was he?
5. Who discovered natural radioactivity in Uranium ore?
6. In 1908, he developed a counter for detecting radioactivity. Who was he?
7. He developed the concept of Light Quanta. Who was he?
8. Birth country of this Scientist who did the first determination of a radioactive half-life?

9. In 1917, he estimated the galaxy had a diameter of 100,000 parsces. Who was he?
10. He developed the Quantum Theory of Atomic Orbits. Who was he?
11. He is well-known for his 'Exclusion Principle'. Who was this quantum mechanics pioneer?
12. Which high frequency electromagnetic waves were re-discovered by Robert Millikan in the upper atmosphere in 1925?
13. He predicted the wave nature of particles. Who was he?
14. Although his name sounds French, this Englishman outlined the distinction between bosons and fermions. He also discussed the symmetry and anti-symmetry of wave function. Who was he?
15. These two scientists observed fission in 1934, the first was Otto Hahn who was the second?

**Answers to History of Physics V**

1. William Thomson or Lord Kelvin, hence the Kelvin Scale.
2. The Angstrom. The Scientist was Anders Angstrom.
3. Hermann von Helmholtz.
4. Ernest Rutherford.
5. Henri Becquerel.
6. Hans Geiger.
7. Max Planck.
8. New Zealand. The Scientist was Ernest Rutherford.
9. Harlow Shapley.
10. Niels Bohr.
11. Wolfgang Pauli.
12. Cosmic Waves.
13. Louis de Broglie.
14. Paul Dirac.
15. Enrico Fermi.

# 100. History of Boxing

1. Who wrote the rules on which Modern Boxing is based?
2. Which famous boxer's real name was Walker Smith?
3. What was the nickname of Tommy Hearns?
4. His nickname was 'Boom Boom'. Who was he?
5. Put the following boxers in chronological order (earliest to latest) taking into account the first time they won the World Heavyweight Crown: Joe Louis, Jack Dempsey, Gene Tunney, Floyd Patterson, and Ezzard Charles?
6. How many times did Mohammed Ali and Joe Frazier meet in the rink?
7. What does the IBF stand for?
8. Who did Cassius Clay/Muhammad Ali beat to win each of his three World Heavyweight Titles?
9. Who was South Africa's only heavyweight boxing champion?
10. Put the following divisions in order from lightest to heaviest weight: Bantamweight, Featherweight and Flyweight?
11. Which boxer ended Larry Holmes' unbeaten run?
12. Who is considered as Boxing's First Heavyweight Champion?
13. How did Rocky Marciano die?
14. This Panamanian fighter was probably Sugar Ray Leonard's greatest rival. Who was he?
15. Who dethroned Mike Tyson as Heavyweight Champion in 1990?

### Answers to Boxing History

1. Sir John Sholto Douglas, 8th Marquis of Queensberry.
2. Sugar Ray Robinson.
3. The Hitman or the Detroit Hitman.
4. Ray Mancini.
5. Jack Dempsey (1919), Gene Tunney (1926), Joe Louis (1937), Ezzard Charles (1949), and Floyd Patterson (1956).
6. Three times. Ali won two and lost one. The third fight was the renowned 'Thriller in Manila'.

7. International Boxing Federation. One of several governing bodies. The other governing bodies of boxing are the World Boxing Council (WBC), World Boxing Association (WBA), and the World Boxing Organization (WBO).
8. Sonny Liston (1964), George Foreman (1974), and Leon Spinks (1978).
9. Gerrie Coetzee (1983—WBA Champion).
10. Flyweight, Bantamweight, and Featherweight.
11. Michael Spinks.
12. John L Sullivan.
13. He was killed in a plane crash in 1969. Marciano fought 49 fights during his professional career, winning all of them (43 by knockout). He was nicknamed the 'Rock from Brockton'.
14. Roberto Duran.
15. James 'Buster' Douglas.

## 101. History of the Life Sciences I

1. Proponents of this now disproved theory argued that all life consisted of a critical essence. What were these proponents called?
2. Known scientifically as Abiogenesis. It was more commonly known as what?
3. In medieval Europe, which profession was also responsible for surgery?
4. This Swede is regarded as the Father of Biological Classification. Who was he?
5. This pair developed The Modern Cell Theory that states that 'the cell is the common structural and functional unit of all living organisms'. Who were they?
6. Medieval Europeans spoke of the four humors that controlled our moods and health. What are they?
7. He was the leading champion of 'animal magnetism'. Who was he?
8. Of what pseudo-science was Franz Gall a Practitioner?
9. What did Gregory Pincus, Min Chuch Chang, John Rock and Carl Djerassi develop in 1961?

10. What theory can be described by the following sentence, 'infectious diseases are caused by living agents transmitted from person to person'?
11. He was the first man to see bacteria. Who was he?
12. What bacterium did Robert Koch identify in 1883?
13. He was Father of the Aqualung. Who was he?
14. Which Frenchman was the leading advocate for comparative anatomy c. 1799-1805?
15. Also known as Epinephrine, it was discovered by John Abel in 1897. What is it?

**Answers to History of the Life Sciences I**

1. Vitalists. They believed that all of nature contained a vital force that gave it the essence of life.
2. Spontaneous Generation.
3. The Barbers. The Red and White pole often located outside barber shops symbolizes the bandages and blood of yester-year.
4. Carolus Linneaus.
5. Theodor Schwann and Matthias Schleiden.
6. Yellow Bile (choler—in excess it makes one angry), phlegm (in excess it makes one indifferent), Black Bile (in excess it makes one melancholic) and blood (in excess it makes one happy).
7. Anton Mesmer, a Hypnotist from whose name is derived the word 'mesmerize'.
8. Phrenology—the Science of examining the bumps on the skull to determine personality traits.
9. The first oral contraceptive.
10. The Contagion Theory as outlined by Girlolamo Fracastoro in 1546.
11. Anton von Leeuwenhoek in 1683.
12. The cholera bacterium.
13. Jacques-Yves Cousteau.
14. Georges Cuvier.
15. Adrenaline

## 102. History of the Life Sciences II

1. Francis Crick and James Watson showed in 1953 that DNA has what kind of structure?
2. Against which disease did the American Virologist, John F. Enders, develop a vaccine?
3. Who is considered to be the father of the Immunization Vaccination?
4. Who reduced the number of birth deaths by infection by encouraging the medical students to wash their hands prior to delivery and after they had finished an autopsy?
5. What is the modern name of the disease consumption?
6. In 1962, Thomas Weller developed a vaccine to protect pregnant women against which disease?
7. From which part of the pancreas did Frederick Banting and Charles Best isolate the hormone insulin in 1921?
8. Which pioneer in the field of Anesthetics once said, "A man laid on the operating table in one of our surgical hospitals is exposed to more chances of death than the English soldier on the field of Waterloo?"
9. What is the scientific name for the practice of cutting a hole in the head to treat an illness?
10. From the bark of which tree was aspirin derived?
11. Who is regarded as the Father of Germ Theory?
12. In 1897, the British Doctor, Ronald Ross, showed that malaria is transmitted by the female of which type of mosquito?
13. Who invented the Stethoscope?
14. Which 16th Century Doctor branded as a heretic in his time pioneered the use of Chemistry in Medicine? He also argued that small doses of what ever makes people ill could also cure them.
15. To what did George Papanicolaou give his name?

### Answer to the History of the Life Sciences II

1. A double helix structure.
2. Measles

3. Englishman, Edward Jenner, who developed a vaccine against smallpox in 1796.
4. The Hungarian Obstetrician Ignaz Semmelweis.
5. Tuberculosis
6. Rubella (German measles).
7. The Islets of Langerhans, named after their discoverer, the German Physician, Paul Langerhans.
8. James Simpson.
9. Trepanning or Trephining. Earliest reports of this practice go back to 5000 BC in Neolithic Germany.
10. The willow tree. The active chemical in the willow bark is salicin. It is believed today that the world consumes over 120 billion aspirin tablets per year.
11. Louis Pasteur.
12. The Anopheles Mosquito.
13. The French Doctor, Rene Laennec. Apparently, he invented it because he was too modest to put his ear up against a woman's chest to hear her heart beat.
14. Paracelsus
15. The pap smear, a technique used to examine exfoliated cells for the early detection of cervical and other forms of cancer.

## 103. History of the Life Sciences III

1. These two Scientists won a Nobel Prize in 1981 for their work in describing how the brain controls vision. Who were they?
2. What was invented in 1887 by A.E. Fick to assist the vision of a man with cancerous eyelids?
3. Who discovered the cure for syphilis?
4. What was the Spaniard Miguel Severetus' principle gift to the Life Sciences?
5. An account of the Foxglove (published in 1785), deals with which heart stimulating drug?
6. Which Englishman elucidated the nature of the Circulatory System?
7. What was the Roentgenoscope an earlier type of?

8. In 1984, a heart transplant took place at the Loma Linda Medical Center in California and a baby girl was given the heart of a baboon. By which name was this baby girl known?
9. What procedure developed in 1941 enabled doctors to more accurately measure the flow of blood in the lungs, the volume and pressure of blood in the heart, the pressure of blood flowing through a heart valve and the oxygen content of blood in the heart and major vessels?
10. Which cardiac diagnostic tool was developed by Mason Sones in 1958?
11. It is called the brain's engram, but what in reality is it?
12. In 1938, he published a book, *The Behaviour of Organisms.* Who was he?
13. Which Scientist in the 1920's evoked memories of epileptic patients by stimulating their brain's electrically?
14. Which drug originally developed in 1972 has the chemical name fluoxetine?
15. This drug was the first oral antihistamine to be sold over the counter. It offered relief from the symptoms of hayfever and became freely available in 1946. What was this drug?

### Answers to the History of Life Sciences III

1. David Hubel and Torsten Wiesel.
2. Contact lenses. Hard plastic lenses were invented in 1947 by Kevin Tuohy. Soft plastic lenses were invented in 1960 by O. Wichterle.
3. Paul Ehrlich. He would win the Nobel Prize for his work in 1908.
4. He discovered pulmonary circulation ie. he accurately described the flow of blood between the lungs and the heart. For his efforts in contradicting religious orthodoxy, he was burned at the stake in 1553.
5. Digitalis (named after the digit like flowers of the plant).
6. William Harvey.
7. X-ray machine.
8. Baby Fae.

9. Catheterization, developed by the American Cardiologists A. Cournand and D.W. Richards.
10. Coronary angiography.
11. The brain's permanent traces of memory.
12. B.F. Skinner of the Skinner Box Fame.
13. The Neurosurgeon, Wilder Penfield.
14. Prozac
15. Benadryl

## 104. History of the Life Sciences IV

1. What was the first virus to be implicated in human cancer?
2. Which anti-virus protein compound was shown by Israeli doctors to be successful in treating hepatitis?
3. What does the acronym 'MAB' stand for in medical terms?
4. In what animal was Mycobacterium leprae (the bacterium that causes leprosy) grown to provide sufficient quantities to make the first vaccine?
5. Who was the first test tube baby?
6. What is the primary use of the drug Cyclosporin A, which was developed in the late 1970s?
7. Which deadly disease broke out in Northern Africa and Southern Sudan in 1977? It is related to the green monkey disease that erupted in Marburg, Germany in 1968.
8. This neurotransmitter was thought by Cambridge University scientists in the mid 70's to be related to the cause of schizophrenia?
9. Which type of ulcer was shown to be preventable by the usage of the drug Cimetidine (Tagamet)?
10. Which metal did Professor Derek Bryce Smith argue in 1974 might result in behaviour disturbances and irrational violence, even if it is only present in trace amounts?
11. Invented in 1972, the CAT Scan has proved to be invaluable in medical diagnostics. What does the acronym stand for?
12. Which important growth hormone, that can be used to treat pituitary dwarfism in children, was synthesized by Choh Hao Li?

13. What important life molecule was shown by Dr. Max Perutz to be made up of four chains?
14. Which Central Nervous System disease broke out amongst American GI's in 1968?
15. Discovered in 1967, to which group of sufferers did the drug Intal offer relief to?

## Answers to the History of the Life Sciences IV

1. The Epstein Barr Virus present in Burkitt's Lymphoma, a highly malignant cancer found in African children.
2. Interferon
3. Monoclonal antibody. These are antibodies that are used to react to specific agents in the body. They can be used to detect the presence of infectious diseases and cancer at an early stage.
4. Believe it or not, the nine banded armadillo. Credit for such insight should go to the English Scientist, Dick Rees, at the National Institute for Medical Research in London.
5. Louise Brown, born in 1978.
6. It is an immunosuppressive drug that is nonsteroidal. It is used to fight transplant rejection and removes the need for long term steroid treatment which has many side effects.
7. Lassa Fever.
8. Dopamine
9. The peptic ulcer.
10. Lead. Another Scientist, Henry Warrem, of British Columbia would later link the metal to both higher than normal rates of still births and incidences of multiple sclerosis.
11. CAT—Computerized Axial Tomography.
12. Somatotrophin
13. Hemoglobin
14. Meningitis
15. Asthmatics (as an Asthmatic myself, I am ever thankful for such drugs).

## 105. History of the Life Sciences V

1. Who was the first man to receive a heart transplant?
2. Which three-letter acronym indicates the common tuberculosis vaccine?
3. Which popular pain-killer was shown in 1966 to cause liver damage in certain cases?
4. Which renal treatment offering the patient more personal freedom was developed in 1964?
5. Which world famous Houston Surgeon was the first to graft a length of the artificial material Dacron to replace a diseased section of the aorta?
6. Which widely used tranquilizer drug was introduced in 1963?
7. What disease was reduced by injecting anti-rhesus serum from Rhesus negative mothers, following delivery of a first baby?
8. Which diagnostic technique was pioneered by Dr. Ian Donald in 1958?
9. Introduced in 1956, which type of drug was halothane?
10. Which common treatment of premature babies was later shown to cause blindness?
11. Which congenital defect is often treated with the Holtzer shunt?
12. Which technique was developed by Solomon Berson and Rosalyn Yalow to detect low amounts of hormones?
13. Which two pituitary hormones were synthesized by Vincent de Vigneud in 1954? Hint: The one hormone raises blood pressure and stimulates the kidney to retrain water and the other causes the uterine muscles to contract during childbirth.
14. Which was the first organ ever to be used in a human transplant?
15. Which fetal diagnostic tool was developed by Douglas Bevis in 1952?

### Answers to History of the Life Sciences V

1. Louis Washkansky. He received the heart of a 24-year-old woman who had died in a traffic accident. The operation was performed

by South African Surgeon, Christian Barnard, in Cape Town. He lived for 18 days following this operation.

2. BCG. The vaccine was shown to not only be effective against tuberculosis, but against leprosy as well.
3. Paracetamol
4. Home dialysis.
5. Michael DeBakey.
6. Valium. It was also marketed for its muscle-relaxant and anti-convulsant action.
7. Hemolytic disease of the newborn.
8. Ultrasound
9. An Anaesthetic. It is potent, easily manageable, and non-flammable.
10. The treatment of the babies at birth with high doses of oxygen.
11. Hydrocephalus
12. The Radio-Immuno Assay. This technique tags elusive chemicals with radio-isotopes. The invention marked a great breakthrough in the fight against hormonal disorders.
13. Vasopressin and oxytocin.
14. The kidney, first transplanted in 1953.
15. Amniocentesis

## 106. History of the Life Sciences VI

1. Which machine revolutionized modern heart surgery?
2. To fight against which type of cancer was the drug Methotrexate introduced?
3. Which cellular body discovered in the early 50's would later be used in tests for distinguishing sex?
4. For which purpose was Methadone introduced on the market?
5. Who wrote, *The Common Sense Book of Baby and Child Care*?
6. What dangerous First World War gas was later used to treat Hodgkin's Disease?
7. What biochemical technique that involves separating amino acids of a protein using a solvent was developed by A.J.P. Martin and R.L.M. Synge in 1952?

8. What controversial chemical brought to a halt the 1944 Typhus Epidemic in Italy?
9. Which chemical compound isolated from microscopic soil fungus by Selman Waksman in 1942 was the first real cure for tuberculosis?
10. Which type of disease is Leishmaniasis?
11. Who was the third member of the team of Howard Florey and Ernst Chain?
12. In 1939, these two Scientists Hendrik Dam and Edward Doisy isolated a vitamin that is essential for clotting. What is this vitamin?
13. Which neurological technique goes by the acronym ECT?
14. Which organic acid that prevents blood clotting was first used in 1929 to prevent thrombosis in the veins?
15. Which Zoologist established that it is the chromosome that carries hereditary traits?

## Answers to History of the Life Sciences VI

1. The Heart-Lung Machine.
2. Uterine cancer, in particular the chorion carcinoma.
3. The Barr Body discovered by Murray Barr.
4. As a painkiller equal in strength to Morphine. Its' use as a treatment for Morphine and Heroin addicts would only come later.
5. Dr. Benjamin Spock.
6. Mustard Gas.
7. Paper chromatography.
8. DDT—it killed the lice that carry the pathogen.
9. Streptomycin
10. A parasitic disease. The insect carrier of the parasite is the sandfly.
11. Alexander Fleming—the three isolated the drug from the Penicillum notarum mould.
12. Vitamin K.
13. ECT stands for electro-convulsive treatment. This technique was developed by the two Italian doctors, Ugo Cerletti and Lucio Bini, to treat the symptoms of schizophrenia.
14. Heparin
15. Thomas Hunt Morgan.

## 107. History of the Life Sciences VII

1. Which surgical tool patented in 1915 by its 23-year-old Inventor, Morgan Parker, revolutionized Surgery?
2. Which disease, first identified in 1934, can now be detected in newborn infants by a blood test and successfully treated? Left alone, it can lead to mental retardation.
3. Which now common Anaesthetic was popularized by J.S. Lundy in the mid 1930's?
4. First performed in 1933 by Evarts Graham, what is a pneumonectomy?
5. Which device, developed in 1932, allowed for better diagnosis of gastrointestinal problems?
6. The deficiency of which vitamin was shown in 1925 to cause night-blindness?
7. Which high protein crop was gathered for the first time in the U.S. by a combine harvester in 1924?
8. Against which disease did Gaston Ramon develop a vaccine in 1923?
9. Which disease took over from tuberculosis as the leading cause of death in the U.S. c. 1921?
10. Which country was the first to legalize abortion?
11. Which membrane around the heart did Ludwig Rehn remove from a patient in 1920 to allow the heart room to work?
12. Which leg disease did many soldiers suffer from during the First World War?
13. Which hormone, whose insufficiency causes hypothyroidism, was isolated by Edward Kendall at the Mayo Clinic in 1914?
14. Against which disease did Bela Schick develop a test to determine susceptibility?
15. Which substance was discovered by Frank Woodbury in 1910 to be a very effective surgical disinfectant and antiseptic?

### Answers to the History of the Life Sciences VII

1. The Disposable Scalpel.
2. Phenylketonuria
3. Sodium pentothal.
4. The removal of a diseased lung.
5. The semi-flexible gastroscope.
6. Vitamin A.
7. Soybeans
8. Tetanus
9. Heart disease.
10. Russia in 1920.
11. The pericardium. The operation is carried out to alleviate those suffering from constrictive pericarditis.
12. Trench Foot. It is caused by standing for long periods of time in water using footwear which restricts the blood supply. If not treated the condition can lead to gangarene.
13. Thyroxin
14. Diphtheria. This test was of course the Schick test.
15. Iodine

## 108. Space Exploration I

1. What was the name of the U.S.'s first human-in-space project?
2. In which capsule did Alan Shepard Jr. make a suborbital flight in 1961?
3. Which planet was targeted by the Viking missions?
4. What was the first space vehicle to reach the moon?
5. Why was the Space Probe Giotto sent up in 1986?
6. What is the claim to fame of Vostok 3 and Vostok 4?
7. Who was the first person to walk in space?
8. How did Virgil Grissom, Edward White, and Roger Chaffee die in 1967?
9. Which year did Valentina Tereshkova become the first woman in space?

10. Who was the first American to walk in space?
11. Which planet did Venera 5 explore in 1969?
12. On December 6, 1958, Pioneer 3 discovered which part of the Earth's atmosphere?
13. Which astronaut is missing from this Group of Seven: Scott Carpenter, Gordon Cooper Jr., John Glenn Jr., Virgil Grissom, Walter Schirra Jr., and Alan Shepard Jr.?
14. Which ship made the first manned flight round the moon?
15. Who were the pilots of the First Space Shuttle Mission in 1981?

**Answers to Space Exploration I**

1. Project Mercury.
2. Freedom 7
3. Mars. There were 2 Viking Missions.
4. The Russian Ship—Luna 2. It collided with the moon on September 14, 1959.
5. To study Halley's Comet. It was a European Space Agency Probe.
6. In 1962, they became the first simultaneous space flights.
7. The Russian, Alexei Leonov, in 1965.
8. During a practice countdown for Apollo 1, the cockpit they were in caught fire.
9. 1963 (June 16th) aboard Vostok 6.
10. Edward White on June 3, 1965. His ship was Gemini 4.
11. Venus
12. The Outer Van Allen Belts.
13. Donald Slayton. There were the original Seven Mercury Astronauts.
14. Apollo 8.
15. John Young and Robert Crippen aboard the Space Shuttle Columbia.

## 109. Space Exploration II

1. What was the name of the First Space Station launched?
2. What was the date (day, month, year) of the First-manned moon landing?

3. Which two ships took part in the first international space docking between July 16-18, 1975?
4. Who captained the ill-fated Apollo 13?
5. What U.S. Space Project immediately preceded the Apollo Project?
6. Who was the first woman to pilot a Space shuttle?
7. Which space shuttle was built to replace the Challenger?
8. With which space station did the Space Shuttle Atlantis link up with in 1995?
9. What crashed onto earth on July 11, 1979?
10. On which body was frozen water found at the North and South Poles in 1998?
11. Which planet is targeted by the Galileo missions?
12. In which year was the Deep Space Probe Voyager 2 launched?
13. What was the last Apollo mission?
14. In which year did Sally Ride become the first American woman to go up in space?
15. What was significant about Soyuz 4 and Soyuz 5 in 1969?

**Answers to Space Exploration II**

1. Salyut I. It was manned for 23 days, however all three of its crew, Georgi Dobrovolsky, Victor Patseyev, and Vladislav Volkov were killed on the return flight home in Soyuz 11.
2. July 21, 1969.
3. Soyuz 19 and Apollo 18.
4. James Lowell Jr.
5. The Gemini Project.
6. Eileen Collins. She also later became the first woman to command a Space Shuttle in July 1999.
7. The Endeavour.
8. The Mir.
9. Skylab. It landed in parts of Australia and the Indian Ocean.
10. On the moon by Lunar Prospector.
11. Jupiter
12. 1977 (on August 20$^{th}$).

13. Apollo 17 in 1972.
14. 1983. Twenty years or so after the first Russian woman, Valentina Tereshkova.
15. The first transfer of crew members from one spacecraft to another took place between these vessels on January 16, 1969.

## 110. History of Psychiatry and Psychology

1. Who is regarded as the founder of Psychology?
2. Who argued that emotions were caused by physical changes in the body ie. we feel sorry because we cry not the other way around?
3. Who is the Father of the IQ Test?
4. Which university adapted the IQ Test for use in the English world?
5. Who pioneered the long term study of gifted children?
6. Into which three parts did Sigmund Freud divide human personality?
7. This Scientist developed the concept of the inferiority complex, who was he?
8. Which School of Psychology argues that behaviour and experience must be treated as a whole rather than as a collection of specific patterns or response to stimuli?
9. Who is the Father of the School of Behaviourism?
10. What is defined as an inherited part of the unconscious mind found in all members of a race or species?
11. Who developed the concept of the Personality Types: extrovert and introvert?
12. What was the name of Sir Frederic Bartlett's 1932 book in which he showed that a person tends to remember things that fit into his existing system of knowledge?
13. Which female disciple of Sigmund Freud became the first to use the content and style of children's play to understand their mental process?
14. This Psychologist was known for his work on Motivation. His most famous works were *Escape From Freedom* and *The Sane Society*. Who was he?
15. This Psychologist introduced such concepts as the need hierarchy,

self-actualization and peak experience. Who was he?

### Answer to History of Psychiatry and Psychology

1. Wilhelm Wundt. He set up the first experimental laboratory in 1879. His actions helped separate the discipline from its mother field of Philosophy.
2. William James.
3. Alfred Binet.
4. Stanford University.
5. Lewis Terman.
6. The id, the ego, and the super-ego.
7. Alfred Adler. He founded the School of Individual Psychology.
8. The Gestalt School.
9. John Watson.
10. The collective unconscious.
11. Carl Jung.
12. Remembering
13. Melanie Klein.
14. Erich Fromm.
15. Abraham Maslow. The founder of Humanistic Psychology.

## 111. Baseball History

1. How many career home runs did Hank Aaron hit?
2. Which player holds the record for the most games played?
3. Which pitcher has won the Cy Young Title the most times?
4. How many World Series have the New York Yankees won as of December 2000?
5. Who pitched a perfect game on July 18, 1999?
6. With which team did Connie Mack make a name for himself as manager?
7. In which city did the Braves franchise start out?
8. What was the nickname of Mordechai Brown?
9. When did the Cleveland Indians last win the World Series?

10. Which team has won the World Series the most times out of all National League teams?
11. Who was known as the 'Splendid Splinter'?
12. With which team did Harmon Killebrew win the Home Run Championship five times?
13. Who managed the Miracle Mets?
14. With which two teams did Sparky Anderson win World Series Championships as a manager?
15. What was the nickname of pitcher 'Charles Ruffing'?

**Answers to Baseball History**

1. 755
2. Pete Rose at 3562.
3. Roger Clemens.
4. Twenty-six.
5. David Cone.
6. Philadelphia Athletics.
7. Boston
8. As a pitcher, he was known as, 'Three-Finger Brown'. Despite his handicap, he managed a fantastic career ERA of 2.06.
9. In 1948. They beat the Boston Braves 4-2.
10. The St. Louis Cardinals with 9 wins out of 15 finals.
11. Ted Williams.
12. Minnesota Twins.
13. Gil Hodges.
14. The Cincinatti Reds in 1975 and 1976 and the Detroit Tigers in 1984.
15. Red as in Red Ruffing.

## 112. Saints

1. What are the three stages involved in conferring Sainthood?
2. Which pope has canonized more saints than any other?
3. What day is the Feast Day of John the Baptist?

4. Which saint's real name was Simon Bar Jona?
5. Who is regarded as the first Christian Martyr?
6. Who is known as the Apostle of India?
7. What is rumored to have sprung up when St. Paul was beheaded?
8. Which Saint was throne into the sea with an anchor around his neck?
9. Who is the Patron Saint of mothers and infertile women?
10. Which Saint was grilled over hot coals?
11. Who is the boy Saint who is often invoked against epilepsy?
12. If you have a throat ailment you might invoke this saint. Who is this saint?
13. Who is the Patron Saint of travelers?
14. Who is the Patron Saint of Norway? His symbol is a battle-axe.
15. Who is the Patron Saint of animals?

**Answers to Saints**

1. Veneration, beatification, and canonization.
2. Pope John Paul II.
3. June 24th.
4. St. Peter.
5. St. Stephen.
6. St. Bartholomew.
7. Three fountains.
8. St. Clement.
9. St. Felicity.
10. St. Lawrence.
11. St. Vitus.
12. St. Blaise.
13. St. Christopher.
14. St. Olaf.
15. St. Francis of Assisi.

# 113. History of Tennis

1. He was the last Englishman to have won the Wimbledon Singles title. Who was he?
2. At which Stadium is the French Open played?
3. Before Michael Chang won the French Open in 1989, who was the last American player to have won it?
4. Put the following players in order from least to most with respect to the number of Grand Slam Singles Titles won: Bjorn Borg, Jimmy Connors, Bill Tilden, Pete Sampras, and Roy Emerson?
5. In which country was John McEnroe born?
6. Which modern doubles pairing is considered to be the greatest of all time, in terms of money and Grand Slams won?
7. Who did Bjorn Borg defeat in 1979 to win his fourth Wimbledon singles title?
8. What is the nationality of the following players: Raul Ramirez, Stefan Edberg, Dick Savitt, Guillermo Vilas, and Lew Hoad ?
9. Who is the all time Grand Slam Women's Singles Title Winner?
10. Who is the youngest Men's Wimbledon Singles Champion ever?
11. How many Wimbledon Singles Titles were won by Martina Navratilova?
12. What is the nationality of the following players: Sue Barker, Manuela Maleeva, Conchita Martinez, Gabriela Sabatini, and Betty Stove?
13. Who did Billie Jean King beat in 1973's Battle of the Sexes?
14. What is the Female version of The Davis Cup?
15. Who has won more Grand Slam Singles Titles: Chris Evert or Martina Navratilova?

### Answers to History of Tennis

1. Fred Perry. Perry won the Wimbledon title three years running from 1934-1936. He also was a Champion Table Tennis Player. In later years, he became a U.S. Citizen.
2. Roland Garros Stadium in Paris.
3. Tony Trabert in 1955.

4. Jimmy Connors (8), Bill Tilden (10), Bjorn Borg (11), Roy Emerson (12), and Pete Sampras (13 and counting).
5. A great trivia question—the answer is West Germany, now of course just plain Germany
6. Todd Woodbridge and Mark Woodforde of Australia.
7. The hard hitting Texan, Roscoe Tanner.
8. Ramirez—Mexican, Edberg—Swedish, Savitt—American, Vilas—Argentinian, Hoad—Australian.
   Give yourself 1 point if you got four or more of these correct.
9. Margaret Court. Twenty-four altogether, including 10 Australian titles.
10. Boris Becker.
11. Nine (1978-1979, 1982-1987, and 1990).
12. Barker—British, Maleeva—Bulgarian, Martinez—Spanish, Sabatini—Argentinian, Stove—Dutch.
    Give yourself 1 point if you got 4 or more of these correct.
13. Bobby Riggs.
14. Federation Cup—A tournament played between different nation states.
15. Neither. They are both tied with 18 Grand Slam Singles Titles.

## 114. Track and Field

1. Which of these is not an Olympic event for men: 200m, 400m, 800m, 1000m, 3000m, 10000m?
2. How many Gold Medals in discus throwing were won by the American, Al Oerter?
3. With which sport do we associate the Czech Jan Zelezny?
4. Which new Field Sport was introduced into the Women's Program at the 1996 Olympic Games?
5. Which two events were won by the French Athlete, Marie-Jose Perec, at the 1996 Olympic Games?
6. Which three distances do Athletes compete for in the Men's Walking Program?
7. Who was the last man to win back-to-back Olympic Marathon Titles?

8. In which Olympics did Emil Zatopek immortalize himself?
9. Which American woman won the 100m and 200m in the 1960 Olympics?
10. Which nationality was the Olympic Champion, Fanny Blankers-Koen?
11. Which 1988 winner of the Women's Olympic Long Jump is widely regarded as the Greatest Female Athlete of all-time?
12. With which event would you associate the American, Robert Mathias?
13. How heavy is the hammer thrown in the men's event?
14. Between 1900 and 1908, he dominated the now defunct Standing High Jump. Who was he?
15. How many Olympic Gold Medals has Carl Lewis won in his career?

## Answers to Track and Field

1. 1000m and 3000m.
2. Four golds. In the Olympics between 1956 and 1968.
3. Javelin Throwing. He has won the Gold Medal in 1992, 1996, and 2000.
4. The Triple Jump. The First Gold Medal was won by Inessa Kravets of the Ukraine.
5. The 200 and 400 meter dashes.
6. 10km, 20km and 50km walks.
7. Walter Cierpinski in 1976 and 1980, running for East Germany.
8. In the 1952 Games in Helsinki. Zatopek won the 5000m, 10000m, and the Marathon?
9. Wilma Rudolph.
10. She was Dutch. Koen won Gold in the 100m, 200m, and 80m hurdle races in the 1948 London Olympics.
11. Jackie Joyner Kersee, who also won the 1988 Pentathlon and the 1992 Heptathlon.
12. The Decathlon. He won it in the 1948 and 1952 Olympic Games.
13. 16 lbs.
14. Ray Ewry.

15. Two in the 100m (1984 and 1988), four in the Long Jump (1984, 1988, 1992 and 1996), two in the 4 x 100 Relay (1984 and 1992), and one Gold in the 200m (1984), for a grand total of nine. He also won the silver in the 1988 200m dash.

## 115. Olympic Games

1. Place the Following Summer Olympic Games in order of earliest to latest: Amsterdam, Helsinki, Antwerp, Stockholm, Rome, and Melbourne?
2. Who was the first ever winner of the Men's 50-meter Freestyle Swimming Event?
3. How many Gold Medals did the Finn Paavo Nurmi win in his Olympic career?
4. Between 1956 and 1980, the Soviet Union finished first in number of medals won in each of the Summer Olympics, except for one Olympic Games. Which one was this?
5. Who was the last white Athlete to win the 100m sprint?
6. Which two Americans gave the Black Power salute at the 1968 Olympic Games?
7. At which Olympic Games did Olga Korbut make a name for herself?
8. Who was known as the Flying Finn?
9. Why did many African countries boycott the 1976 Summer Olympic Games?
10. Which athlete was known as the 'Horse'?
11. He won the Men's Slalom, Giant Slalom, and Downhill in 1968. Who was he?
12. These two competed in figure skating at 'The Battle of the Brians' in Calgary in 1988. Who were they?
13. What was the nation of origin of Sonja Henie who won the Women's Figure Skating Olympic Championship in 1928, 1932, and 1936?
14. Place the following Winter Olympic Games in the order they occurred (earliest to latest): Sapporo, Chamonix, Squaw Valley, Grenoble, and Cortina d'Ampezzo?

15. How many 500m and 1000m Speed Skating Olympic Gold Medals has Bonnie Blair won?

**Answers to Olympic Games**

1. Stockholm (1912), Antwerp (1920), Amsterdam (1928), Helsinki (1952), Melbourne (1956), and Rome (1960).
2. Matt Biondi in 1988.
3. Nine
4. Mexico City in 1968.
5. Scotsman, Alan Wells in Moscow in 1980.
6. Tommie Smith and John Carlos. They finished 1st and 3rd in the 200m dash.
7. A brilliant Gymnast Korbut's Olympics were in Munich in 1972.
8. Lasse Viren, winner of the 5000m and 1000m, in both the 1972 and 1976 Olympic Games.
9. To protest New Zealand's continued rugby links with South Africa.
10. Cuban, Albert Juantorena, winner of both the 400m and 800m races in Montreal in 1976.
11. Jean-Claude Killy.
12. Brian Boitano and Brian Orser.
13. Norway
14. Chamonix (1924), Cortina d'Ampezzo (1956), Squaw Valley (1960), Grenoble (1968), and Sapporo (1972).
15. Five (three 500m titles and two 1000m titles).

## 116. Soccer History

1. Which country hosted Soccer's First World Cup?
2. Which Team has won the European Cup or the Champion's League the most number of times?
3. How many times have each of these teams won the World Cup: a) Brazil; b) Germany (including West Germany); c) Italy; and d) England?
4. Who was known as the 'Wizard of Dribble'?
5. For which two club teams did Pele play for during his career?

6. Who holds the record for the most goals scored during a single World Cup?
7. Who captained the French side to World Cup Victory in 1998?
8. Which Hungarian star was known as the 'Galloping Major'?
9. From which country do the following club teams originate from: a) Anderlecht; b) Go Ahead Eagles; c) Barry Town; d) Vasco Da Gama; e) River Plate; and f) Orlando Pirates?
10. What is the home nation of the following players: a) John Toshack; b) Luis Figo; c) Nat Lofthouse; d) Garrincha; e) Hernan Crespo?
11. Which club has been Italy's most decorated in the Domestic League and Cup?
12. Which of the clubs has never won the English League and FA Cup Double: a) Everton; b) Liverpool; c) Arsenal; d) Tottenham Hotspur; and e) Aston Villa?
13. From which African Country did the Portuguese star, Eusebio, originally come from?
14. How many European Footballer of the Year titles were won by Johan Cruyff?
15. Which country first won the European Championship in 1960?

### Answers to Soccer History

1. Uruguay. Who also won the tournament beating Argentina 4-2 in the final.
2. Real Madrid. They have won the tournament nine times, AC Milan at five, Liverpool, Bayern Munich and Ajax Amsterdam at four, follow behind.
3. a) Brazil (four times 1958, 1962, 1970, and 1994); b) Germany/ West Germany (three times 1954, 1974, and 1990); c) Italy (3 times 1934, 1938 and 1982); d) England (one time 1966). Give yourself one point if you got three or more of these correct.
4. Sir Stanley Matthews.
5. Santos of Brazil and later New York Cosmos.
6. Just Fontaine.
7. Didier Deschampes.

8. Ferenc Puskas.
9. a) Belgium; b) The Netherlands; c) Wales; d) Brazil; e) Argentina; and f) South Africa. Give yourself one point if you got four or more of these correct.
10. a) Wales; b) Portugal; c) England; d) Brazil; and e) Argentina. Give yourself one point if you got four or more of these correct.
11. Juventus of Turin.
12. a) Everton. They came close in 1984/85 when they won the League, but were beaten 1-0 by Manchester United in the Final of the FA Cup.
13. Mozambique (formerly Portuguese East Africa).
14. Two
15. The Soviet Union.

## 117. General Sports History II

1. In which sport did Geoff Hunt of Australia earn his fame from?
2. How many Formula One Driver's Championships were won by the Argentinian, Juan Manuel Fangio?
3. What is the nationality of the legendary Swimmer, Dawn Fraser?
4. Who 'guaranteed' Super Bowl III?
5. Which two types of wrestling are featured at the Olympic Games?
6. What are the three types of fencing disciplines?
7. Which American cleaned up in the Speedskating event in the 1980 Olympic Games?
8. With which two English schools do you associate the Games of Fives?
9. In which sport is the Sheffield Shield competed for?
10. What is the name of the trophy given for Rugby Union's World Cup?
11. What was Michael Jordan's college basketball team?
12. From which city did the Athletics baseball franchise originate?
13. Who is considered to be France's greatest Jockey?
14. Which Swedish fighter once beat Floyd Patterson?
15. In which sport does Rusty Wallace compete?

### Answers to General Sports History II

1. Squash
2. Five Titles.
3. Australian
4. Joe Naimith. The Quarterback for the New York Jets.
5. Greco-Roman and Freestyle.
6. The sabre, the epee and the foil.
7. Eric Heiden.
8. Rugby and Eaton Schools.
9. Cricket. It is the National Championship of Australia
10. The William Webb Ellis Trophy (named after the sport's founder).
11. University of North Carolina.
12. From Philadelphia.
13. Yves Saint-Martin.
14. Ingemar Johanssen.
15. NASCAR

## 118. General Sports History III

1. With which sport do you associate Naim Suleymanoglü?
2. Which stroke developed from a loophole in the rules governing breaststroke?
3. With which sport would you associate Koichi Nakano?
4. How many times have the Boston Celtics won the NBA titles (within 1)?
5. Which three NFL Teams hold the record for most wins in a season (15)?
6. Who is the oldest winner of the U.S. Open Golf Title?
7. Which country won the first Women's Olympic Ice Hockey Title?
8. Which Cross-Country Skier holds the Men's Record for the most World Cup Titles at 6?
9. With which sport do you associate Aleksandr Karelin?
10. To the nearest 2 wins, how many games did the Chicago Bulls win in the 1995/96 regular season?

11. Which French Rugby star played 111 times for his country between 1982 and 1995?
12. In which city is Soccer's World Club Championship normally held?
13. With which water sport do you associate Kelly Slater?
14. Which country has won the most Four-man Bobsled Titles?
15. What are Golf's Four Majors?

**Answers to General Sports History III**

1. Weightlifting. This Turkish superstar has won 10 World Titles. He is known as the 'Pocket Hercules'.
2. Butterfly
3. Cycling. He won 10 Professional Sprint Titles in a row between 1977 and 1986.
4. Sixteen times, including nine times in the 1960's.
5. San Francisco 49ers in 1984, Chicago Bears in 1985, and Minnesota Vikings in 1998. Give yourself one point if you got two or more of these correct.
6. Hale Irwin. He won it in 1990 at age 45 years 15 days.
7. U.S.A. in 1998 in Nagano, Japan. They beat Canada 3-1 in the Final.
8. Bjørn Daehlie of Norway.
9. Greco-Roman Wrestling. He is a legend, having won three Gold Medals in a row in the 30 kg Class.
10. Seventy-two—a record number within a single NBA Season.
11. Phillipe Sella.
12. Tokyo between the South American and European Champions.
13. Surfing
14. Switzerland
15. The U.S. Open, The British Open, U.S. Masters, and the U.S. PGA.

# 119. Ancient General History III

1. Which enemy of Ancient Israel are often described as the 'Sea People'?
2. Which very ancient culture developed what is now known as 'the lost-wax process of casting copper and bronze'?
3. Who defeated the Egyptians at Carchemish in 605 BC?
4. The Samnites were an Italian tribe? True or False?
5. Esarhaddon was King of which civilization?
6. Into which three periods is the Stone Age traditionally divided?
7. Who introduced Athen's first Written Law? Hint: These were known for their severity.
8. Three, four, or five? What was the number of kingdoms that Egypt was divided up into between 828-712 BC?
9. In which valley does one find the prehistoric human rich, Olduvai Gorge?
10. Which relative of Abraham was an ancestor of the Moabite and Ammonite people?
11. Which Greek Island was known for its shrine to Apollo?
12. What was the Assyrian capital c. 1150 BC? Starts with an 'A'.
13. What was the Akkadian Capital built by Sargon? Starts with an 'A' as well.
14. Which Roman Emperor built the Colosseum?
15. Which Gaulish city was known as Lutetia?

### Answers to Ancient General History III

1. The Philistines.
2. The Mesopotamians.
3. The Babylonians.
4. True
5. Assyria
6. The Paleolithic Age (300000—8000 BC), The Mesolithic Age (8000—2700 BC) and the Neolithic Age (2700-1900 BC).
7. Dracon. From which the word 'Draconian' arises.

8. Five
9. The East African Rift Valley.
10. Lot
11. Delos
12. Assur
13. Agade
14. Vespasian
15. Paris

## 120. Ancient Rome VII

1. Which Iberian City was called Olispo by the Romans?
2. What is meant by pater familias?
3. Which literary technique was Juvenal the master of?
4. What were the Comitia curiata and the Comitia centuriata?
5. Which famous poet was originally a Carthaginian slave? He was known for his humour.
6. What was a figidarium?
7. Which instrument did the Romans use to write with?
8. Which insect was thought by the Romans to be a messenger of the Gods?
9. What was the population (more or less of Rome) at the time of Augustus?
10. Which Emperor tried to revive paganism in Rome between 361-363 AD?
11. Which temple was dedicated in Rome in 509 BC?
12. Which Ancient Scientist died while investigating the eruption of Mount Vesuvius?
13. Which common Roman engineering structure was first built in 312 BC?
14. Which church father began to write a new version of the Bible in Rome in 382 AD?
15. Which problem did the Roman currency face during the Empire's decline?

### Answers to Ancient Rome VII

1. Lisbon
2. Head or Father of the Family.
3. Satire
4. Two assemblies that together with the Senate formed the Government of Republican Rome.
5. Terence
6. A cold bath. A tepidarium was a warm bath and a calidarium a hot bath.
7. A stylus.
8. The Bee.
9. One million
10. Julian the Apostate.
11. The Temple of Jupiter.
12. Pliny the Elder.
13. The Aqueduct.
14. St. Jerome.
15. It was debased to pay the army and payoff the barbarian chieftains.

## 121. Vietnam War I

1. Which political organization did Ho Chi Minh find in 1941?
2. Whose forces were defeated at the Battle of Dien Bien Phu in 1954?
3. Which agreement signed in 1954 temporarily divided Vietnam?
4. Which organization did Hanoi form in 1960 to operate in South Vietnam?
5. Which South Vietnamese President, elected in 1955, rejected re-unification?
6. What was the DMZ?
7. Which Policy was the U.S. following when it engaged itself in Vietnam?
8. What was the name of the American ship that was attacked in the Gulf of Tongking Crisis?
9. Troops from which country arrived in South Vietnam in 1962?

10. Which U.S. Marine Base was attacked in January-April 1968?
11. What did ARVN stand for?
12. Who was the North Vietnamese Military Leader throughout the war?
13. Which book did he write that has become a textbook for revolutionaries?
14. Which year was the Tet Offensive?
15. Which leader declared Cambodia to be neutral in 1956?

**Answers to Vietnam War I**

1. The Viet Minh (The League for the Independence of Vietnam).
2. The French.
3. The Geneva Agreement.
4. National Liberation Front (NLF).
5. Ngo Dinh Diem.
6. The demilitarized zone between South and North Vietnam that was allowed for by the Geneva Agreement.
7. The Policy of Containment (Containment of Communism).
8. USS Maddox.
9. Australia
10. Khe Sanh.
11. Army of the Republic of South Vietnam.
12. Vo Nguyen Giap.
13. People's War, People's Army
14. 1968 (January-February).

## 122. Vietnam War II

1. Of 540,000, 520,000 or 580,000, what was the maximum size of the U.S. Force in Vietnam in 1968?
2. Which trail began in Ne Pe Pass?
3. What was Linebacker II?
4. Which South East Asian Country adopted a strong policy of anti-communism in 1958 with the backing of the U.S.?

5. What is Vietnam's most important river?
6. Which country attacked Vietnam in 1979?
7. More or less, which proportion of the Cambodian population were killed in the mass genocide between 1975-79?
8. Which Guerrilla Group seized power in Laos in 1975?
9. What was the name of the policy followed by Richard Nixon where military contribution was aimed at directly boosting the ARVN?
10. In 1965, which site in Vietnam did U.S. Troops first land?
11. Who succeeded Ho Chi Minh as North Vietnamese Leader in 1969?
12. Which infamous event happened in March 1968?
13. Which two political figures signed the Paris Peace Agreement?
14. In which year did the last U.S. Troops leave Vietnam?
15. Which South-East Asian Country, with towns such as Don Muang and U Tapao, was hit with significant anti-government demonstrations in 1973?

## Answers to Vietnam War II

1. 540,000
2. The Ho Chi Minh Trail.
3. The U.S. Air War designed to destroy the transportation systems of North Vietnam.
4. Laos
5. The Mekong.
6. China
7. One Quarter (2,500,000 lives).
8. The Pathet Lao.
9. Vietnamization
10. Da Nang.
11. Le Duan.
12. My Lai Massacre.
13. Henry Kissinger and Lu Duc Tho.
14. 1973
15. Thailand

# 123. Vietnam War III

1. Which year did Saigon fall to the NVN?
2. What was significant about the Tet Offensive?
3. Which war villain was paroled in March 1974?
4. Which country was led at one stage by Lon Nol?
5. What was ordered to be mined in December 1972?
6. Which South Vietnamese City fell to the North Vietnamese forces in the Easter uprising in 1972?
7. To the closest 10,000, how many Americans died in the Vietnam War?
8. Which major blow to the Vietnam War effort did President Ford incur in 1975?
9. Who led the Khmer Rouge to power in 1975?
10. Who drove the Khmer Rouge out of power in Cambodia in 1979?
11. Which type of Society did the Khmer Rouge seek to create in Cambodia?
12. What was the name of the U.S. Merchant Ship that was seized by Cambodian troops in 1975?
13. Who was the last President of South Vietnam?
14. Who made the famous, "peace is at hand" statement in November 1972?
15. Which year did the killing of the four at Kent State University take place?

### Answers to Vietnam War III

1. 1975
2. It showed that the American Government had been overly optimistic about the progress in the war and the war might take longer than expected. It also played a significant role in turning public opinion against the continuation of the war.
3. Lieutenant William Calley Jr. who was convicted for his involvement in the My Lai Massacre.
4. Cambodia.

5. North Vietnamese harbours.
6. Quang Tri City. It was later taken by the U.S.
7. Fifty thousand. Some say the number is closer to 60,000. Give yourself one point if you have either.
8. His request for further aid to South Vietnam was rejected by the U.S. Congress.
9. Pol Pot.
10. Vietnam
11. A Marxist Agrarian Society.
12. The Mayaguez. It was eventually regained by U.S. Troops.
13. Nguyen Van Thieu.
14. Henry Kissinger.
15. 1970

## 124. Korean War

1. At which parallel was North and South Korea divided after the Second World War?
2. Which country brought troops into North Korea towards the end of World War II?
3. Who was elected as the Head of Government of South Korea in 1948?
4. Which city was taken by U.S. Troops in September 1950 following a surprise amphibious landing?
5. What was/is the Capital City of North Korea?
6. Who was the North Korean leader throughout the duration of the War?
7. What strategically important site north of Yanguu was captured by U.S. Troops in 1951?
8. Who was commander of the U.S. Position that was attacked by the North Koreans on the first day of the invasion?
9. Who replaced MacArthur as Head of the U.S. and United Nations Command in the Far East, when 'Mac' was dismissed by President Truman?
10. Which factor made it easier for the U.S. to win support in the

United Nations Security Council for a mission in Korea under the U.N. banner?

11. What was the area in the southeast portion of South Korea called where U.S. Troops were under siege for some time in the early part of the war?
12. Which river in the Northern part of the country were the Chinese afraid the U.N. Troops would cross?
13. Which U.S. Army fought in Korea (ie. what was its' number)?
14. Where was the Korean War Armistice signed?
15. What was the nationality of the 52 POW's killed in a prison riot on Cheju Island in October 1952?

**Answers to Korean War**

1. 38th Parallel.
2. The Soviet Union.
3. Syngman Rhee.
4. Inchon
5. Pyongyang
6. Kim Il Sung.
7. Heartbreak Ridge.
8. Colonel Charles 'Brad' Smith.
9. Matthew Ridgway.
10. The Soviets were boycotting the Security Council at the time, thereby negating all significant opposition the U.S. would normally have experienced in the Council.
11. The Pusan Perimeter.
12. The Yalu River.
13. The Eighth Army.
14. Panmunjom
15. Chinese. They were killed by U.S. Guards during a violent demonstration.

## 125. Australian History

1. Who was the first Prime Minister of Australia?

2. Which policy was established in Australia to block immigration from Asia?
3. Which two parties combined with each other in a coalition in 1904 to oust the Labour Party?
4. Which Australian Prime Minister was known as 'Ming the Merciless'?
5. Where was the Australian Parliament located between 1901-1927?
6. Over which large territory did Australia win a mandate at The Treaty of Versailles in 1919?
7. Which Prime Minister was dismissed by the Governor General Sir John Kerr?
8. Which party was Prime Minister Harold Holt a member of?
9. What was the old name for Tasmania?
10. What was the first colony to be established in Australia?
11. What city was once called Port Jackson?
12. To the nearest 10,000 years, when did the Aborigines come to Australia?
13. Which change did Prime Minister Bob Hawke usher in with respect to the Australian dollar?
14. Which Prime Minister nationalized the Airline Qantas?
15. Prime Minister Malcolm Fraser worked to drop the Preferential Trade Tariffs for goods of this country. What was the country?

**Answers to Australian History**

1. Edmund Barton (1901-1903).
2. White Australia Policy.
3. The Free Traders and the Protectionists (now there is a match made in heaven).
4. Robert Menzies who served for a total of 18 years as Australian Prime Minister.
5. Melbourne
6. German New Guinea.
7. Gough Whitlam in 1975.
8. The Liberal Party.

9. Van Dieman's Land.
10. New South Wales in 1786.
11. Sydney
12. Forty-thousand years ago.
13. He allowed it to float freely, ending the Fixed Exchange Rate Policies of earlier prime ministers.
14. Joseph 'Ben' Chifley.
15. Britain

## 126. Early American History I

1. This Editor of *The New York Journal* went to trial for seditious libel, but was acquitted. The case represented a landmark in the struggle for freedom of the press. Who was the Editor?
2. What was the name given to the outburst of religious fervor which swept several colonies in the 1740s?
3. He wrote, *Memorable Providences Relating to Witchcraft and Possessions.* Who was he?
4. What was the name of the West Indian slave who was first to be wrongly accused of being an evil witch?
5. This document was signed in December 1620. What was it?
6. What was the name of the Indian Chief whose braves sat down to the first Thanksgiving dinner with the pilgrims?
7. This was set up in Virginia in 1619 by Governor Yeardley. What was it?
8. Miles Standish and John Alden were puritans? True or False?
9. In which year was Jamestown founded?
10. Which City was once called Naumkeag?
11. What was the name of the woman who was banished from Boston in 1638 as a heretic? She would settle near Providence and start Portsmouth.
12. What was the name of the Union formed between Connecticut, New Haven, Plymouth, and Massachusetts Bay Colonies?
13. Who was the founder of Providence, Rhode Island?
14. This Indian Chief led a rebellion in 1676. Who was he?

15. This man is said to be the Father of Virginia's Modern Tobacco Industry. Who was he?

## Answers to Early American History I

1. John Peter Zenger.
2. The Great Awakening.
3. Cotton Mather, who was highly influential in the Salem witch-hunt.
4. Tituba. She was a slave to the Parrish Family.
5. The Mayflower Compact. The first written Constitution of North America.
6. Massasoit or Wasamegin. His tribe was the Wampanoags.
7. The House of Burgesses. An elected Legislative Assembly.
8. False. Although they sailed to the New World aboard the Mayflower, both were loyal to the Church of England and were not Puritans. Puritan figures included: William Brewster, John Carver, William Bradford, and Edward Winslow. Of the 102 people aboard the Mayflower, 50 were Puritans.
9. 1607. It was the first permanent English settlement in the New World.
10. Salem
11. Anne Hutchinson.
12. The New England Confederation. It was founded in 1643 to alleviate border disputes between the colonies.
13. Roger Smith. Smith favoured a separation of Church and State and the payment of the Indians for land. His colony at Rhode Island was reckoned to be one of the freest communities on the planet.
14. King Philip. His rebellion failed and he was beheaded and his relatives sold into slavery.
15. John Rolfe. He crossed Virginian tobacco with a milder type of Jamaican leaf to produce a tobacco product that would soon be selling in vast amounts throughout Europe.

# 127. Early American History II

1. She was later known as Lady Rebecca, but what was she more well known as?
2. Which word was inscribed on a tree at the site of the lost Roanoke colony?
3. Although at times a Military Dictator, he saved Jamestown from an early demise. Who was he?
4. This European group settled heavily along the Delaware. Who were they?
5. Name the five Middle Colonies?
6. What did the Rebel Leader Nat Bacon die of in 1676?
7. Which city did Bacon capture and burn?
8. This man is considered the Father of Paper Currency in America. Who was he?
9. Which University did Thomas Jefferson attend?
10. He started a Journal called, *The Saturday Evening Post*. Who was he?
11. Who founded Maryland in 1632?
12. With which Colony is James Oglethorpe associated?
13. He was Leader of the 1624 Settlement on Manhattan. Who was he?
14. How did William Penn gain possession of the Territory of Pennsylvania?
15. He was the last Dutch Governor of New Amsterdam. Who was he?

### Answers to Early American History II

1. Pocahontas
2. CROATOAN. An Indian name for a nearby island.
3. Captain John Smith,
4. The Swedes. A settlement near Wilmington Delaware was once known as New Sweden.
5. New York, Pennsylvania, New Jersey, Delaware, and Maryland.

6. Dysentery. He died of the disease just before his capture. Bacon was a relative of the Philosopher, Sir Francis Bacon.
7. Jamestown
8. John Winthrop (1606-1675). Not to be confused with the elder John Winthrop (1588-1649), the original Chief Officer of the Massachusetts Bay Company and Governor of the Massachusetts Bay Colony.
9. William and Mary in Virginia.
10. Benjamin Franklin.
11. Lord Baltimore.
12. Georgia, which he helped found in 1732.
13. The Dutchman Peter Minuit. He purchased the island for goods valued at 2400 English cents.
14. He was given it by the Duke of York who owed money to Penn's father.
15. Peter Stuyvesant.

## 128. American Revolution I

1. In which two towns did hostilities break out on April 19, 1775?
2. Who led the American Forces that captured Fort Ticonaroga in May 1775?
3. Where did the Second Continental Congress meet?
4. Who led the American forces at the Battle of Bunker Hill?
5. Which lower hill did the Americans initially choose to fortify to fight off the British attack at Bunker Hill?
6. What did George III issue on August 23, 1775, with respect to the Revolution?
7. Who was sent by Congress to France in December 1776 to secure aid from the French?
8. Who was the first person to read the Declaration of Independence in Public?
9. Between July 1776 and September 1776, which City was the focus of hostility in the Revolutionary War?
10. Which New Jersey City was the site of a critical battle on December 26, 1776?

11. What was the 'Turtle'?
12. Who was the author of the American Crisis?
13. In which Battle did Molly Pitcher make a name for herself?
14. Which General was the Victor at the Battle of Saratoga?
15. Which 'atrocity' happened on the July 27, 1777, angering the Americans and stiffening their resolve against the British?

**Answers to American Revolution I**

1. Concorde and Lexington.
2. Benedict Arnold and Ethan Allen.
3. Philadelphia on May 5, 1775.
4. Colonel William Prescott.
5. Breeds Hill.
6. Proclamation of Rebellion.
7. Benjamin Franklin.
8. Colonel John Nixon in Philadelphia's Independence Square on July 8, 1776.
9. New York.
10. Trenton. Washington defeated the Hessians at this battle.
11. The first attack submarine in history. It was used against the HMS Eagle on September 6, 1776.
12. Thomas Paine.
13. The Battle of Monmouth Courthouse. She took her husband's place at a cannon when he was wounded.
14. General Horatio Gates.
15. The butchering of Jane McRae.

## 129. American Revolution II

1. Complete the missing word in these three Battle names: a) S____ Point; b) B____ Heights; c) F____Farm.
2. It is said, "The Stile of this Confederacy shall be The United States of America." What document is being referred to here?
3. In which year did Washington and his army enter their Winter Quarters at Valley Forge?

4. This South Carolina City fell to the British on May 12, 1780. What was it?
5. What did Benedict Arnold plan to hand over to the British?
6. Which Admiral commanded the French Fleet that arrived in American waters in 1781?
7. Complete the missing word in these three Battle names: a)____ Creek; b) K____Mountain; c) G____Courthouse.
8. This man was appointed Superintendent of Finance in the Continental Congress in 1781. Who was he?
9. This General brought order to North Carolina in 1781 by driving out the British. Who was he?
10. Which Battle was fought between October 6th—20th 1782?
11. Which Treaty ended the American War of Independence?
12. Which French General arrived with a force of 5500 to assist the Americans in 1780?
13. In which state was The Battle of Cowpens fought on January 17, 1781?
14. Who defeated Horatio Gates at The Battle of Camden?
15. This Georgia City was captured by the British in 1778. What was its name?

**Answers to American Revolution II**

1. a) Stony Point; b) Bemis Heights; c) Freeman's Farm. Give yourself one point if you got two or more of these correct
2. The Articles of Confederation.
3. 1777
4. Charlestown
5. West Point.
6. Admiral deGrasse.
7. a) Brandywine Creek; b) King's Mountain; c) Guilford Courthouse. Give yourself one point if you got two or more of these correct.
8. Robert Morris.
9. Nathaniel Greene.
10. Battle (Siege) of Yorktown.

11. The Peace of Paris signed September 3, 1783.
12. Comte de Rochambeau.
13. South Carolina.
14. General Cornwallis.
15. Savannah

## 130. American Revolution III

1. Who defended the soldiers of the Boston Massacre?
2. What was the name of the Black American killed at the Boston Massacre?
3. Who pressurized the Boston Meeting to set up the Committee of Correspondence?
4. This event occurred on December 16, 1773. What was it?
5. How many intolerable Acts were passed by the British Parliament?
6. What was another name for the Intolerable Acts?
7. What did the Administration of Justice Act of May 20, 1774 state?
8. What was the chief focus of the Massachusetts Government Act?
9. Who said "Give me Liberty or Give me Death"?
10. This Act implemented in January 1765 caused great resentment within the colonies. What was it?
11. What was defined by George III in 1764 as the boundary of expansion for the American colonies?
12. Why did British troops arrive in Boston in 1768?
13. These taxes were placed on lead, glass, paper, and tea in 1767. What were these duties known as?
14. What was the main focus of the Declaratory Acts?
15. What body produced a series of Declaration and Resolves on October 14, 1774?

### Answer to American Revolution III

1. John Adams.
2. Crispus Attucks. A total of five people were killed and six wounded in the massacre.

3. Samuel Adams.
4. The Boston Tea Party.
5. Five
6. The Coercive Acts.
7. That British Officials could not be tried in provincial courts for capital crimes.
8. It annulled the Charter of the Colonies, and it took control of the town meetings away from the colonists and gave it to the British Governor.
9. Patrick Henry.
10. The Stamp Act.
11. The Appalachian Mountains. Expansion was limited to East of the Mountains.
12. To enforce the customs laws.
13. The Townshend Duties.
14. The British Parliament reasserted its right to make laws that were enforceable in the colonies.
15. The First Continental Congress.

## 131. U.S. Civics

1. Which amendment was bought in as a reaction to the British Quartering Act?
2. Who signed the U.S. Constitution on behalf of New York?
3. Which was the last of the 13 original states to ratify the constitution?
4. Who is 4th in line of succession to the President?
5. What is Francis Bellamy known for?
6. Which state had the most members sign The Declaration of Independence?
7. What are the first seven words of The Declaration of Independence?
8. Amendment XX is often given a nickname. What is it?
9. How many Amendments make up The Bill of Rights?
10. In what year did 18 year olds win the vote in the U.S.?
11. Which state currently sends 15 votes to the Electoral College?
12. Which two states can split their Electoral College votes?

13. How many members of The House of Representatives are there?
14. What is significant about July 30, 1956?
15. What number Congress was elected in 2000?

**Answers to U.S. Civics**

1. The Fourth Amendment. It says that soldiers cannot be housed in a private home without the owner's agreement.
2. Alexander Hamilton.
3. Rhode Island.
4. Secretary of State after the Vice President, Speaker of the House and the President pro tempore of the Senate.
5. He wrote The Pledge of Allegiance to the Flag in 1892.
6. Pennsylvania with 9. One of which was Ben Franklin.
7. When in the Course of human events . . .
8. The Lame Duck Amendment.
9. Ten. Amendments I-X.
10. 1971, through Amendment XXVI.
11. New Jersey.
12. Maine and Nebraska.
13. 435
14. On this day, "In God We Trust" became the national motto.
15. The 107$^{th}$ Congress.

## 132. Economic History

Name the economic law that states:

1. Supply creates its own demand.
2. In an organization, every employee tends to rise to his level of incompetence so that all important work is done by those who have not reached that level.
3. Bad money drives out good.
4. An increase in supply tends to lead to a lower price for any particular product unless there is an increase in demand, and vice versa.
5. Work expands to fill the time available for its completion.

Name the Economist most associated with the following ideas:

6. The value of any product is roughly equal to the value of labour which has gone into producing it.
7. Unemployment is reduced, not by cutting wages, but by stimulating purchasing power. Therefore, there is a need for heavy state investment in public works to provide jobs and increase purchasing power.
8. Government spending in excess of income produces inflation and leads to higher level of unemployment.
9. This Canadian-born Economist wrote *The Affluent Society*. Who was he?
10. What is the currency of the following countries: a) Greece; b) Jamaica; c) Thailand
11. There are three factors of production ie. factors needed to produce a commodity. What are they?
12. In what field would you find the corporation: McCann-Erickson world group?
13. What do the initials DJIA stand for?
14. Based on current U.S. Dollars, who according to the American Heritage Magazine was/is the wealthiest American of all-time?
15. Of 1968, 1969, 1970, 1971, and 1972, in which year was the Nobel Prize for Economics first offered?

**Answers to Economic History**

1. Say's Law.
2. Peter's Principle.
3. Gresham's Law.
4. Law of Supply and Demand.
5. Parkinson's Law.
6. David Ricardo.
7. John Maynard Keynes.
8. Milton Friedman.

9. John Kenneth Galbraith.
10. a) The Drachma b) The Jamaican Dollar c) The Baht. Give yourself one mark if you got two or more of these correct.
11. Labour, Land, and Capital.
12. Advertising
13. Dow Jones Industrial Average.
14. John D. Rockefeller—valued at $189.6 billion dollars—three times that of Bill Gates.
15. 1969. It was won that year by Ragnar Anton Kittil Frisch and Jan Tinbergen.

## 133. Political Terms I

What political term is best described by the following definitions:

1. Rule by a small executive class.
2. Harmony, without law.
3. Acknowledgment that a government holds power as of right.
4. Joint control of a territory by two or more countries.
5. Government agent who incites others to break the law.
6. Land administered by country on behalf of the United Nations.
7. Political system where all have equal power.
8. System of mutual assistance with a defensive purpose.
9. Easing of a political situation.
10. The Right to Vote.
11. Renunciation of nationality by an individual.
12. Division of government among Executive, Legislative and Judicial branches as in the U.S.
13. State ownership of industry or business.
14. Attempt by one state to attain a position of pre-eminence in its relations with other states.
15. To manipulate voting districts, facts, or arguments in favour of a particular political party.

### Answers to Political Terms I

1. Oligarchy
2. Anarchy
3. De Jure recognition.
4. Condominium
5. Agent provocateur.
6. Trust Territory.
7. Isocracy
8. Collective security.
9. Détente
10. Franchise
11. Expatriation
12. Separation of powers.
13. Nationalization
14. Hegemony
15. Gerrymander

## 134. Political Terms II

What do the Following abbreviations stand for:

1. EURATOM
2. COMECON
3. UPU
4. ITU
5. FAO
6. GATT
7. UNESCO

Which political term is best described by the following definitions:

8. Stoppage of Movement of people or property.
9. Pressure group within a political party, or a meeting of such a group.

10. Acknowledgment that a government actually holds power.
11. Rule by women.
12. Independent investigator who protects citizens against maladministration by civil servants.
13. Belief in right to vote.
14. Rule by divine guidance.
15. Reconciliation of conflicting claims by some Third Party.

**Answers to Political Terms II**

1. European Atomic Energy Community.
2. Council for Mutual Economic Aid.
3. Universal Postal Union.
4. International Telecommunications Union.
5. Food and Agriculture Organization.
6. General Agreement on Tariffs and Trade.
7. United Nations Educational Scientific and Cultural Organization.
8. Embargo
9. Caucus
10. De facto recognition.
11. Gynocracy
12. Ombudsman
13. Suffragism
14. Theocracy
15. Mediation

## 135. Religion

What Religious Movement/Term is defined below:

1. An act of repentance or sacrifice that wills a person back to God.
2. Islamic official who conducts mosque prayers.
3. Primitive religion, objects (charms) are attributed with special power.
4. Christian sacrament that celebrates the Lords' supper.

5. Belief that after death the soul enters the body of another living creature.
6. Religion that originated in Cuba. Known as 'the way of the saints'.
7. All things are inhabited by a soul or spirit.
8. Principal of self-denial to obtain a state of heightened spiritual awareness.
9. Hindu Philosophy involving union with the Absolute Being.
10. Spiritual leader of the Rastafarians.
11. Identification of God with the Universe.
12. Regular form of service at a church.
13. Theory that the earth is a living, self-regulating super-organism. Name derives from Greek mythology
14. Encyclopedia of Jewish Law and Tradition. Supplements Pentateuch.
15. Law that a man's deeds determines his destiny.

**Answers to Religion**

1. Atonement
2. Imam
3. Fetishism
4. Eucharist
5. Transmigration of the soul.
6. Santería
7. Animism
8. Asceticism
9. Yoga
10. Haile Selassie I, former Emperor of Ethiopia.
11. Pantheism
12. Liturgy
13. Gaia Hypothesis.
14. The Talmud.
15. Karma

# 136. Disasters

Name or describe the disaster from the date given:

1. January 28, 1986.
2. March 27, 1977.
3. May 6, 1937.
4. April 15, 1911.
5. February 6, 1958.
6. December 21, 1987.
7. Which river flooded its banks killing 900,000 people in October 1887?
8. Which type of disaster struck Hong Kong on September 18, 1906?
9. What was the name of the hurricane that hit Central America in late 1998, causing 9745 deaths?
10. Why is Chelabinsk, Russia notorious?
11. In what type of disaster did 1426 people die in Saudi Arabia in 1991?
12. What happened in Ramstein, Germany on August 28, 1988?
13. Name the largest European city that is at present still threatened by a volcano?
14. This Asian country has the worst road fatality rate. Name the country?
15. Two hundred and twenty-two people died in Sinceljo, Colombia when a stand collapsed. What sport were the people watching?

### Answers to Disasters

1. Explosion of the Space Shuttle Challenger 51L.
2. Collision of two Boeing 747, one operated by Pan Am the other by KLM on the runway at Los Rodeos Airport, Canary Islands. Five hundred and eighty-three people were killed. This is the largest air accident of all-time.
3. Hindenburg Airship Disaster.
4. The S.S. Ttitanic sunk.

5. Munich Air Disaster. A plane carrying the Manchester United Soccer Team and reporters crashes.
6. Ferry Dona Paz collided with the tanker Victor off the Philippines coast. In the worst ferry disaster ever.
7. The Yellow River.
8. A typhoon with winds up to 100 mph. Ten thousand people died.
9. Hurricane Mitch.
10. It is the most radioactive place on Earth. There have been three nuclear disasters in this area. Five hundred thousand people in the region have been affected by radiation equivalent to Chernobyl.
11. A mass panic stampede in a tunnel between Mecca and Medina.
12. An airplane disaster at an air show. Three Italian jets collided, one jet exploded killing 70 people and injuring 400.
13. Naples
14. India. It has 1% of the world's roads but 6% of its accidents.
15. Bullfighting (if it is indeed a sport).

## 137. U.S. Civil War I

1. Which was the first state to secede from the Union?
2. Who was President of the Confederacy?
3. In which city was the First White House of the Confederacy located?
4. Who was the greatest naval figure to emerge from the war?
5. Which ship sunk the Merrimac?
6. Why did Robert E. Lee side with the Confederacy?
7. Which noted abolitionist founded *The New York Tribune*?
8. Which city was the site of a major battle fought on July 22, 1864?
9. Which General was known as 'Fighting Joe'?
10. Who said, "It is well that war is so terrible—we should grow too fond of it?"
11. How many men died in the Confederate attack on Fort Sumter?
12. Which General was described as Robert E. Lee's war horse?
13. Which city in Virginia was General Grant's headquarters from 1864-1865?

14. What were 'Popskull' and 'Rifle Rock Knee'?
15. With which side did the Five Civilized tribes ally with?

**Answers to U.S. Civil War I**

1. South Carolina.
2. Jefferson Davis.
3. Montgomery, Alabama.
4. David Farragut.
5. The Monitor. It beat the Merrimac at the Battle of Hampton Roads.
6. He could not bare to take up arms against his home state, Virginia.
7. Horace Greeley.
8. Atlanta
9. General Joseph Hooker.
10. Robert E. Lee.
11. Although this event initiated the war, there were no casualties on either side.
12. The Confederate General James Longstreet.
13. Hopewell
14. Civil War terms for 'liquor'.
15. The Confederacy.

## 138. U.S. Civil War II

1. Gettysburg was the costliest Battle in the Civil War in terms of lives. Which was the second most costliest battle?
2. Which state had the distinction of being the birthplace of 64 Union Generals?
3. In which state was Gettysburg fought?
4. What distinction did Danville, Virginia have?
5. Who said, "War is cruelty and you cannot refine it?"
6. Who led the Union Forces at Gettyburg?
7. POWs of which side were held at Andersonville?
8. What is the claim to fame of Edmund Ruffin?
9. What year was the inconclusive Battle of Antietam fought in?

10. Where did Robert Lee surrender?
11. Which troops were first used in The Battle of Island Mount in Missouri?
12. In which city was Jefferson Davis captured in 1865?
13. How many states made up The Confederacy?
14. At which Battle did General Thomas Jonathan Jackson earn his nickname 'Stonewall'?
15. Who led the Union Forces at Spotsylvania, Cold Harbour, and Petersburg?

**Answer to U.S. Civil War II**

1. The Vicksburg Campaign, 35,825 died. At Gettysburg 51,112 died. In the entire Vietnam War between 50,000 to 60,000 Americans died.
2. Ohio
3. Pennsylvania
4. It was the last Capital of The Confederacy.
5. General William Tecumseh Sherman.
6. General Gordon Meade.
7. The Union. Andersonville is in Georgia.
8. He fired the first shot of the Civil War.
9. 1862
10. At the Appomattox Court House. Lee did not offer his word to Grant as is customary, but neither did Grant request it.
11. Black Troops.
12. Irwinsville, Georgia
13. Eleven
14. First Manassas.
15. Lt. General Ulysses Grant.

## 139. U.S. Civil War III

1. What transportation device was known as 'The General'?
2. Which city was beset by well-documented draft riots in 1863?

3. At which famous plantation in Nashville, Tennessee was there a skirmish on December 15, 1864?
4. In which State did the Union win The Battle of Vicksburg?

For Questions 5 and 6 guess the name of the Battle from the following clues:

5. Two words, one of four letters. The other contains eight. The sum of 19,455 soldiers died in this mid-western battle?
6. One word, six letters. This battle was fought on the April 6th—7th 1862?
7. Stonewall Jackson died from pneumonia that set in after his left arm was amputated because of a wound he received. Just before which Battle, that was fought between May 2-4th 1863, did he receive the wound?
8. For which side did the following Generals fight for:
a) Ambrose Burnside b) John Bell Hood c) George Sykes d) Jubal Anderson
9. Who led the ill-fated Confederate Charge at The Battle of Gettysburg?
10. Who led an anti-slavery revolt at Harper's Ferry, West Virginia?
11. Of 2, 2.5, 3, or 3.5 million dollars, what was the cost per day of the war to the U.S. Government?
12. What was the most famous phrase that Southerner's often described The Civil War as?
13. Who wrote the famous Civil War novel entitled, *The Red Badge of Courage*?
14. She was known as 'Moses', but what was her real name?
15. What is memorable about November 19, 1863?

**Answers to U.S. Civil War III**

1. A locomotive that was captured by the Union on April 12, 1862. It can be seen today at the Big Shanty Museum in Kennesaw, Georgia.
2. New York.

3. The Belle Meade Plantation.
4. Mississippi
5. Fort Donelson.
6. Shiloh
7. Chancellorsville. In this battle 30,099 people died. a) Union b) Confederacy c) Union d) Confederacy. Give yourself one point if you got three or more of these correct.
8. George Pickett.
9. John Brown.
10. $2.5 million
11. The War of Northern Aggression.
12. Stephen Crane.
13. Harriet Tubman.
14. It was the day Abraham Lincoln delivered the Gettysburg Address. Ironically, it was ill-regarded at the time.

## 140. British History in the 19th Century I

1. What was the real name of the Duke of Wellington?
2. Who represented Britain at the Congress of Vienna in 1815?
3. What terms describe the security felt by Britain after the Napoleonic Wars as a result of her unique geographic and political position in Europe?
4. Who assassinated the British Prime Minister, Spencer Perceval?
5. This political figure carried through the Catholic Emancipation Act and reshaped London's police force. Who was he?
6. Which Law was repealed in 1846?
7. Who was Prime Minister of Britain when Queen Victoria ascended to the throne?
8. Who was the famous wife of the politician referred to in Question 7?
9. Where in the British Empire was slavery abolished in 1807?
10. In which year was slavery finally abolished in the British colonies?
11. Born in 1759, he encouraged the aristocracy to practice real Christianity. An ardent abolitionist he died one month before The Slavery Abolition Act. Who was he?

12. The initials of these 19th Century freetraders are R.C. and J.B. What were there full names?
13. Which massacre took place in 1819?
14. Which assassination conspiracy in Britain failed in 1820?
15. Who was the King of Britain between 1820 and 1830?

**Answers to British History in the 19th Century I**

1. Arthur Wellesley.
2. Robert Castlereagh. Like Wellington, he was also Irish.
3. Splendid Isolation.
4. A bankrupt London broker, John Bellingham, who was later hanged.
5. Robert Peel. The police force would become known as the Peelers or Bobbies.
6. The Corn Law.
7. William Melbourne. He served as her mentor during the early years of her reign.
8. The Novelist Lady Caroline Lamb. An ardent 'devotee' of Lord Byron.
9. British West Indies.
10. 1833
11. William Wilberforce.
12. Richard Cobden and John Bright. Both were opposed to The Corn Law and were instrumental in the success of The Anti-Corn Law League fight against agricultural protectionism.
13. The Peterloo Massacre.
14. The Cato Street Conspiracy. The conspirators wanted to seize London after assassinating the Prime Minister, Lord Liverpool. They failed on both accounts.
15. George IV.

## 141. British History in the 19th Century II

1. What was presented to Parliament in 1839 and 1842?
2. Why did Britain refuse to take part in the post-Napoleonic Era of The Concert of Europe?

3. A favorite with the public, this Queen died in 1821. Who was she?
4. Associated with the Political Reform Movement, this Irish-born Politician died in 1855 in a state of insanity. He championed working class rights through his newspaper, *The Leeds Northern Star*. Who was he?
5. Which Reform Act gave the vote to most of the middle class?
6. Who did Queen Victoria succeed to the throne in 1837?
7. With which group do we associate the Preacher, George Loveless?
8. This Catholic woman secretly married the Prince of Wales in 1785, and the Prince later denied this marriage. Their connection was broken off with the Pope's consent in 1803. Who was she?
9. How old was Victoria when she became Queen?
10. How long did she reign?
11. Which nobleman greatly influenced Queen Victoria's mother The Duchess of Kent?
12. What was a 'Rotton Borough'?
13. Name one of the two Standards of Wealth regulated by the Bank Charter Act of the 1840's?
14. Children under 13 had their work-week limited to no more than how many hours by The Factory Act of 1833?
15. Which nobleman is most associated with The Factory Acts of 1847 and 1859?

## Answers to British History in the 19th Century II

1. The People's Charter. It called for universal manhood suffrage, voting by secret ballot, the abolition of property qualification for MPs, payment of MPs, equally sized constituencies and annually elected parliaments. All of these except the last demand would eventually be won.
2. Britain did not agree with the anti-liberalism and anti-nationalism flavour of the concert.
3. Princess Caroline of Brunswick, whose marriage to George IV was declared invalid under dubious circumstances.
4. Feargus O'Connor.

5. The 1832 Reform Act introduced by Earl Grey.
6. Her Uncle, William IV known as the Sailor King because of his earlier naval career.
7. The Tolpuddle Martyrs. One of the earlier trade unions that were eventually crushed. Loveless organized the Martyrs into a Trade Union.
8. Maria Anne Fitzherbert.
9. Eighteen years old.
10. Sixty-four years.
11. Sir John Conroy. One of Victoria's first acts as Queen was to exclude Conroy from the court.
12. Former towns which had lost almost all of their population, but still elected members to parliament as a constituency. They were abolished by The Reform Act of 1832.
13. The Act regulated the number of bank notes that could be printed, as well as gold stocks.
14. Forty-eight hours. By the same Act, children under nine were banned from working.
15. The 7th Earl of Shaftesbury.

## 142. British History in the 19th Century III

1. This Politician once fought a duel with Castlereagh. He held a variety of positions in public service which included: Treasurer of the Navy (1804-1806), Minister of Foreign Affairs (1807, 1822-1827), and President of the Board of Control (1816). He was the first British Politician to recognize the Free Spanish American States. He died in 1827. Who was he?
2. Which disease was Queen Victoria a carrier of?
3. Who planned and managed the Great Exhibition of 1851?
4. Which Prime Minister was known as 'Firebrand'?
5. What 1850 incident affair involved the British Government vigorously defending the rights of British citizens abroad?
6. Between which two years was the Crimean War fought?
7. Who were Britain's allies in this war?
8. Whose ambiguous order led to the ill-fated Charge of the Light Brigade at Balaclava?

9. Who led the Actual Charge of the Light Brigade?
10. Which reporter gained fame in *The Times* for his Crimean War reports?
11. The fall of which Russian fortress during the Crimean war encouraged peace negotiations?
12. Which Prime Minister was associated with The Ministry of All Talents?
13. Which group most benefited from the 1867 Reform Act?
14. What did The Trade Union Act of 1875 allow?
15. Under whose Prime Ministership was Queen Victoria proclaimed Empress of India?

### Answers to British History in the 19th Century III

1. George Canning.
2. Hemophilia. This X-chromosome-related disease has attacked the Russian lineage of the Queen, but not the British side.
3. Prince Albert.
4. Viscount Palmerston for his fervent support of British interests worldwide.
5. The Don Pacifico Affair.
6. 1854-1856.
7. France, Turkey, and Sardinia.
8. Lord Raglan's.
9. Earl of Cardigan. As you guessed it, the Crimean War, was a breeding place for new clothing types.
10. W.H. Russell.
11. Sevastopol
12. Lord Grenville. The ministry was composed of the best men from all political parties.
13. Urban Labourers.
14. Peaceful Picketing.
15. Benjamin Disraeli.

## 143. British History in the 19$^{th}$ Century IV

1. Whose government was brought down by a vote of no confidence for their handling of the Crimean War?
2. What did The Climbing Boys Act of 1875 ban?
3. What was established as the loading limit for ships by The Merchant Shipping Act of 1876?
4. From whom did Disraeli purchase shares to allow Britain to gain control of The Suez Canal?
5. How many times was William Gladstone Prime Minister of Britain?
6. In which city was Lord Frederick Cavendish assassinated in 1882?
7. Under whose term at 10 Downing Street was The Local Government Act of 1888 introduced?
8. What was the main feature of The 1872 Ballot Act?
9. Why did Gladstone resign as Prime Minister in 1886?
10. Who were the Chief Franchise Beneficiaries of The 1884 Reform Act?
11. What was William Gladstone's middle name?
12. Which Political Party was founded in 1893?
13. Who formed the British South Africa Company in 1889?
14. The Upper part of which South East Asian Country did Britain annex in 1886?
15. Born in 1854, this Irish Conservative Politician gained fame for his persecution of Oscar Wilde. Later on in life, he organized the Ulster Volunteers and opposed Home Rule. Who was he?

### Answers to British History in the 19$^{th}$ Century IV

1. The Earl of Aberdeen's Tory Government in 1855.
2. The employment of children as chimney sweeps.
3. The Plimsoll Line.
4. The Khedive of Egypt.
5. Four Times.
6. Dublin. He was the Viceroy of Ireland. He was killed in Phoenix Park together with his Under-Secretary, Thomas Henry Burke, by

'The Invincibles', a Nationalist Terror Group. Five of the murderers were later arrested and hung.

7. Marquess of Salisbury.
8. It made voting secret.
9. His Home Rule Bill for Ireland was defeated.
10. Rural and Mining workers.
11. Ewart
12. The Independent Labour Party by the Socialist Keir Hardie.
13. Cecil John Rhodes of Rhodes scholarship fame,
14. Burma. After The Third Anglo-Burmese War.
15. Baron Edward Henry Carson.

## 144. British Authors

Who wrote the following works of fiction?

1. The Tenant of Wildfell Hall
2. Prisoner of Zenda
3. The Old Curiosity Shop
4. Kidnapped
5. She
6. Persuasion
7. Forsythe Saga
8. Scoop
9. To the Lighthouse
10. The End of the Affair
11. Ivanhoe
12. The History of Tom Jones
13. Jude the Obscure
14. Lucky Jim
15. Black Beauty

### Answers to British Authors

1. Anne Brontë (as Acton Bell).

2. Anthony Hope.
3. Charles Dickens.
4. Robert Louis Stevenson.
5. Henry Rider Haggard.
6. Jane Austen.
7. John Galsworthy.
8. Evelyn Waugh.
9. Virginia Woolf.
10. Graham Greene.
11. Walter Scott.
12. Henry Fielding.
13. Thomas Hardy.
14. Kingsley Amis.
15. Anne Sewell.

## 145. Pseudonyms

Which writers used the following pseudonyms?

1. Maxim Gorky.
2. Boz
3. Lewis Carroll.
4. Mary Westmacott.
5. O. Henry.
6. Currer Bell.
7. George Sand.
8. Mark Twain.
9. George Orwell.
10. Nicholas Blake.
11. Elia
12. John le Carré.
13. Voltaire
14. Ellery Queen.
15. Stendahl

**Answers to Pseudonyms**

1. Alexy Peshov.
2. Charles Dickens.
3. Charles Dodgson.
4. Agatha Christie.
5. William Sydney Porter.
6. Charlotte Brönte.
7. Amandine Dupin.
8. Samuel Longhorne Clemens (apparently, he obtained the name 'Twain' from the cry of the Mississippi Boatmen).
9. Eric Blair.
10. Cecil Day Lewis.
11. Charles Lamb.
12. David Cornwell.
13. François-Marie Arouet.
14. Co-authors Frederic Dannay and his Cousin Manfred Lee.
15. Marie Henri Beyle.

## 146. American Authors

Which Authors wrote the following works?

1. The Good Earth.
2. A Connecticut Yankee in King Arthur's Court.
3. Zuckerman Bound.
4. The Beautiful and the Damned.
5. Herzog
6. The Witches of Eastwick.
7. Tar Baby.
8. The Bostonians.
9. Snow Image.
10. Tropic of Cancer.
11. Arrowsmith.
12. The Murders in the Rue Morgue.

13. Sophie's Choice.
14. The Pathfinder.
15. Junkie

**Answers to American Authors**

1. Pearl Buck.
2. Mark Twain.
3. Philip Roth.
4. Francis Scott Fitzgerald.
5. Saul Bellow (actually, he was born in Canada).
6. John Updike.
7. Toni Morrison.
8. Henry James.
9. Nathanial Hawthorne.
10. Henry Miller.
11. Sinclair Lewis.
12. Edgar Allan Poe.
13. William Styron.
14. James Fenimore Cooper.
15. William Burroughs.

## 147. Woman Only

Pick the famous female personality from the clues provided"

1. Critic, she wrote, *The Style of the Radical Will and Illness as Metaphor.*
2. Italian Educationist. Opened her first children's house in 1907.
3. Co-founder of the Women's Action Alliance and Champion of Women's Issues through *Ms. Magazine.*
4. The Taj Mahal was built in honour of this woman.
5. A writer, her works include, *Three Lives, Tender Buttons* and *The Autobiography of Alice B. Toklas.* Who was she?
6. Her real name was Margaret Hookham, but most people knew her as . . . . ?

7. An opponent of Apartheid and a member of the South African Communist Party, she was assassinated by a parcel bomb in 1982.
8. An American Poet. She wrote over 1000 poems in seclusion whilst living in Amherst.
9. Composer of the ever-popular 'Happy Birthday to You'.
10. Saint, Mother of Constantine, and Founder of the Basilicas on the Mt. of Olives and Bethlehem.
11. Theosophist of Russian origin. She had many followers, one of which was Annie Besant.
12. Englishwoman, renowned for a daring sea rescue near the Farne Islands in 1838.
13. Actress. Famous for her role as 'Phèdre'.
14. Founder of the Christian Science Movement.
15. Expert Marksman in The Wild West. Lived in several mining camps and in Deadwood S. Dakota.

### Answers to Woman Only

1. Susan Sontag.
2. Marie Montessori.
3. Gloria Steinem.
4. Mumtaz Mahal.
5. Gertrude Stein.
6. Margot Fonteyn (the Ballet Dancer).
7. Ruth First.
8. Emily Dickinson (almost all of her work was published after her death).
9. Patty Smith Hill.
10. St. Helena.
11. Helena Blavatsky (aka Madame Blavatsky).
12. Grace Darling.
13. Sarah Bernhardt.
14. Mary Baker Eddy.
15. Calamity Jane (Martha Jane Cannary).

# 148. Philosophy—Schools of Thought

From the descriptions supplied, give the school of thought that would be most associated with this doctrine:

1. Virtue is a mean or a middle way between opposing extremes.
2. Everything is open to doubt.
3. The events of our lives are determined.
4. Virtue is the only aim in life. A virtuous man will always achieve happiness regardless of his circumstance.
5. Good involves creating the most happiness for the most number of people.
6. All knowledge is derived from sensory experience.
7. Good is pleasure and that evil is pain.
8. All belief in the supernatural must be rejected.
9. The strength of an idea lies in its practical consequence.
10. Reason is the only source of knowledge.
11. The world has no absolute meaning; we are therefore free to make choices providing we accept the consequences.
12. History is a struggle between opposing economic forces.
13. Matter is an illusion; reality is that which exists mentally.
14. Self-sufficiency is the best way of achieving happiness. Mankind should be scorned for anything else.
15. Knowledge is a product of sense-experience. Observations must be governed by Scientific methods.

### Answers to Philiosophy Schools of Thought

1. Aristotlelianism
2. Sceptism
3. Predestination
4. Stoicism
5. Utilitarianism
6. Empiricism
7. Epicureanism (although in moderation of course).

8. Humanism
9. Pragmatism
10. Rationalism
11. Existentialism
12. Dialetic Materialism (aka Marxism).
13. Idealism
14. Cynicism
15. Logical Positivism.

## 149. Philosopher' s Works

Who wrote the following works of Philosophy:

1. Summa Theologiae.
2. The Discourses.
3. The Philosophy of Right.
4. Vindication of the Right's of Woman.
5. Leviathan
6. Essay Concerning Human Understanding.
7. Critique of Pure Reason.
8. Discourse on Method.
9. Principia Mathematica.
10. History and Class Conscious.
11. Tractatus Logico-Philosophicus.
12. The World as Will and Idea.
13. The Second Sex.
14. On Liberty.
15. Stages in Life's Way.

### Answers to Philosopher's Works

1. St. Thomas Aquinas.
2. Niccolò Machiavelli.
3. G.W.F. Hegel.
4. Mary Wollstonecraft.

5. Thomas Hobbes.
6. John Locke.
7. Immanuel Kant.
8. Rene Descartes.
9. Bertrand Russell with A.N. Whitehead.
10. George Lukacs.
11. Ludwig Wittgenstein.
12. Arthur Schopenhauer.
13. Simone de Beauvoir.
14. John Stuart Mill.
15. Søren Kierkegaard.

## 150. Artists I

From the following clues identify the artist. All Artists painted during the Period 1300-1850.

1. Venetian Painter. Born c. 1490. Works include the *Assumption of the Virgin*, *Bacchus and Ariadne* and *The Fall of Man*.
2. Married Saskia van Uylenburgh. Painted 650 oil paintings, created 1400 drawings and studies and 300 etchings. He was also known for his self-portraits.
3. Painted *The Birth of Venus*
4. Another Venetian artist. Lived 1697-1768. Famous for his paintings of *The Canals of Venice*.
5. Baroque painter. Painted several altarpieces and religious paintings. Often contrasted light and dark. Made several paintings of St. Matthew. He also painted *Christ at Emmaus*.
6. Painter. Known for his full-figured women.
7. Flemish portrait painter. Lived later in London where he carried out much work on behalf of the Stuart Royal Family.
8. Once asked to prove he was an Artist, he drew freehand, a perfect circle.
9. British landscape Painter. Most famous works were *Haywain* and *The White Horse*.

10. Painted *The Virgin of the Rocks* and wrote a famous treatise on painting known as *Trattato della Piture.*
11. Venetian Artist combined the glowing colour of Titian with the energy of Michelangelo. Painted *The Last Judgement*, *The Paradiso* and *The Annunciation.*
12. Born in Caprse, Italy in 1475, he studied with Ghirlandaio in Florence. He preferred form over colour. His early work was *The Cupid.* In 1496, he was summoned to Rome.
13. Dutch Painter, 1632-75, noted for his domestic interior paintings and his use of perspective and daylight tone. Works include *The Allegory of Painting* and *Women Reading a Letter.*
14. Painted *The Laughing Cavalier.*
15. Italian Painter much influenced by Da Vinci and Michelangelo. Paintings include *The Crucifixion*, *The Holy Family* and *The Reposition.* He also served as an Architect of St. Peter's. His last work was *The Transfiguration.*

**Answers to Artists I**

1. Titian or Tiziano Vecellio.
2. Rembrandt van Rijn.
3. Sandro Botticelli.
4. Canaletto or Giovanni Antonio Canal.
5. Caravaggio or Michelangelo Merisi.
6. Peter Paul Rubens.
7. Anthony van Dyck.
8. Giotto
9. John Constable.
10. Leonardo Da Vinci.
11. Tintoretto or Jacopo Robusti.
12. Michelangelo or Michelangelo di Lodovico Buonarroti Simoni.
13. Jan Vermeer.
14. Frans Hals.
15. Raphael or Raffaello Sanzio.

## 151. Art Schools

Which School of Art are the following Artists most associated with?

1. Roy Lichtenstein.
2. Edvard Munch.
3. Paul Cézanne.
4. Henry Moore.
5. Pablo Picasso.
6. Salvador Dali.
7. Edgar Degas.
8. Jackson Pollock.
9. Jacques Louis David.
10. Henri Matisse.
11. Dante Gabriel Rossetti.
12. Giovanni Bellini.
13. Edward Hopper.
14. Piet Mondrian.
15. Marcel Duchamp.

### Answers to Art Schools

1. Pop Art.
2. Expressionism
3. Post-Impressionism.
4. Abstract Art.
5. Cubism
6. Surrealism
7. Impressionism
8. Abstract Expressionism or Action Painting.
9. Romanticism
10. Fauvism
11. Pre-Raphaelite.
12. Renaissance
13. Realism/New Realism.

14. The De Stijl Movement and Neoplasticism.
15. Dadaism/Futurism/cubism. Give yourself one point if you answered any of these.

## 152. Artists II

From the clues provided identify the Artist:

1. French Cubist. Lived between 1882-1963. Paintings include, *The Port of La Ciotat* and *The Black Birds.*
2. This Pittsburgh-born Painter redefined the soup can.
3. A leading master of the Vienna Sezession, his portraits often combine realistically painted heads with flat abstract backgrounds.
4. Avant-Garde Bulgarian Artist. Has been known to wrap an island or two.
5. A member of the Blue Reiter Group. This Swiss-born Artist lived between 1879 and 1940. He worked in oils producing pictures such as *The Twittering Machine.*
6. This Belgian Surrealist produced such works as, *The Wind and the Song* and *The Human Condition.*
7. A pioneer of Abstract Art in the U.S., she painted a great amount in New Mexico.
8. He illustrated *Alice's Adventures* in *Wonderland* and *Through the Looking-Glass.*
9. A Russian Surrealist and Abstract Expressionist, he often stained huge canvases with rectangular blocks of pure colour.
10. This Austrian Expressionist was known for his stark naked slim figures that were drawn with a hard outline. They often filled the entire canvass and showed gestures of anguish.
11. Belorussian Artist who moved to the U.S. during World War II. A one-time ballet set and costume designer, he is known for his paintings of animals, dreams, Russian folklore and objects. Some say he was the first Surrealist.
12. Italian artist. Lived life to the fullest between 1884-1920. He often

combined the African art of the elongated face with rich colours, promoting the nude at the same time.

13. British non-figurative Sculptor. Known for her formal carving, one of her greatest works was *Contrapuntal Forms.*
14. Mexican Painter. Work blends Folklore with Revolutionary Propaganda.
15. This Abstract Expressionist founded a school known as the 'Subject of the Artist'. His style was simple and involved a single-image.

**Answers to Artists II**

1. Georges Braque.
2. Andy Warhol.
3. Gustav Klimt.
4. Christo (real name is Christo Javacheff).
5. Paul Klee.
6. René Magritte.
7. Georgia O'Keefe.
8. John Tenniel.
9. Mark Rothko.
10. Egon Schiele.
11. Marc Chagall.
12. Amedeo Modigliani.
13. Barbara Hepworth.
14. Diego Rivera.
15. Barnett Newman.

## 153. Franklin Delano Roosevelt

How much do you know about FDR?

1. Where was Franklin Delano Roosevelt born? Give the City and the State.
2. Which Law School did he attend?
3. Which position did he hold between 1913 and 1920?

4. In which year did he become stricken with polio?
5. Who did Roosevelt support for Governor of New York in 1924?
6. Who nominated FDR as his running mate in 1920?
7. Which State was his defeated 1936 presidential opponent Alfred Landon from?
8. Who did FDR defeat for the presidency in 1940?
9. Who was FDR's Secretary of the Interior?
10. Who was his Secretary of the Treasury from 1934 onward?
11. What was FDR's wife's maiden name?
12. What did Roosevelt shelve in 1942 in an effort to win the cooperation of business in the war effort?
13. Who was FDR's running mate in 1932?
14. What did FDR die of?
15. Where did he die?

### Answers to Franklin Delano Roosevelt

1. Hyde Park, New York.
2. Columbia Law School.
3. Assistant Secretary of the Navy.
4. 1921
5. Alfred E. Smith.
6. James M. Cox.
7. Kansas
8. Wendell Wilkie.
9. Harold Ickes.
10. Henry Morgenthau Jr.
11. Roosevelt (as well).
12. The New Deal.
13. John N.Garner.
14. A cerebral hemorrhage.
15. Warm Springs, Georgia.

## 154. Artists III

From the clues given pick the Artist:

1. He painted *Cornfields with Flight of Birds* and *The Potato Eaters.*
2. This Impressionist Painter was a midget.
3. American Painter. Often painted poor people, rustic landscapes of America. He liked oils and tempera. One of his famous works is *Christina's World.*
4. He often painted the countryside around Paris. This Impressionist is famous for his *Boulevard Montmartre.* His son's first name was Lucien. The son was also a painter.
5. His mother might not approve of him being a West Point dropout. He painted *Old Battersea Bridge.*
6. He painted *Liberty Guiding the People.*
7. Spanish Artist. He painted remarkable scenes of the Spanish uprising against Napoleon.
8. This one-time Stockbroker landed up in Tahiti.
9. 17th Century Spanish Painter. Work includes, *Las Hilanderas* and *Venus and Cupid.*
10. American Artist from Port Arthur, Texas. Created collages using rusty metal, old tyres, and clothing strips.
11. Impressionist Landscape Painter. He loved the valleys of the Seine, Loire and Thames. Although French, he came from English ancestry.
12. This French Impressionist loved colour and the action of sunlight. Paintings include the series of *Bathers* and *The Moulin de la Galette.*
13. Mexican Painter. A Surrealist, she used vibrant imagery that showed the suffering of women. She was once described as 'a ribbon around a bomb'.
14. An Original Impressionist, he painted such works as *Haystacks* and *Water Lilies.*
15. A Catalan, he loved painting using curvilinear and fantastical forms. He also worked on ballet sets and created sculptures, murals, and tapestries.

**Answers to Artists III**

1. Vincent van Gogh.
2. Henri de Toulouse-Lautrec.
3. Andrew Wyeth.
4. Camille Pissarro.
5. James Whistler.
6. Eugene Delacroix.
7. Francisco Goya.
8. Paul Gauguin.
9. Diego Velázquez.
10. Robert Rauschenberg.
11. Alfred Sisley.
12. Pierre Renoir.
13. Frida Kahlo.
14. Claude Monet.
15. Joán Miró.

# 155. George Washington

Please note these are difficult questions. If you get five correct, you seem to be on pretty solid ground with respect to this subject. With ten correct, you are a Washington know-it-all.

1. Under whose leadership did George Washington fight in the campaign against Fort Duquesne?
2. What was the full name of his wife before marriage to him?
3. In which city did Washington take command of the Continental Army during the American Revolution?
4. Which Political Party was he a member of?
5. What most angered Washington about the British during his earlier service in their army?
6. Did Washington make it into the 19th Century?
7. What did Washington warn against creating permanent alliances with in his farewell address?

8. Which political body was Washington a member of between 1758 and 1765?
9. What were the twin aims of the Annapolis Convention of 1786?
10. What was Washington elected President of in 1787?
11. Which fleet suprisingly fired a 20-gun salute at Washington's death?
12. Which women twice refused marriage to George Washington?
13. Who was Washington's Treasury Secretary?
14. Why was a convention called in Philadelphia soon after the 1787 Annapolis Convention?
15. What was the name of the Virginia County where Washington was born in?

**Answers to George Washington**

1. General Edward Braddock.
2. Martha Dandridge Custis.
3. Cambridge, Massachusetts.
4. The Federalist Party.
5. The Arrogance of the British Officers.
6. No, he died in 1799.
7. Foreign Powers.
8. Virginia House of Burgess.
9. To eliminate boundary disputes and trade wars between states.
10. The Constitutional Convention.
11. The British Channel Fleet.
12. Betsy Fauntleroy.
13. Alexander Hamilton.
14. To amend the ineffectual Articles of Confederation adopted in 1781.
15. Westmoreland County.

## 156. Jazz Music

1. Name one of the two Musicians, who according to legend, invented Jazz?
2. Which early Jazz group toured England in 1919?

3. What was Louis Armstrong's nickname?
4. Who was the 'King of Swing'?
5. Which instrument did Coleman Hawkins play?
6. Which recordings did Louis Armstrong produce between 1925 and 1928?
7. Who is regarded as the Virtual Symbol of Kansas City Jazz?
8. Which type of Jazz is associated with John Coltrane?
9. Who became the first jazzer to integrate hot jazz solos within the framework of a written score?
10. Which instrument did Thelonious Monk play?
11. With which Jazz style is Max Roach associated?
12. Who had an album called 'Bitches Brew'?
13. What is the home city of Wynton Marsalis?
14. What was the nickname of Charlie Parker?
15. Name this Jazz style from the clue given. Six letters beginning with the letter 'F'?.

**Answers to Jazz Music**

1. Buddy Bolden and Jelly Roll Morton.
2. Original Dixieland Jazz Band.
3. Satchmo
4. Benny Goodman.
5. The saxophone.
6. The Hot Five and Hot Seven recordings.
7. Count Basie.
8. Free Jazz.
9. Duke Ellington.
10. The piano.
11. Bebop
12. Miles Davis.
13. New Orleans.
14. Charlie Bird.
15. Fusion

# 157. Winston Churchill

1. Where was Churchill born?
2. What was his mother's maiden name?
3. Against which forces did he fight in Sudan?
4. During which war was he captured, imprisoned, and then escaped?
5. What constituency was he elected to represent in Parliament in 1900?
6. Which party did Churchill join in 1904?
7. Which position did Churchill hold between 1924 and 1929?
8. Why was Churchill excluded from The War Cabinet in 1915?
9. Which position did he assume when war broke out with Germany on September 3, 1939?
10. What Charter did Churchill help shape in 1941?
11. How many volumes make up his series of books, *The Second World War*?
12. What did Churchill receive in 1963?
13. Of which famous military figure did Churchill write a biography of during the period 1929-1939?
14. How old was Churchill when he died?
15. There was another Winston Churchill who lived between 1871 and 1947. What was the profession of this other Winston Churchill?

### Answers to Winston Churchill

1. Blenheim Palace, Woodstock, Oxfordshire, England.
2. Jennie Jerome.
3. The Dervishes.
4. The Anglo-Boer War.
5. Oldham
6. The Liberals.
7. Chancellor of the Exchequer.
8. He was held responsible for the failed attempt to open the Dardanelles and the ruinous Galipoli Campaign.
9. First Lord of the Admiralty.

10. The Atlantic Charter with the U.S.
11. Six Volumes.
12. United States Citizenship through an act of Congress.
13. John Churchill, his ancestor (aka Duke of Marlborough).
14. Ninety-one.
15. He was a Historical Novelist.

## 158. Musicals

1. Which musical are the songs *Summertime* and *It Ain't Necessarily so* associated with?
2. Who wrote the lyrics to *Showboat*?
3. He composed the music to *Kiss Me Kate* and *The Can-Can*. Who was he?
4. What were the first names of Lerner and Loewe?
5. For which Musical did Oscar Hammerstein win the Pulitzer Prize in 1943?
6. Which Musical is the odd one out: *My Fair Lady*, *Brigadoon*, *South Pacific* and *Gigi*?
7. Who composed the music to *Annie Get Your Gun*?
8. Credit this British Composer with the musical *Lock up your Daughters*. Who was he?
9. What was the name of Irving Berlin's renowned Christmas Musical produced in 1942?
10. He wrote, *On the Town*, *The Age of Anxiety*, and *The Ballet Dybbuk*. Who was he?
11. Which Musician went by the pseudonym 'Arthur Francis'? Clue: He is remembered for the hit, *I Got Rhythm*?
12. Place these five Andrew Lloyd Webber Musicals in the order they were produced, starting with the earliest: *Jesus Christ Superstar, Chess, Evita, Joseph and the Amazing Technicolour Dreamcoat and Cricket*?
13. Who wrote the Lyrics for the Musicals mentioned in Question 12?
14. This Red Petticoat Composer also wrote the Hit Songs, *The Way You Look Tonight* and *Smoke Gets in Your Eyes*. Who was he?
15. Moss Hart combined with Kurt Weill and Ira Gershwin to write which Musical in 1941?

### Answers to Musicals

1. Porgy and Bess (1935).
2. Oscar Hammerstein.
3. Cole Porter.
4. Alan and Frederick.
5. Oklahoma!
6. South Pacific was the product of Rogers and Hammerstein. The other Musicals are the works of Lerner and Loewe.
7. Irving Berlin.
8. Lionel Bart.
9. *White Christmas.* An ironical Musical in a way if you consider the fact that Berlin was Jewish.
10. Leonard Bernstein. Who is of course most famous for *The West Side Story.*
11. Ira Gershwin. Older brother of George Gershwin.
12. *Joseph and the Amazing Technicolour Dreamcoat* (1968), *Jesus Christ Superstar* (1971), *Evita* (1978), *Chess* (1984), and *Cricket* (1986).
13. Tim Rice.
14. Jerome Kern.
15. *Lady in the Dark.*

## 159. Science Fiction Writers

Who wrote the following Books or series of Books?

1. Foundation and Empire
2. Martian Chronicles
3. The Lensman Series
4. Rendezvous with Rama
5. Ringworld
6. Fire Time
7. Friday
8. A Canticle for Leibowitz
9. Timescape

10. The Long Dark Tea-Time of the Soul
11. Children of Dune
12. A Man of the People
13. Moving Mars
14. Do Androids Dream of Electric Sleep?
15. The Space Merchants

### Answers to Science Fiction Writers

1. Isaac Asimov.
2. Ben Bova.
3. Doc E. Smith.
4. Arthur C. Clarke.
5. Larry Niven.
6. Poul Anderson.
7. Robert Heinlein.
8. Walter Miller.
9. Gregory Benford.
10. Douglas Adams.
11. Frank Herbert.
12. Ursula K. le Guin.
13. Greg Bear.
14. Philip K. Dick.
15. Frederick Pohl.

## 160. Famous Historians

Who wrote the following Books or series of Books?

1. Hitler and Stalin—Parallel Lives
2. The Guns of August
3. A Thousand Days: John F. Kennedy in The White House
4. The Trouble Makers
5. History of England from the Accession of James II
6. The Creators

7. The Decline of the West
8. Conquest of Mexico
9. The Rise of Christian Europe
10. D-Day and Citizen Soldiers
11. The Mediterranean and The Mediterranean World at the Time of Philip II
12. The History of the Decline and Fall of the Roman Empire
13. The Rise and Fall of the Third Reich
14. On Heroes, Hero—Worship and the Heroic in History
15. The Holocaust—The Destruction of European Jewry 1933-1945

**Answers to Famous Historians**

1. Alan Bullock.
2. Barbara Tuchman.
3. Arthur Schlesinger, Jr.
4. A. J. P. Taylor.
5. Thomas Macauley.
6. Daniel Boorstin.
7. Oswald Spengler.
8. William Prescott.
9. Hugh Trevor-Roper.
10. Stephen Ambrose.
11. Fernand Braudel.
12. Edward Gibbon.
13. William Shirer.
14. Thomas Carlyle.
15. Nora Levin.

## 161. The New Testament

1. Who was the brother of Peter?
2. Who was Mary's sister?
3. How many letters did Paul write to Timothy?
4. Who was chosen to replace Judas Iscariot?

5. Who was described as 'the disciple that Jesus loved'?
6. Who was the mother of John the Baptist?
7. In which Book does the archangel Michael appear?
8. Who was the author of *The 13 Epistles*?
9. What did 'Doubting Thomas' doubt?
10. Which Angel announced the birth of John the Baptist and Jesus?
11. Which Herod ruled when Jesus was born?
12. Who authored the Second Gospel?
13. What was Peter's original name?
14. Who was Caiaphas?
15. Who carried Jesus' cross?

### Answers to The New Testament

1. Andrew
2. Martha
3. Two
4. Matthias
5. John
6. Elisabeth
7. Revelation
8. Paul
9. The Resurrection of Christ.
10. Gabriel
11. Herod the Great. There are four Herods in the New Testament: Herod the Great; Herod Antipas, his son who ruled during the murder of John the Baptist; Herod Agrippa who killed John's brother, James; and Herod Agripp II who tried Paul.
12. Mark
13. Simon
14. The High Priest who Jesus was taken to after his arrest.
15. Simon of Cyrene.

## 162. Greek Mythology

1. What is Calliope the muse of?
2. Which beautiful youth, who fell in love with Aphrodite, was killed by a boar?
3. Who was the Greek version of Vulcan?
4. Which people did Polyphemus lead?
5. Who fell to his death off his horse, Pegasus, trying to reach Olympus?
6. Over which Kingdom was Odysseus the King?
7. Which instrument did Orpheus play?
8. Who was the God of Sleep?
9. Who is the Greek equivalent of the Roman Dis?
10. Who was the Goddess of the Dawn?
11. What was Heracles' first task?
12. Who was the first woman on Earth?
13. What were the Satyrs?
14. Who was the Father of Hector?
15. How many Fates were there?

### Answers to Greek Mythology

1. Epic Poetry.
2. Adonis
3. Hephestus
4. The Cyclopses.
5. Bellerophon
6. Ithaca
7. The Lyre.
8. Hypnos
9. Hades
10. Eos
11. The Killing of the Nemean Lion.
12. Pandora
13. Hoofed Demigods of the forests, streams and fields.
14. Priam
15. Three

## 163. Some more Mythology

1. Who was the Norse God of Evil?
2. Where in Norse Mythology is the home of the Gods?
3. What is the Roman name for Pan?
4. Who is the Greek God of Physicians, Traders and Thieves?
5. Which stables did Hercules clean in his Fifth Labour?
6. Who is the Roman equivalent of Helios?
7. Who conducted the Warriors to Valhalla?
8. Who in Norse Mythology is the Goddess of the Dead?
9. How did Balder die?
10. What collective noun defines all the Chief Norse Gods?
11. Who was Odin's eldest son?
12. Who is the Roman Goddess of Wisdom?
13. Who was Odin's wife?
14. What was Plutus the Greek God of?
15. In Greek Mythology, into which paradise did heroes pass through without dying?

### Answers to Some more Mythology

1. Loki
2. Asgard
3. Faunus
4. Hermes
5. The Augean Stables.
6. Sol
7. The Valkyries.
8. Hel
9. He was killed by a mistletoe arrow.
10. Aesir
11. Thor
12. Minerva
13. Frigga, Goddess of Married Love.
14. Wealth
15. Elysium

## 164. History of Technology I

1. Available for the first time to the mass market in 1975, it is known by the acronym, LCD. What is its full name?
2. What was the major advantage of the Synchromesh Gearbox that was first offered in 1929?
3. This Engineer designed a revolutionary engine that obtained its power from a rotating piston. Who was he?
4. What communication device was set up in New Bedford, MA in 1900?
5. What was developed by Corning Glass Works in 1915?
6. In which City were red, green, and amber traffic lights introduced for the first time in 1918?
7. Which high-speed British train made its debut in 1924?
8. Once a Hallmark of the Gramophone, it disappeared in 1925?
9. Which part of the atmosphere do short waves bounce off repeatedly?
10. Which type of locomotives were first introduced in Switzerland in 1941?
11. What was the main problem with cellulose nitrate film?
12. What was noteworthy about the ship the HMS Hermes that was launched in 1919?
13. Which Science Fiction Writer first proposed the idea of Geostationary Satellites?
14. Which monitoring device did the Electronic Company EMI install for the first time in Guy's Hospital, England in 1948?
15. This Hungarian invented the ballpoint pen. Who was he?

### Answer to History of Technology I

1. Liquid Crystal Display.
2. It made gear-changing smoother.
3. Felix Wankel.
4. The first telephone exchange. It consisted of 10,000 lines.
5. Pyrex
6. New York City.

7. The Flying Scotsman.
8. The loudspeaker horn. It was replaced by a built-in cabinet loudspeaker.
9. The ionosphere.
10. Gas turbine powered locomotives.
11. It was flammable. It was replaced in 1948 by a safety film made up of cellulose trinitrate.
12. It was the first ship to be designed specifically as an aircraft carrier.
13. Arthur C. Clarke in 1945. This is the foundation of modern space communication.
14. Closed-circuit T.V.
15. Laszlo Biro.

## 165. History of Technology II

1. Which devises were first used in a T.V. in 1959?
2. Who designed the first working hovercraft?
3. What type of weapon was Atlas?
4. What 1957 invention made vegetable preparation easier?
5. Which type of books became cheaper and easier to read as a result of Solid Dot Printing?
6. Which type of pen was Pentel the first kind of?
7. Tiros I, performed what type of function as a satellite?
8. The oil tanker, Wandel, was the first motorship to make use of which type of engine to power it in 1904?
9. What 1929 invention revolutionized Track Running?
10. Which company designed the engine for the first supersonic combat fighter?
11. What was/is the International Telecommunications Satellite Organization more commonly known as?
12. Which type of fastener was invented in 1955?
13. Which company produced the first stick-on bandage?
14. What was the major advantage of quartz crystal in radio technology?
15. Tools, of a certain makeup, greatly increased lathe-cutting speeds when introduced in 1926. What was this makeup?

### Answers to History of Technology II

1. Transistors. Sony made the first transistorized T.V.
2. Christopher Cockerill. The idea however was first developed by Emanuel Swedenborg in 1716.
3. An intercontinental ballistic missile (ICBM). It was the first American ICBM.
4. The Shredder.
5. Braille Books.
6. Felt Tip Pen.
7. Launched in 1960, it was the first weather satellite.
8. A Diesel Engine.
9. Starting Blocks.
10. Pratt and Whitney. They fitted the J57 to the F-100 A to create the fighter in 1953.
11. Intelsat
12. The Velcro Fastener.
13. Johnson & Johnson. The bandage was known as 'Band-Aid'.
14. It maintains a steady carrier frequency and acts to reduce frequency overlaps in the receiver.
15. Tungsten-carbide.

## 166. History of Computers

1. This Englishman invented the Analytical Engine and the Difference Engine. Who was he?
2. It cost the U.S. Army $500,000 in 1943, weighed 30 tons and contained 19,000 vacuum tubes. What was it?
3. With which test are the questions "Do you have feeling?" and "Do you have pain?" associated with?
4. What was the name of the first commercial computer created?
5. With what is Jack Kilby most associated with?
6. Which company is associated with The Palo Alto Research Center?
7. Which company developed UNIX?
8. What is the claim to fame of the Intel 4004 Chip?

9. With which computer languages do you associate the following developers:
   a) Niklaus Wirth b) John Kemeny and Thomas Kurtz c) Brian Kernighan and Dennis Ritchie?
10. Robert Noyce and this man were the founders of INTEL. Who is the 'missing' person?
11. Bob Metcalfe is associated with which Connectivity System?
12. Which two Steve's formed Apple Computers on April Fool's Day 1976?
13. Which company is associated with the SPARC System?
14. Which company was bought by Compaq in 1998 for $9.6 billion?
15. Which event that occurred in 1991 would allow the internet to expand significantly?

## Answers to History of Computers

1. Charles Babbage.
2. The first electronic general use computer (aka ENIAC).
3. The Turing Test, developed in 1937 by Alan Turing.
4. UNIVAC
5. The building of the first integrated circuit. It contained five components on a sliver of Germanium half an inch long and thinner than a toothpick.
6. Xerox (aka Xerox PARC).
7. AT&T at their Bell Labs.
8. It was the first Microprocessor.
9. a) Pascal b) BASIC c) C. Score one point if you get two or more of these correct.
10. Gordon Moore of Moore's Law Fame.
11. Ethernet
12. Steve Jobs and Steve Wozniak.
13. Sun Microsystems.
14. Digital Equipment.
15. The ban on business through the internet was lifted.

# 167. Eccentrics

Name the Eccentric/s from the following clues:

1. This Psychiatrist wrote about the energy of the orgasm, which he termed 'Orgone Energy'.
2. French Author, some say he was the illegitimate son of Flaubert. He died in a state of madness, cursed by syphilis. A famous storybook of his was *Le Horla.*
3. Wealthy Heiress. She kept building on to her California home to keep the ghosts of the gunshot dead from haunting her.
4. She was known as The Witch of Wall Street.
5. Family name of the identical twins whom for years would only communicate with each other.
6. Occultist. Practitioner of Magick. Founded The Order of the Silver Star.
7. Esoteric American. Argued that the Earth was hollow and that gravity was an illusion. He and his followers founded a colony in Naples, Florida and named it 'Estero'.
8. Movie Director. Films include: *Crossroads of Laredo* and *Glen or Glenda.* Made movie scenes often using only one take.
9. Innovative Dancer. She died when her shawl became trapped in the rear wheel of her car, snapping her neck instantly.
10. Magician. His real name was Erik Weisz. He died in 1926 from peritonitis after being punched in the stomach. What was his stage name?
11. Fitness Freak. Claimed to have built a multi-million dollar empire on Carrots and Sex.
12. A 'native' hero of The Wild West. This Englishman's real name was Archie Belaney. What was he more commonly known as?
13. Canadian Prime Minister. Communicated with such deceased individuals as his mother, Louis Pasteur and Lorenzo De Medici.
14. Genius. Had an estimated IQ between 250-300. He wrote about collapsed stars, decades before the concept entered the field of

astronomy. Had several unpublished books on various topics. Wrote a book on Streetcar Transfers.

15. Japanese Officer. He was still fighting World War II in 1974.

**Answers to Eccentrics**

1. Wilhelm Reich.
2. Guy de Maupassant.
3. Sarah Winchester.
4. Henrietta Green.
5. The Gibbons Twins, June and Jennifer.
6. Aleister Crowley.
7. Cyrus R. Teed.
8. Ed Wood Jr.
9. Isadora Duncan.
10. Harry Houdini.
11. Bernarr MacFadden.
12. Grey Owl.
13. William Lyon Mackenzie King.
14. William Sidis.
15. Lt. Onoda.

## 168. Abraham Lincoln

1. Where in Kentucky was Lincoln born?
2. Which state did the family settle in, in 1830?
3. For which party was Lincoln elected to the Illinois General Assembly as a member of?
4. Who did he become engaged to in 1840?
5. Which mental disease did Lincoln suffer from?
6. What was the Christian name of his first child?
7. For which politician in Illinois did Lincoln campaign for in 1844?
8. What was Lincoln elected to in 1846?
9. Which Act did Lincoln oppose in 1854?
10. Which famous speech did Lincoln give in 1858?

11. What percentage of the popular vote did Lincoln win in 1860: 40%, 43% or 48%?
12. Which political rival of Lincoln died of acute rheumatism on June 3, 1861?
13. Which Law approved by Lincoln in 1862 gave 160 acres of publicly owned land to anyone who would claim and work the property for five years?
14. Which Play was Lincoln watching when he was assassinated at Ford's Theater?
15. In which City is Lincoln buried?

### Answers to Abraham Lincoln

1. Nolin Creek in a log cabin.
2. Illinois
3. The Whig Party. He would become Floor Leader in 1838.
4. Mary Todd. They broke off their engagement in 1841, but got married in 1842.
5. Depression
6. Robert
7. Henry Clay
8. The U.S. House of Representatives.
9. The Kansas-Nebraska Act.
10. The 'House Divided' Speech.
11. Forty percent. He however took 180 out of the 303 electoral votes that were up for grabs.
12. Stephen A. Douglas. He of the 1858 Great Debates Fame.
13. Federal Homestead Law. Encouraged the conquest of The Wild West.
14. Our American Cousin.
15. Springfield, Illinois.

# 169. History of Rock Music

1. Which year did Bill Haley and the Comets release, *(We're Gonna) Rock Around the Clock*?
2. Which song was Elvis Presley's first No.1 Hit?
3. Who sang, *That'll Be the Day*?
4. What first started on August 4, 1958?
5. What was Ray Charles' nickname?
6. He sung, *Only the Lonely*. Who was he?
7. This group hit #1 with *Please Mr. Postman* in 1961. Who were they?
8. When was the Year of 'The Twist'?
9. Which era of Rock was the song, *Denise by Randy and the Rainbows* a part of?
10. This group did the 'Wild Thing'. Who were they?
11. Which 1967 Festival featured The Mamas and The Papas, The Who, Janis Joplin and Jimi Hendrix?
12. Which barrier did the Beatles' *Hey Jude* break when it reached the Top of the U.S. Charts in 1968?
13. Who duo split up in March 1970?
14. Which Beatles song, which was a hit in the U.S. in 1965, only became a U.K. Single in 1976?
15. This group produced, *Good Vibrations*. Who were they?

### Answers to History of Rock Music

1. 1955. It reached #1 on July 9th, staying there for eight weeks.
2. *Heartbreak Hotel*
3. Buddy Holly.
4. The Billboard Top 100.
5. The Genius.
6. Roy Orbison.
7. The Marvelettes.
8. 1962
9. The Doo Wop Era.

10. The Troggs.
11. Monterey Pop Festival.
12. The Song Length Barrier. *Hey Jude* was over seven minutes in duration.
13. Simon and Garfunkel.
14. Yesterday
15. The Beach Boys.

## 170. Pop Music

Name the Singer/Group associated with each of these songs or albums:

1. *Killing Me Softly with His Song*
2. Rumours Album
3. *Crazy Little Thing Called Love*
4. *Video Killed the Radio Star*
5. The Sports Album
6. Breakfast in America Album
7. Maneater
8. Permanent Vacation Album
9. Volume 1 Album
10. Supernatural Album
11. American Pie
12. *Money for Nothing*
13. In the Year 2525
14. Mack the Knife
15. *Like a Rolling Stone*

### Answers to Pop Music

1. Roberta Flack.
2. Fleetwood Mac.
3. Queen
4. The Buggles (this song was the first music video).
5. Huey Lewis and the News.

6. Supertramp
7. Hall and Oates.
8. Aerosmith
9. Traveling Wilburys.
10. Carlos Santana.
11. Don McLean.
12. Dire Straits (background vocals supplied by Sting).
13. Zager and Evans.
14. Bobby Darin.
15. Bob Dylan.

## 171. Capitals of the Modern Country

What is the modern day Capital City of the following countries?

1. Brunei Darussalam.
2. Republic of Yemen.
3. Niger
4. Mauritius
5. Croatia
6. Guyana
7. Tajikistan
8. Liechtenstein
9. Ecuador
10. Botswana
11. Costa Rica
12. Guinea-Bissau.
13. Mali
14. Turkmenistan
15. Fiji

### Answers to Capitals of the Modern Country

1. Bandar Seri Begawan.
2. Sanaá

3. Niamey
4. Port Louis.
5. Zagreb
6. Georgetown
7. Dushanbe
8. Vaduz
9. Quito
10. Gaborone
11. San José
12. Bissau
13. Bamako
14. Ashgabat
15. Suva

## 172. Famous Explorers

Match the achievement with the Explorer who was the first Westerner to do this:

1. Discovered Alaska in 1728.
2. Discovered the Mouth of the River Congo.
3. Sighted Antarctica in 1820.
4. Discovered Tierra del Fuego in 1520.
5. Reached North Pole in 1909.
6. Discovered Brazil in 1499.

For which exploration feats are the following individuals most noted for:

7. Eric the Red.
8. Henry Hudson.
9. Ferdinand Richthofen.
10. Mungo Park.
11. St. Francis Xavier.
12. Vivian Fuchs.

13. Heinrich Barth.
14. Robert Burke and William Wills.
15. David Livingstone.

**Answers to Famous Explorers**

1. Vitus Bering. A Danish Explorer who was working for the Russians.
2. Diogo Cão of Portugal c. 1483.
3. American Nathaniel Palmer.
4. Ferdinand Magellan.
5. American Robert Peary.
6. Pedro Alvares Cabral of Portugal.
7. Explored Greenland c. 982.
8. First European to discover Hudson Bay (1610).
9. Explored China in 1868.
10. Explored River Niger in 1795.
11. Visited Japan in 1549.
12. Crossed Antarctica in 1957-58.
13. Explored Sudan between 1852-55.
14. Crossed Australia South to North between 1860 to 1861.
15. He was the first European to discover the Zambezi River and the Victoria Falls.

## 173. Contemporary History

1. With which Company do you associate the Haas Family?
2. To the nearest two percent, how much of the world's greenhouse gases were produced in the U.S.A. in 1998?
3. Which Art Gallery holds the record for the most visitors in a year?
4. Which Supermodel represented Calvin Klein for ten years until she left catwalk modeling in 1995?
5. Which Actor held the record for the most leading roles?
6. What is the largest Crime Organization in the world today?
7. Which transport-related safety device was invented by William Carey?

8. What is the most successful Latin record of all-time?
9. Which City has the biggest underground shopping complex in the world?
10. This Computer Game is the best-selling ever. What was it?
11. What is Rap producer, Sean Coombs' more popular name?
12. With which death-defying sport do you associate the Italian, Reinhold Messner?
13. Which Computer boasts the shortest instruction manual?
14. Which Country has the most industrial robots?
15. This Book spent 694 weeks on the Bestseller List before dropping off on April 6, 1997. What was it?

**Answers to Contemporary History**

1. Levi Strauss Co.—The Jeans People.
2. Twenty-five percent. Considering the U.S. makes up only 4 % of the world's population, this is quite a number.
3. The Centre Pompidou in Paris, France in the Year 1995.
4. Christy Turlington. She started modeling at 13. Working full-time from the age of 17.
5. John Wayne. He played the leading role in 142 of the 153 movies he made.
6. Six Great Triads of China. They have about 100,000 members worldwide.
7. The Airbag. It has saved over 4000 lives in the U.S. alone.
8. The Marcarena by Los Del Rio which spent 60 weeks on the U.S. Charts and 12 weeks at the Top in 1996.
9. Toronto, Canada. Its PATH Walkway has 16 miles of shopping arcade.
10. Nintendo's Super Mario. It has sold over 40 million copies worldwide.
11. Puff Daddy.
12. Mountain climbing. He was the first person to climb the world's three highest mountains: Everest, K2 and Kachenjunga. He has scaled 14 of the world's mountains that are over 26, 250 ft without using oxygen.

13. The Apple iMac. Its instruction manual has six pictures and 36 words.
14. Japan
15. *The Road Less Traveled,* by M. Scott Peck.

## 174. The Academy Awards

Given the person's name and year they won the Oscar provide the name of the film they won the Oscar for:

1. Richard Dreyfuss—1977.
2. Vivien Leigh—1951.
3. Fredrich March—1946.
4. Clark Gable—1934.
5. Jodie Foster—1988.
6. Sally Field—1979.
7. Paul Newman—1986.
8. Yul Brynner—1956.
9. Grace Kelly—1954.
10. Jeremy Irons—1990.
11. Julie Christie—1965.
12. John Wayne—1969.
13. Bette Davis—1938.
14. William Hurt—1985.
15. Holly Hunter—1993.

### Answers to The Academy Awards

1. The Goodbye Girl
2. A Streetcar Named Desire
3. The Best Years of Our Lives
4. It Happened One Night
5. The Accused
6. Norma Rae
7. The Color of Money
8. The King and I
9. The Country Girl

10. Reversal of Fortune
11. Darling
12. True Grit
13. Jezebel
14. Kiss of the Spider Woman
15. The Piano

## 175. Famous Directors

Given the movie—name the Director:

1. La Dolce Vita (1960).
2. Cabaret (1972).
3. East of Eden (1954).
4. Apocalypse Now (1979).
5. Hannah and Her Sisters (1986).
6. The Last Emperor (1987).
7. One Flew over the Cuckoo's Nest (1975).
8. Gone with the Wind (1939).
9. Reds (1981).
10. Taxi Driver (1976).
11. Casablanca (1943).
12. The Shining (1980).
13. The Color Purple (1985).
14. Gandhi (1982).
15. Gigi (1958).

### Answers to Famous Directors

1. Federico Fellini.
2. Bob Fosse.
3. Elia Kazan.
4. Francis Ford Coppola.
5. Woody Allen.
6. Bernardo Bertolucci.

7. Milos Forman.
8. Victor Fleming.
9. Warren Beatty.
10. Martin Scorsese.
11. Michael Curtiz.
12. Stanley Kubrick.
13. Steven Spielberg.
14. Richard Attenborough.
15. Vincente Minnelli.

## 176. Famous Composers

Given the name of the Classical work—identify the Composer:

1. The Magic Flute (1791).
2. Variations on a Theme by Hayden (1861).
3. Choral Symphony No. 9 (1824).
4. The Tales of Hoffmann (produced in 1881 after composer's death).
5. The Song of the Earth (1908-09).
6. Messiah (1742).
7. Enigma Variations (1899).
8. The Rite of Spring (1913).
9. Wozzeck (1925).
10. The Blue Danube (1867).
11. Peter and the Wolf (1936).
12. Appalachian Spring (1944).
13. Finlandia (1899).
14. The Wooden Prince.
15. Tosca (1900).

### Answers to Famous Composers

1. Wolfgang Amadeus Mozart.
2. Johannes Brahms.
3. Ludwig van Beethoven.

4. Jacques Offenbach.
5. Gustav Mahler.
6. George Handel.
7. Edward Elgar.
8. Igor Stravinsky.
9. Alban Berg.
10. Johann Strauss.
11. Sergey Prokofiev.
12. Aaron Copeland.
13. Jean Sibelius.
14. Béla Bartók.
15. Giacomo Puccini.

## 177. Famous Composers II

Given the name of the Classical work—identify the Composer:

1. The Barber of Seville (1816).
2. The Nutcracker (1892).
3. The Flying Dutchman (1843).
4. Rhapsody on a Theme of Paganini (1934).
5. The Four Seasons (1725).
6. Peter Grimes (1945).
7. El Capitan (1896).
8. The Golden Kestrel (1907).
9. The Student Prince (1924).
10. Rigoletto (1851).
11. Peer Gynt (1876).

From the following clues—choose the composer:

12. Soviet Composer. Produced 15 symphonies. Ran into problems with the government when he failed to observe the principles of ' Soviet Realism'.
13. Piano player. Amongst his many works were 50 mazurkas.

14. His works include St. Paul (1836) and Elijah (1846).
15. Born in Austria in 1732, he wrote 104 symphonies. His innovations include the Four-Movement String Quartet and The Classical Symphony.

**Answers to Famous Composers II**

1. Gioacchino (Antonio) Rossini.
2. Piotr Tchaikovsky.
3. Richard Wagner.
4. Sergey Rachmaninov.
5. Antonio Vivaldi.
6. Benjamin Britten.
7. John Philip Sousa.
8. Nikolai Rimsky-Korsakov.
9. Sigmund Romberg.
10. Giuseppe Verdi.
11. Edvard Grieg.
12. Dmitri Shostakovich.
13. Frédéric Chopin.
14. Felix Mendelssohn.
15. Franz Haydn.

## 178. The Wild West

1. Who killed William Bonney Jr.?
2. Who were Wyatt Earp's and Doc Holliday's adversaries in the famous gunfight at the OK Corral?
3. What did Doc Holliday die of?
4. Whose head did Harry Love bring back to collect a reward?
5. What did Clay Allison answer with when asked why he would eat dinner with a man who wanted to kill him?
6. What is the claim to fame of Bob Ford?
7. Where were the Donner Party traveling to during their well-renowned cannibalistic journey?

8. What was the name of the vengeance monger who took to killing and eating the liver of Crow Indians after his wife and child had been murdered by braves of the tribe?
9. His dime novels redefined the way we view the Wild West. Who was he?
10. He was the law in Vinegaroon. Who was he?
11. What piece of clothing, which if worn, was believed by certain members of the Sioux to protect one against bullets?
12. This Yankee tried to establish a Republic with himself as President in Baha and Sonara, Mexico. It failed and he was driven out as somewhat of a joke. Who was he?
13. What were the first names of the two Younger Brothers?
14. Which Native American tribe were largely at the receiving end of the 'scalp for a scalp' policy negotiated between the Mexican authorities and American mercenaries?
15. A free Black cowboy, Jim Beckwourth became an honorary chief in which native tribe?

## Answers to The Wild West

1. William Bonney Jr. (aka Billy the Kid) was killed by Pat Garrett in 1881. The Kid had been a killer since the age of 12.
2. The Clanton Gang.
3. Tuberculosis in 1887.
4. Joaquin Murieta. Love also bought back the hand of Murieta's partner—Three-Fingered Jack Garcia. The head and hand were eventually destroyed in the San Francisco Earthquake of 1906.
5. "I didn't want to send a man to hell on an empty stomach."
6. He shot Jesse James in the back killing the legendary outlaw.
7. California
8. John Johnson (aka Liver-eatin' Johnson).
9. Ned Buntline.
10. Judge Roy Bean.
11. The Ghost Dancer's Shirt. It inspired the lll-fated Ghost Dancer's rebellion which ended in defeat for the Sioux.

12. William Walker.
13. Cole and Bob.
14. The Apache. The most ruthless scalper was a John Joel Scranton, who was active in the 1840's. He himself would later be scalped.
15. The Crow. Beckwourth led the tribe to many military victories.

## 179. Architectural History

1. This Architectural style dominated European building design between the 8th and 12th Century AD. What was it called?
2. This was the name of the tower that stood in the center of a Norman Lord's Castle. What was it called?
3. Name two of the three elements that Gothic Architecture exploited?
4. This type of vault was developed by the Romans. It consisted of four vaults that supported one another. What was this called?
5. What was the average medieval house's roof covered with?
6. This architect was famous for his work on proportion. He saw beauty as harmony with geometry. He designed the Santa Maria Novella church in Florence. Who was he?
7. This Italian Architect saw a building as an extension of the human form. A theatre in London is named after him. He also wrote four books on architectural design and theory. Who was he?
8. This architectural style was popular between 1600 and 1750. What was it called?
9. What is the prime difference between Classical and Romantic styles of Architecture?
10. Walter Gropius is associated with this school of Architecture that was popular in the Weimar Republic. What was it called?
11. This 1920's school of design has often been described as repetitive, cold, mathematical, and rational. What is this style known as?
12. This late Renaissance style encouraged the relaxation of the rules of Classicism. It was popular in the 16th Century. What was it called?
13. What was the Greek equivalent of the Roman Forum?

14. This Architect once said that there would be 'one single building for all nations and climates'. Who was he?
15. He designed the Imperial Hotel in Tokyo and the Guggenheim Museum of Art in New York. Who was he?

**Answers to Architectural History**

1. Romanesque
2. The Keep.
3. The Pointed Arch, the Flying Buttress and the Ribbed Vault.
4. The Groin Vault. It reduced the need to support a regular vault with thick walls.
5. Thatch
6. Leone Battista Alberti.
7. Andrea Palladio. The theatre is the Palladium.
8. Baroque Architecture.
9. In Classical Architecture, man is concerned with imposing order on nature. Mathematics and symmetry are therefore key. In Romantic Architecture, man chooses to integrate with nature. Asymmetry is therefore encouraged.
10. The Bauhaus School.
11. Functionalism—which argues that if one fulfils the function then form will follow automatically.
12. Mannerism
13. The Agora (or marketplace).
14. Le Corbusier.
15. Frank Lloyd Wright.

## 180. Albert Einstein

1. To which city did Albert's parents move to a year after his birth?
2. From which school did Albert graduate in Physics and Mathematics in 1900?
3. What was the first name of his first wife?
4. What Theory did Einstein write about in a paper published in 1916?

5. Who did Einstein partner with in 1933 to write *Warum Krieg (Why War)*?
6. Where did Einstein work between 1902 and 1909?
7. What did Einstein do with the money he won for his Nobel Prize?
8. At which prestigious Berlin Institute did Einstein work between 1914 and 1933?
9. In which journal were several of Einstein's groundbreaking papers published in 1905?
10. What force according to Einstein could bend light?
11. What relation was Einstein's second wife Elsa to him (besides being his wife of course)?
12. In which year did Einstein write a letter to President Roosevelt warning the President of the possibility that German would be making an Atomic bomb?
13. As a musician, Einstein was accomplished in the playing of this instrument. What was it?
14. Who encouraged Einstein, as a child, to follow into the field of mathematics?
15. What two theories did Einstein hope to link with his Unified Field Theory?

**Answers to Albert Einstein**

1. Munich
2. The Federal Polytechnic in Zurich.
3. Mileva as in Mileva Maric. They married in 1903. She too was a gifted Physicist.
4. The Foundations of the General Theory of Relativity.
5. Sigmund Freud.
6. At the Swiss Patent Office as an Examiner.
7. He gave it to his ex-wife Mileva who had given up Physics to look after their son Edward.
8. The Kaiser Wilhem Physical Institute.
9. *The Annalen der Physik* (including his special theory of relativity).
10. Gravity. It curves space. Light follows the curvature.

11. She was his first cousin.
12. 1939 (September).
13. The violin. His mother Pauline Koch persuaded him to study music.
14. His uncle, Jakob Einstein.
15. The General Theory of Relativity and Quantum Theory.

## 181. Irish History

1. What was the name of the people who settled Ireland between 600 and 150 BC?
2. What was the tuatha?
3. Which people attacked Ireland between 800-850 AD?
4. Which English Monarch encouraged settlement of Ireland in the 1550s?
5. Why did many Irish chieftains flee the country in 1607?
6. Which immigrants bought land in the 17th Century at six pence per acre?
7. To which British colonies did Cromwell order many Irishmen and women to be transported to as labour?
8. What did the Treaty of Limerick signed in 1691 penalize?
9. A decline in which material trade spurred Irish immigration to the U.S. between 1772 and 1777?
10. True or False: The Irish formed between a third to a half of all patriots in the American Revolutionary War?
11. Which Irish Society uprising was destroyed by the British in 1798?
12. What hit Ireland between 1840-1850?
13. Which organization was founded in 1850 to fight for fair rent, fixity of tenure and free sale?
14. Who was deprived of property and authority by The Disestablishment Act of 1869?
15. In which year did Ireland become a free country independent of Britain?

### Answers to Irish History

1. A Celtic people known as 'The Gaels'.
2. Petty kingdoms which dominated Ireland between the 7th Century BC and the 5th Century AD.
3. The Vikings.
4. Mary Tudor.
5. They were nor prepared to live under an administration where they were largely nobles as opposed to petty kings.
6. Scottish Immigrants.
7. The West Indies.
8. Public worship for Catholics and Presbyterians. It was reversed by the Emancipation Act of 1829.
9. The Linen Trade.
10. True. Including 1492 officers and 26 generals.
11. Society of United Irishmen.
12. The Great Famine. 1,000,000 Irish left Ireland, of which 80% came to the U.S.
13. The Tenant-Right League.
14. The Irish Church.
15. 1948

## 182. Publications

Guess the publication from these cryptic clues:

1. Magazine once edited by Michael Kinsley and Charles Krauthammer.
2. Brainchild of Bill Buckley.
3. Leftist Magazine—named after a letter in the Alphabet.
4. Kristol's mag.
5. British Political magazine—initials N.S.
6. J of FA (not the expletive).
7. Opposite of Father Smith.
8. Its Bazaar.
9. Temporal Luce Booth Creation.

10. Maybe somebody should write a Spanish language version called 'Jorge'.
11. One should always live by this.
12. Canadian Magazine—same as a toothpaste.
13. Similar to Things.
14. Medical Journal—begins with the letter 'L' (one word).
15. Means the same as 'original seeker of knowledge'.

**Answers to Publications**

1. *New Republic*
2. *National Review*
3. *Z Magazine*
4. *American Spectator*
5. *New Statesman*
6. *Journal of Foreign Affairs*
7. *Mother Jones*
8. *Harpers*
9. *Time Magazine*
10. *George*
11. *Maxim*
12. *Macleans*
13. *Stuff*
14. *Lancet*
15. *New Scientist*

## 183. Modern Palestinian History

1. What is the name of the largest faction within the PLO?
2. In which city was the PLO founded?
3. What was the trained profession of Yasser Arafat?
4. Against which rival Palestinian group did Arafat fight against c. 1982-1983 in Lebanon?
5. Who is the head of the PFLP?
6. Who is the head of the DFLP?

7. When did Yasser Arafat claim to first recognize the State of Israel—Give the year?
8. Who was Arafat's predecessor as Head of the PLO?
9. Ahmed Jibril headed which organization?
10. Which country did Arafat study in?
11. Where did Arafat flee to after being expelled from Lebanon in the early 1980s?
12. Which group carried out the Munich Olympics massacre?
13. What was the name of the ocean going liner that was hijacked by Palestinian terrorists?
14. In which year did Jordan clamp down on the Palestinians?
15. What does 'Abu' mean?

**Answers to Modern Palestinian History**

1. Al-Fatah.
2. Cairo
3. Civil Engineer.
4. A Syrian backed faction led by Abu Musa.
5. George Habash.
6. Naif Hawatmah.
7. 1988
8. Ahmed Sekourary.
9. PFLP-GC. The Popular Front for the Liberation of Palestine General Command.
10. Kuwait
11. Tunis, Tunisia.
12. Black September.
13. Achille Lauro.
14. 1971
15. Father of—as used in the names of the PLO leaders Abu Iyad, Abu Jihad etc.

# 184. Adolph Hitler and The Early Days of The Nazis

1. In which town was Adolph Hitler born?
2. True or False: Hitler was the illegimate son of Maria Ann Shicklgruber.
3. Hitler failed the entrance exam for which city's Art School?
4. What role did he carry out as a soldier during World War I?
5. Which Mayor and Head of the Christian Social Party greatly influenced Hitler?
6. Why was Hitler never promoted to Sergeant?
7. Which party did Hitler join after the First World War?
8. Who actually founded the party?
9. Where was Hitler imprisoned after the failed Beer Hall Putsch?
10. This man helped Hitler write his book, Mein Kampf in Prison. Who was he?
11. This Newspaper of the Nazi party was banned in early 1925. What was it called?
12. What was the name of the district units that the Nazis divided Germany into?
13. What was the Bund Deutscher Meidel?
14. By the mid 1920's, what factor hindered the progress of the Nazi Party?
15. In the Nazi Party, what was the difference between PO I and PO II?

## Answers to Adolph Hitler and The Early Days of The Nazis

1. Braunau Am Inn in Upper Austria in 1889.
2. False: His father, Alois was the illegitimate son of Maria Ann Shicklgruber.
3. Vienna's
4. He was a dispatch runner.
5. Karl Lueger of Vienna—a noted anti-semite.
6. His superiors felt that his strange personality and unkempt nature would not allow him to command respect from his men.

7. The German Workers' Party (it was not yet the Nazi Party).
8. Anton Dexler. Hitler would become leader of the Nazi Party on July 29, 1921. Despite earlier attempts to oust him from the party.
9. Landsberg Prison.
10. Rudolph Hess. Hess wrote as Hitler dictated.
11. *The Völkischer Beobachter* (Peoples' Observer).
12. The Gau. Each one would be headed by a leader known as the Gauleiter. There would be 34 Gaue altogether.
13. A Nazi Youth organization for Young Woman. Not to be confused with the Frauenschaffen, which was a Nazi organization for Women in general.
14. The improvement in the economy and the introduction of the Dawes plan which stabilized the German Mark. Also the German Army appeared to have made peace with the Weimar Republic.
15. PO I and PO II were two organizations into which the Nazi Party was divided. The former focused on undermining and weakening the Weimar Republic, the latter would act as a Government in waiting.

## 185. The Rise of Hitler

1. This man was sent to Berlin in October 1926 to be its Gauleiter. Who was he?
2. He headed a faction within the Nazi party that believed strongly in socialism (an issue which was somewhat anathema to Hitler). Who was this person?
3. Hitler had an affair with this niece of his. She would later commit suicide. What was her first name?
4. What powers did Chancellor Heinrich Bruening ask President von Hindenburg to give him?
5. How many seats did the Nazis win in the September 14, 1930 election? Was it: 45, 98, 107, 188, 129, or 143?
6. What was the name of the Nazi Headquarters in Munich?
7. This organization, led by Ernst R Röhm had 400,000 members by 1932. What was it called?

8 What position did Hitler fail to win in an April 10, 1932 election?
9 Newspaper articles leaked by the Social Democrats in 1932 linked this leading Nazi to homosexual activity. Who was the Nazi leader?
10 This man had a secret meeting with Hitler in May 1932. He had already helped to undermine a pro-republic general Wilhelm Groener and now set his focus with Hitler to undermine Bruening's Administration. Who was this arch-manipulator?
11 Who succeeded Bruening as chancellor?
12 When Hitler became Chancellor in January, 1933, how many of the 11 cabinet posts did the Nazis obtain?
13 Why did many wealthy industrialists support Hitler?
14. This man and former ally of Hitler sent von Hindenburg a letter saying by appointing Hitler Chancellor of the Reich, you have handed over our sacred German Fatherland to one of the greatest demagogues of all time. I prophesy to you this evil man will plunge our Reich into the abyss and will inflict immeasurable woe on our nation. Future generations will curse you in your grave for this action'. Who was he?
15. With which Third Reich Organization do you associate Kurt Gruber?

## Answers to The Rise of Hitler

1. Josef Goebbels.
2. Gregor Strasser.
3. Geli. Daughter of Hitler's half sister Angela. Speculation though is that Geli might have been murdered.
4. The ability to rule by decree, through Article 48. He felt he needed these powers to push through legislation to establish a financial program in Germany. Earlier efforts had met with much opposition. This move by Bruening was severely criticized. Bruening then asked von Hindenburg to dissolve the Reichstag and call for new elections.
5. One hundred and seven or just over 18 percent of the popular vote. The Nazis were now the Second largest party in Germany.
6. The Brown House.

7. The SA (Brownshirts).
8. President of the Republic. He was defeated by von Hindenburg.
9. Ernst R Röhm
10. Kurt von Schleicher.
11. Franz von Papen.
12. Three. Goebbels as Minister without Portfolio and Minister of the Interior of Prussia and Wilhem Flick as Minister of the Interior. It was thought that limiting the Nazis to three cabinet positions and having von Papen as Vice-Chancellor would control Hitler's power.
13. They saw him as a bulwark against Communism and the growing power of the Trade Unions.
14. General Erich Ludendorff.
15. The Hitler Youth. He became the organization's head in 1923.

## 186. The Second World War I

1. What was the exact date that Germany invaded Poland?
2. Which country presented territorial demands to Finland on October 11, 1939?
3. Where was the Graf Spee scuttled in December 1939?
4. What were the two most common types of U-Boats used by the Germans in The Battle of the Atlantic?
5. What was the name of the Treaty signed between the Soviets and the Germans in September 1939?
6. This man served as Field Marshal of the Finnish Army. After the war, he became Finland's President. Who was he?
7. This American Secretary of State went to Europe in Early 1940 with the hope of negotiating an end to the war. Who was he?
8. What was the name of the British-Polish team that broke Germany's 'Enigma' code?
9. What is the portion of the war following the defeat of Poland more commonly known as?
10. Which Northern European country fell to Germany in April 1940?
11. This General is often considered the Father of 'Blitzkrieg'. Who was he?

12. Which Dutch City was bombed into near oblivion in May 1940 in an attempt to weaken the Allied will?
13. This individual gave his name to a word that is now synonymous with being a traitor. Who was he?
14. What did the initials BEF stand for?
15. Which Navy sank the French Warships at Mers El Kebir in Algeria?

**Answers to The Second World War I**

1. September 1, 1939.
2. The Soviet Union.
3. Montevideo Harbour by its Captain Hans Langdorff following The Battle of River Plate.
4. The Type VII and the Type IX.
5. The Treaty of Friendship.
6. Baron Carl Gustaf von Mannerheim.
7. Sumner Welles.
8. The 'Ultra' Team. The breaking of the Enigma code would allow the Allies to read much of the German radio correspondence concerning operation strategy.
9. The Phony War.
10. Denmark
11. General Heinz Guaderian.
12. Rotterdam
13. Vidkun Quisling who headed Germany's Puppet Government in Norway.
14. British Expeditionary Force.
15. The British Navy. They did not want the ships to fall into German hands.

## 187. The Second World War II

1. This man became head of the Vichy Government on July 11, 1940. Who was he?

2. At which town did the French sign an armistice with Germany in June 1940?
3. Between which days were the Allied forces evacuated from Dunkirk?
4. Which two Welsh cities were bombed by the Germans to start off The Battle of Britain?
5. August 13, 1940 is known by another name when discussing The Battle of Britain. What is this name?
6. These weapons of war were responsible for the so-called 'Happy Time'. What were they?
7. This is also known as Phase 4 of The Battle of Britain. By which name however is it more commonly called?
8. What did the Germans aim Phase 2 of The Battle of Britain at?
9. What was the codename for the planned German invasion of Britain?
10. Which three countries signed the Tripartite Pact on the September 27, 1940?
11. Which African Territory did Italy attack on August 4, 1940?
12. What did the U.S. agree to give Britain in September 1939 in exchange for bases?
13. This European Country refused to join the Axis, at a meeting held on October 23, 1940. What was this Country?
14. Where did Hitler and Mussolini meet on October 4, 1940?
15. Which Country did Italy attack in October 1940?

### Answers to The Second World War II

1. Henri Pétain.
2. Compiegne
3. Between May 26 and June 23, 1940.
4. Cardiff and Swansea. The Germans attacked the docks of these cities; beginning of Phase 1 of The Battle of Britain.
5. Eagle Day or Adlertag. Germany initiated a high intensity bombing campaign to weaken the RAF. Beginning of Phase 3 of The Battle of Britain.
6. The U-boats that plagued the North Atlantic.

7. The London Blitz. Phase 1 of The Battle of Britain was the attack on the docks.
8. Allied shipping in the English Channel.
9. Operation Sea Lion.
10. Germany, Russia, and Italy.
11. British Somaliland. They attacked from Ethiopia.
12. Destroyers
13. Spain
14. The Brenner Pass.
15. Greece. The Italians sent 10 divisions into Greece, but they were not successful.

## 188. The Second World War III

1. This man was Commander of Germany's U-boat army. Who was he?
2. The Bombing of which English City began the 'Night Blitz'?
3. Which Country had a fighter plane known as the Bf-109?
4. What was the main problem with the British Matilda Tank when faced with German opposition?
5. The Luftwaffe first attacked this Island on January 16, 1941. What was this Island
6. This Libyan City fell to the British in late January 1941. What was this city?
7. From which City did the German Afrikakorps enter North Africa?
8. This German Battleship sank seven Allied ships in the Atlantic in February 1941. What was it?
9. Which Act did FDR sign on March 11, 1941?
10. The Germans occupied this Eastern European Capital in March 1941. What was this capital?
11. The Americans occupied this island in April 1941. Name this Island?
12. Why did Germany attack Greece in 1941?
13. What was the ultimate objective of Germany's Afrikakorps?
14. This German Battleship was sunk on May 27, 1941. What was this ship?
15. What was this Battleship's most famous Allied scalp?

### Answers to The Second World War III

1. Admiral Karl Dönitz.
2. Coventry
3. Germany
4. It was too slow and could be easily outflanked by the German Panzers. Even though it was well-armoured, another British tank the Mark VIB would be used in later months against the Germans. The VIB was light-skinned, but quick.
5. Malta
6. Tobruk
7. Tripoli
8. The Hipper.
9. The Lend-Lease Act.
10. Sofia—The Capital of Bulgaria.
11. Greenland
12. To support the Italian Forces who were suffering severe setbacks. Hitler sent 50,000 troops to reinforce the Italians in April 1941.
13. To capture the Suez Canal.
14. The Bismarck.
15. The HMS Hood sunk on May 24, 1941.

## 189. The Second World War IV

1. Which armed force assisted the British in their invasion of Syria in June 1941?
2. What was the codename for the German invasion of the Soviet Union?
3. To the closest half-million, how many troops were used on the attack on the Soviet Union?
4. Three hundred and twenty-four thousand Soviets were captured on July 9, 1941 in the pocket of this Soviet City. What was this city?
5. What was the name of the August 1941 Conference held between Churchill and Roosevelt?

6. This ship was America's first liberty ship (ie. it was built to carry supplies to the Allies). What was this ship's name?
7. Where in the Ukraine were 33,000 Jews massacred by the Germans on September 28-29th 1941?
8. Which City suffered from a 'great panic' on October 16, 1941?
9. What was the claim to fame of the USS Reuben James?
10. This Russian City withstood a German siege for 3 years. What was the city?
11. This Operation was launched by the British on the November 11, 1941 to relieve Tobruk. What was it called?
12. This Country developed the T-34 tank. What was the country?
13. What Act was repealed in the U.S. on November 19, 1941?
14. These three German ships made a drastic run from Brest to the North Sea ports in February 1942. Name one of the three ships?
15. Which General's offense was halted on February 4, 1942 at the Gazala-Bir Hacheim line?

**Answers to The Second World IV**

1. The Free French Forces.
2. Operation Barbarossa.
3. Three million.
4. Minsk
5. The Atlantic Conference. The Atlantic Charter would be issued following the Conference. It outlined the war aims and the foundation of the United Nations.
6. The Patrick Henry.
7. Babi Yar.
8. Moscow. Fear of the arrival of the Germans forced many citizens to flee the city.
9. It was the first American warship to be sunk during the war. It was hit by a U-boat torpedo near Iceland.
10. Leningrad (890-day siege).
11. Operation Crusader.
12. The Soviet Union. Some say the T-34 was the best tank of the war.

13. The 1939 Neutrality Act.
14. The Scharnhorst, Gneisenau, and Prinz Eugen.
15. Erwin Rommel's Offensive.

## 190. The Second World War V

1. In which city was the German invasion of Russia halted?
2. This pocket was relieved by the Germans in April 1942. What was the pocket?
3. In which city was the Nazi Reinhard Heydrich killed?
4. This German City was hit by a 1,000-plane raid in May 1942. What was this city?
5. Which German Army began a drive on Stalingrad on July 1942?
6. This city fell to Rommel's forces in June 1942. What city was it?
7. The doomed British convoy PQ 17 was destined for which Russian City when it was devastated by the Germans?
8. He was appointed Commander, U.S. Forces European Theater in June 1942. Who was he?
9. On August 19, 1942, the Allies attacked this town in France. What was the town?
10. The U.S. Army established this project in September 1942. What was it called?
11. In which Battle was Rommel defeated in on October 23-24th 1942?
12. What was the codename of the allied invasion of North Africa in November 1942?
13. From which region of the Soviet Union did the Germans begin to withdraw from in January 1943?
14. Many American tanks were named after these two Civil War Generals. Who were they?
15. American forces were not successful in this North African Battle fought in February 1943 in Tunisia. Which Battle was this?

**Answers to The Second World War V**

1. Moscow. In the heavy snow, the Germans did not have the right clothing for the weather. The Soviet Winter counter-offensive would last until March 1942.
2. The Demyansk Pocket. Ninety-thousand Germans were encircled by the Soviets.
3. In Prague by Czech Commandos. In retaliation, the Germans destroyed the town of Lidice.
4. Cologne
5. The German 6th Army.
6. Tobruk
7. Archangel
8. General Dwight D. Eisenhower.
9. Dieppe. The attack failed but its lessons would be made use of in later invasions such as 'D-Day'.
10. The Manhattan Project—to build an atomic bomb.
11. The Second Battle of El Alamein. Following this battle, the Germans would gradually be pushed back to Tunisia.
12. Operation Torch.
13. The Caucasus
14. Sherman and Grant.
15. The Battle of Kasserine Pass. The Americans appeared to be disorganized and ill-trained.

## 191. The Second World War VI

1. This General made a name for himself by capturing the Maknassy Pass in Tunisia. Who was he?
2. Which German General surrendered in January 31, 1943 on behalf of his army at Stalingrad?
3. Which allied Conference was held between the January 14-24th 1943?
4. Which event in May 1943 swung the Battle of the Atlantic in favour of the allies?

5. This 'raid' was designed to hit German industry in the Ruhr. It occurred on May 17, 1943. By which more common name was it called?
6. The British seized Pantelleria in June 1943 as a prelude to the invasion of which island?
7. What did the U.S. target in its attack on Ploesti, Romania?
8. This Battle was the largest tank battle of the war. What Battle was it?
9. This leader fell from power in July 1943. Who was he?
10. This City, which fell to a German counter-offensive in February 1943, was recaptured by the Soviets in August 1943. Which city was this?
11. Which straits did the allies cross in September 1943 in their attack on Europe?
12. This plane was America's pre-eminent strategic bomber. It was used in raids against German factories. What was this plane?
13. Over 20,336 variants of this allied fighter were produced. It first entered into service in June 1938. What was this plane?
14. In which city was the Allied Eureka Conference held in 1943?
15. In November 1943, the British attacked this line in Italy. What was the line called?

**Answers to The Second World War VI**

1. General George Smith Patton Jr. on March 31, 1943.
2. Field Marshall Friedrich von Paulus.
3. The Casablanca Conference. Roosevelt and Churchill called it to clear up any differences in strategy and set a coordinated plan for the rest of the war.
4. The sinking of 41 U-boats over a period of less than 20 days by the allies.
5. The Dambuster Raid.
6. Sicily
7. Its oil fields. These were central to the supply of the German Army.
8. The Battle of Kursk. It was won by the Soviets. Two million men,

6000 tanks, and 5000 aircraft were involved in the battle. Losses were heavy on both sides, but the Soviets had an easier time absorbing their losses.

9. Benito Mussolini.
10. Kharkov
11. Strait of Messina. To invade Italy.
12. The Boeing B-17 Flying Fortress.
13. The Supermarine Spitfire.
14. Teheran
15. The Gustav Line. The Allies would break through the line in May 1944.

## 192. The Second World War VII

1. Where in Italy did Allied Forces land on January 22, 1944?
2. This historic abbey was leveled by allied bombers in February 1944. The ruins of the Abbey would provide vital cover for the Germans afterward. What was the name of this Abbey?
3. This aircraft was widely regarded as the best American fighter. What was the name of this plane?
4. What codename was given to the 'D-Day Invasion'?
5. Name all five beaches that were attacked during the 'D-Day Invasion'?
6. Which American General led the U.S. 5th Army?
7. What was Operation Cobra?
8. This type of rocket was first used against the British in June 1944. What was it called?
9. In which month in 1944 did the allies liberate Paris?
10. This Latvian Capital fell to the Soviet forces in October 1944. What was it?
11. What was the intent of Operation Market Garden?
12. This town was relieved by Patton on December 26, 1944. Which town was this?
13. Name the country that was the site of the Battle of Walcheren in November 1944?

14. The Germans launched this offensive in November 1944. What was it called?
15. This man headed the German Abwehr spy network until his arrest in 1944 for taking part in the bomb plot against Hitler. Who was he?

**Answers to The Second World War VII**

1. Anzio
2. Monte Cassino.
3. P-51 Mustang.
4. Operation Overlord.
5. Gold, Juno, Omaha, Sword, and Utah (give yourself one point if you got four or more of these correct).
6. Mark Clark.
7. The Allied Plan to break out of Normandy.
8. The V-1 Rocket. The first V-2 Rocket strikes occurred in September 1944.
9. August ($25^{th}$).
10. Riga
11. It was an allied attempt to seize the Rhine Bridge at Arnheim, however the attempt failed.
12. Bastogne
13. The Netherlands.
14. The Ardennes Offensive or The Battle of the Bulge.
15. Admiral Wilhelm Canaris.

## 193. The Second World War VIII

1. This important Eastern European City fell to Soviet troops on January $17^{th}$ 1945. Which city was this?
2. In which region of the Soviet Union did The Yalta Conference take place?
3. This German City was the site of a devastating allied bombing attack on February $14\text{-}15^{th}$ and also March 2, 1945. Which city was this?

4. Which day was 'VE Day'?
5. In which City did the Germans sign their unconditional surrender?
6. This group known as The ACC took control of the government in Germany in June 1945. What did The ACC stand for?
7. In the gardens of which building were the bodies of Adolph Hitler and Eva Braun cremated?
8. Which three leaders met at the Potsdam Conference in July 1945?
9. What was the name of the charter that was drawn up to try war criminals?
10. In the Second World War alone, what was the best estimate to the nearest 5 million, of the number of people who died in the European /North African/Middle Eastern Theatre of the War?
11. Of the 22 accused at Nuremberg, how many were sentenced to death?
12. What was the fate of Herman Goering?
13. This Romanian leader was dismissed by King Michael in August 1944. Who was he?
14. This country's sector of Berlin contained Spandau, Charlottenburg, and Wilmersdorf. Which country is this?
15. This German was tried in absentia and sentenced to death at Nuremberg. Who was he?

**Answers to The Second World War VIII**

1. Warsaw
2. In the Crimea.
3. Dresden
4. May 8, 1945.
5. Reims
6. Allied Control Council.
7. The Chancellory.
8. Clement Atlee (UK), Josef Stalin (USSR), and Harry S. Truman (U.S.A.).
9. The London Charter.
10. Forty million.

11. 12 were sentenced to death, 3 to life, 4 to terms of 10-20 years, and 3 were acquitted.
12. Sentenced to death at Nuremberg, Goering committed suicide before his execution could take place.
13. Ion Antonescu.
14. Great Britain.
15. Martin Bormann.

## 194. The Second World War IX

1. Troops of these two countries clashed on September 1' 1939 on the Manchurian/Outer Mongolia border. Name these countries?
2. This man was elected President of China in December 1939. Who was he?
3. A Japanese puppet government under Wang Ching-wei was set up in which Chinese City in March 1940?
4. This Chinese Group launched the 'Hundred Regiments' offensive against the Japanese. Which group was this?
5. Which European-controlled Territory in Asia was attacked by the Japanese in September 1940?
6. The British opened this transport artery in October 1940. It had been closed since July of the same year. What was this artery called?
7. This man became Japanese Premier in October 1941. He led the party which favoured war. Who was this man?
8. The Japanese launched an offensive in this Region of China in January 1941. Which Region was this? Clue: Begins with the letter 'H'.
9. This nickname was given to The American Volunteer Group that arrived as pilots to fight in the Far East before the U.S. entered the war. What was this nickname?
10. In July 1941, the Filipino Army was nationalized and placed under the control of this General. Who was this general?
11. This Chinese Nationalist Capital was bombed heavily in July and August 1941. Which Capital City was this?
12. This ship had the most casualties on board during The Pear Harbour Attack?

13. To the nearest 50, how many aircraft did the U.S. lose in The Pearl Harbour Attack?
14. How many U.S. Aircraft Carriers were destroyed at Pearl Harbour?
15. On which island was Pearl Harbour base located?

### Answers to The Second World War IX

1. Japan and The Soviet Union.
2. Chiang Kai-Shek.
3. Nanking
4. The Chinese Communists led by Mao Zedong.
5. French Indochina.
6. The Burma Road.
7. Hideki Tojo. He would be hung at the end of the war for war crimes. Tojo replaced Prince Konoye as Prime Minister.
8. Honan. The Japanese would be defeated there at The Battle of Shagkao in March 1941.
9. The Flying Tigers. Pilots received a $500 bonus for every Japanese plane they shot down.
10. Douglas MacArthur.
11. Chungking
12. The Arizona.
13. Two hundred and fifty.
14. None. The three major U.S. Aircraft Carriers—The Lexington, The Enterprise, and The Saratoga were all at sea and therefore went undamaged.
15. Oahu

## 195. The Second World War X

1. This Japanese Admiral planned and directed the attack on Pearl Harbour. Who was he?
2. This American was appointed Chief of Staff of the Chinese Nationalist Army. Who was he?

3. After being pushed out of Malaya, where did the British forces flee to in early 1942?
4. Who were the victors at The Battle of Java Sea?
5. This Dutch Territory fell to the Japanese in March 1942. What was it?
6. Japanese General Masaharu Homma led the attack on which set of Islands in January 1942?
7. These bombers attacked Tokyo in April 1942. What were they nicknamed?
8. This March followed the surrender of Corregidor. What was this March called?
9. Defeat in this Battle delayed Japan's invasion of Port Moresby (New Guinea). Which Battle was this?
10. These two British ships were both sunk by the Japanese on December 10, 1941. The first was the HMS Prince of Wales. What was the other ship?
11. In which Battle did the Japanese lose four aircraft carriers, as well as the heavy Armed Cruiser, The Mikuma?
12. Where was The Battle of Bloody Ridge fought in September 1942?
13. This band of troops organized by Order Wingate were active in Burma. What were they called?
14. These five American brothers were killed while serving at Guadalcanal. Who were they?
15. This weapon was the standard sidearm of U.S. Military Officers. Which weapon was this?

### Answers to The Second World War X

1. Isoruku Yamamoto. His forces would later be defeated at Midway and he, himself would die in 1943 when his plane was shot down over the Solomon Islands.
2. General Joseph W. Stillwell.
3. Singapore
4. The Japanese.
5. The Dutch East Indies (later Indonesia).

6. The Philippines.
7. The Doolittle Raiders. This represented the first U.S. attack on Tokyo.
8. The Bataan Death March. Seventy thousand allied troops were marched 100 miles to a prison camp. Thousands died enroute. The perpetrators of this incident would later be prosecuted for war crimes.
9. The Battle of the Coral Sea.
10. The Repulse.
11. The Battle of Midway.
12. Guadalcanal. Allied fighting in Guadalcanal would last until February 1943.
13. The Chindits.
14. The Sullivan Brothers. They were all serving on the same ship.
15. The Colt. A 45 caliber automatic.

## 196. The Second World War XI

1. The U.S. F4F Wildcat competed largely against which Japanese plane?
2. In which Islands did the Naval Battles of Kula Gulf and Kolombangara occur?
3. This Northern Australian City was attacked by the Japanese during the war. Which city was this?
4. To which rank was Chester Nimitz promoted to in December 1944?
5. Which Islands did The Battle of Eniwetok Atoll occur on?
6. What was the 'Silent Service'?
7. Starting from earliest to latest—in which order were the following islands re-taken by the allies: New Britain, Gilbert Islands, The Aleutian Islands?
8. This later President's PT-109 ship was sunk by the Japanese on August 1, 1943. Who was this individual?
9. Nicknamed 'The Great Marianas Turkey Shoot', what was the official name of this Battle?

10. What was the name given to the troops led by Frank Dow Merrill in the U.S. Chinese offensive in Burma in February 1944?
11. Who were also known as 'The Divine Wind'?
12. The Japanese lost the carrier the Zuiho and 16 other important ships in this October 1944 Battle. Which battle was this?
13. This Burmese City fell to British Troops in March 1945. Which city was this?
14. The Americans completed capture of this Island in June 1945. Name this island?
15. On which island's Mount Suribachi did the Americans plant the U.S. Flag?

## Answers to The Second World War XI

1. The Japanese Zero.
2. The Solomon Islands.
3. Darwin
4. To the newly created position of Fleet Admiral. Before this, he was Commander in Chief, Pacific Ocean Areas.
5. The Marshall Islands in February 1944.
6. Generally speaking the U.S. Submarine Fleet that waged war against the Japanese in the Pacific.
7. The Aleutian Islands (July 1943), The Gilbert Islands (November 1943), and New Britain (December 1943).
8. John F. Kennedy.
9. The Battle of the Philippine Sea.
10. Merrill's Marauders.
11. The Japanese Kamikaze Pilots.
12. The Battle of Leyte Gulf.
13. Mandalay
14. Okinawa
15. Iwo Jima.

# 197. The Second World War XII

1. This was the nickname of the bomb that was dropped on Hiroshima. What was this nickname?
2. This General bought together The Team of Academics involved in the Manhattan Project. Who was he?
3. In August 1945, the Soviets invaded this former Japanese held Territory on the Asian Mainland. Which territory was this?
4. The Formal Surrender Agreement of the Japanese was signed aboard this ship. Name this ship?
5. When was 'VJ Day' (exact date)?
6. What was a 'Baka' or an 'Okha'?
7. To the nearest 10,000, how many people died at Hiroshima?
8. Which plane dropped the first Atom Bomb?
9. Incendiary raids on this City killed 84,000 people between March 9-10th, 1945. Which city was this?
10. Name the Naval Carrier Expert who said, "Hit hard, hit fast, hit often," when referring to his attack strategies?
11. This plane recorded an 11:1 kill ratio against the Japanese. It was nicknamed 'The Whistling Death'. What was the name of the plane?
12. Which type of plane dropped the Atomic bomb on Nagasaki?
13. How many days in 1945 separated the Atomic Bomb drops on Hiroshima and Nagasaki?
14. This was the last Japanese super battleship to be sunk. What was it?
15. He would eventually have to acknowledge that he was not a god. Who was this individual?

## Answers to The Second World War XII

1. Little Boy.
2. General Leslie Grove.
3. Manchuria
4. The U.S.S. Missouri.
5. August 15,1945.
6. A piloted rocket bomb used by the Japanese against the allies.

7. Eighty thousand. A further 75,000-125,000 would die in the years that followed.
8. The Enola Gay. It was a B-26 Bomber.
9. Tokyo
10. William Frederick Halsey Jr.
11. The Vought F4U Corsair.
12. A B-29 (40,000-70,000 would die at Nagasaki and 50,000-100,000 would die later in the years to follow.)
13. Three Days. August 6, Hiroshima and August 9, Nagasaki.
14. The Yamato during The Battle of Okinawa.
15. Emperor Hirohito.

## 198. The Holocaust I

1. Why was the Reichstag burnt down?
2. What was the first Concentration camp to be set up?
3. This Concentration Camp was opened for women only. Which camp was it?
4. This Act was passed by the German Parliament on March 24, 1933. It gave Hitler dictatorial powers. Which Act was this?
5. This man created the Gestapo. Who was he?
6. Put these 'Prohibition Against Jews' in the order they occurred—earliest to latest :

   Jews are not allowed to own land.

   Jews are banned from the German Labour Front.

   Jews cannot be newspaper editors.

   Jews cannot obtain legal qualifications.

   Jews are not allowed national health insurance
7. Which division was formed in March 1936 to guard concentration camps?
8. These Laws came into being on September 15, 1935. What were they?
9. Why were the Jews fined a billion marks on November 12, 1938?
10. In August 1936, the Nazis set up an office to combat Abortions by healthy women, as well as which other 'deviation'?

11. This ship carrying Jewish refugees was turned away by several countries including the US. It was forced to return to Europe. What was the name of the Ship?
12. Which name did the Nazis force all Jewish women to add to their names on August 17, 1938?
13. Who was appointed Head of the Prague Office of Jewish Emigration on July 21, 1939?
14. These professionals were prohibited from practicing on July 25, 1938. Who were they?
15. What did the Nazis force all Jewish passports to be stamped with on October 5, 1938?

**Answers to the Holocaust I**

1. To create a crisis situation that Hitler would exploit to give himself Emergency Powers in Germany.
2. Dachau Camp outside Munich on March 22, 1933.
3. Ravensbrück
4. The Enabling Act.
5. Hermann Göring.
6. Jews are not allowed to own land (September 29, 1933); Jews cannot be newspaper editors (October 4, 1933); Jews are banned from the German Labour Front (January 24, 1934); Jews are not allowed national health insurance (May 17, 1934); Jews cannot obtain legal qualifications (July 22, 1934).
7. The SS Deathshead Division.
8. The Nuremberg Laws.
9. For Damage resulting from Kristallnacht.
10. Homosexuality
11. The St. Louis.
12. Sarah, men had to add Israel to their names.
13. Adolph Eichmann.
14. Jewish Physicians.
15. A large red 'J'.

## 199. The Holocaust II

1. To which organization was Reinhard Heydrich appointed the head of on September 27, 1939?
2. In October 1939, this group (not an ethnic division), were slated for murder. Who were they?
3. Which section of The Gestapo dealing sole with Jewish affairs did Adolf Eichmann head?
4. On November 23, 1939, Polish Jews over what age were forced to wear the yellow star?
5. This anti-Semite published the Nazi Newspaper, *Der Strürmer*?
6. Over which Concentration Camp was Rudolf Höss chosen to be commander of on May 1, 1940?
7. To which Island did Eichmann intend at one point to deport the Jews to?
8. Of the ghettos in Warsaw, Krakow, and Lodz, which was the first to be sealed off?
9. This man, who was Gauleiter of Poland said, "I ask nothing of the Jews except they should disappear." Who was he?
10. This organization followed on behind the army committing mass murders in their pathway. What was this organization?
11. This 'racial' Philosopher was appointed Reich Minister for the Eastern Occupied Territories on July 17, 1941. Who was he?
12. This gas was first tested on September 3, 1941. What was this gas?
13. This ghetto set up near Prague was to serve as a model for propaganda reasons. What was this ghetto called?
14. The Chelmno Extermination Camp was situated near which Polish City?
15. This ship left Romania for Palestine with 767 Jews on board. It was denied entry into Palestine by the British Authorities and was subsequently sunk by a Soviet Submarine in the Black Sea. What was this ship's name?

**Answers to the Holocaust II**

1. The RHSA (The Reich Main Security Office). The RHSA combined the SS Security Service (SD), the Secret State Police (the Gestapo), and the Criminal Police.
2. The sick and disabled in what the Nazis described as 'euthanasia'.
3. Section IV B4.
4. Age of 10.
5. Julius Streicher.
6. Auschwitz
7. Madagascar
8. Lodz in April 1940. Krakow and Warsaw were sealed off in November 1940.
9. Hans Frank.
10. The SS Einsatzgruppen.
11. Alfred Rosenberg.
12. Zyklon-B.
13. Theresienstadt
14. Lublin. On December 8, 1941 it became operational.
15. The Struma.

## 200. The Holocaust III

1. Name the conference that was called on January 1942 to coordinate the 'Final Solution'?
2. Belzec extermination camp was located in which country?
3. Which gas was at first used for mass executions?
4. Located East of Warsaw, this death camp was opened on July 23, 1942. It contained 10 gas chambers, each of which could hold 200 people. Which camp was this?
5. There was a mass killing of Jews from the Mirocz Ghetto on October 14, 1942. In which country was the Mirocz Ghetto?
6. Jews from this City were sent to the Drancy Internment Camp enroute to Auschwitz, Majdanek or Sobibor. Which city was this?

7. Operation Reinhard involved the mass deportation of Jews from which country?
8. This Eastern European Country, which was an ally with Germany, resisted deportation of the Jews on March 17, 1943. Name this country?
9. The Waffen SS attacked this ghetto in April 1943 to put down a Jewish rebellion.? Which ghetto was this?
10. What was meant by the phrase 'Judenfrei'?
11. To the closest number of years, how long did Treblinka remain open?
12. Which Country did the Danes send their 7220 Jews for safety to?
13. This concentration camp was shut down after a mass breakout of 300 individuals on October 4, 1943. Name this camp?
14. This was the first concentration camp to be liberated by the Soviets. Which camp was this?
15. This name was given to Jewish slave labourers. Which name was this?

**Answers to the Holocaust III**

1. The Wannsee Conference.
2. Poland. Six hundred thousand would die in Belzec alone.
3. Carbon monoxide piped in from engines.
4. Treblinka
5. The Ukraine.
6. Paris
7. Poland
8. Bulgaria
9. The Warsaw Ghetto.
10. Cleansed of Jews—a status given to such cities as Berlin (on May 19, 1943).
11. One year, however 870,000 people died there.
12. Sweden
13. Sobibor. Only 50 would survive the escape. Sobibor would eventually be shut down and all trace of its existence removed; this after 250,000 people had died there.

14. Majdanek
15. Sonderkommando. They revolted at Auschwitz-Birkenau on October 6, 1944 destroying Crematory IV.

## 201. The Holocaust IV

1. She was arrested with her sister, Margot, and shipped to Auschwitz. Who was she?
2. He saved 1200 Jews by relocating them from the Plaszow Labour Camp to his home town of Brunnlitz. Who was he?
3. Troops of which Country liberated the following camps: a) Auschwitz, b) Bergen-Belsen, c) Buchenwald?
4. Which U.S. Army liberated Dachau?
5. To the closest 100,000, how many people died at Auschwitz?
6. Jews from this Country began arriving at Auschwitz in May 15, 1944. Around the same time Eichmann ordered the mass killings at Auschwitz to speed up. Name the country?
7. Who were kidnapped as a result of the Hay Action?
8. This country lost the second most amount of Jews during the Holocaust. Which country was this?
9. What was Himmler's title within the SS?
10. This infamous doctor arrived at Auschwitz in May 1943. Who was he?
11. In which Country was Adolf Eichmann captured by Israeli Secret Service?
12. What is the claim to fame of Mordechai Anielewicz?
13. This Holocaust survivor would win the Nobel Prize for Peace in 1986. Who was he?
14. Known also as the Holocaust Martyrs and Heroes Research Authority, it was established in 1953 by an act of the Knesset. What is being referred to?
15. This area in the Ukraine contained 300,000 Jews. Two-thirds fled the mobile killing squads in 1941. After the German occupation, it would become a destination for deported Romanian Jews. Which area was this?

### Answers to the Holocaust IV

1. Anne Frank.
2. Oskar Schindler.
3. a) Soviet Union; b) Britain; c) U.S.A.
4. The 7th Army.
5. 2,000,000 of which 1,500,000 were Jews.
6. Hungary
7. 40,000 Polish children aged between 10-14 who were to be used as slave labour.
8. The USSR. 1,100,000 Jews died. Poland had the most losses 3,000,000 out of a pre-war Jewish population of 3,300,000.
9. SS Reichsführer.
10. Dr. Josef Mengele.
11. Argentina on May 11,1960.
12. He was leader of the Warsaw Ghetto uprising.
13. Eli Wiesel.
14. Yad Vashem.
15. Transnistria

## 202. European History 19th Century I

1. This Congress was called to settle European affairs after the defeat of Napoleon. Name the Congress?
2. Which two political forces ('isms) were the Concert of Europe system opposed to?
3. Who represented: a) Prussia, b) France, and c) Russia at the Congress mentioned in Question 1?
4. Put these four congresses in the order they occurred, earliest to latest: Troppau, Laibach, Verona, Aix-la-Chapelle?
5. This General forced Ferdinand I of Naples to accept a liberal constitution in 1820. Who was he?
6. This reactionary Russian Writer was assassinated by Karl Ludwig Sand on March 23, 1819. Who was this writer?

7. The Congress of Verona was called to deal with the crisis in which Country?
8. What was the Burschenscraft?
9. Who were the Carbonari?
10. These four countries made up the Holy Alliance. Name the countries?
11. This Country was once described as a mere 'geographical expression'. Which was the country?
12. This first step toward German Unity was undertaken with the formations of a Customs Union. What was this Custom Union called?
13. Giuseppe Mazzini founded a political movement in Paris in 1832. What was the movement called?
14. The Russians crushed a rebellion in this Country in 1831. Name the country?
15. Leopold of Saxe-Coburg-Gotha would become King of this country in 1830-31. Name the country?

## Answer to European History 19th Century I

1. The Congress of Vienna.
2. Nationalism and Liberalism.
3. a) Prince of Hardenberg, b) Charles Talleyrand, c) Tsar Alexander I. Give yourself one point if you got two or more of these correct.
4. Aix-la-Chapelle (1818), Troppau (1820), Laibach (1821), Verona (1822).
5. General Pepe. The constitution would later be abolished when Austrian troops entered Naples after the Congress of Laibach.
6. August von Kotzebue—an opponent of Romanticism, Liberalism and Nationalism.
7. Spain. It was called to put down the rebellion of General Riego, which it did in unmerciful fashion.
8. A liberal student organization in Germany, supportive of revolutionary agitation and opposed to the old order.
9. Secret Societies of Middle Class Liberals in Italy that were active

after the Napoleonic War. They were called a such as their members met in the woods just like charcoal burners.
10. Austria, France, Prussia, and Russia.
11. Italy. It was called this by Klemens von Metternich in 1815.
12. The Zollverein.
13. Young Italy. Mazzini in his lifetime would become a symbol for democratic movements throughout Europe. "He is one of my heroes."
14. Poland
15. Belgium. It won independence from Holland in December 1830 (Conference of London gave recognition to Belgium by the Great Powers). Holland however would only officially acknowledge the existence of an independent Belgium in 1839.

## 203. European History 19th Century II

1. This man ascended to the French Throne in 1824. Who was he?
2. This French Philosopher wrote that 'property is theft'. Who was he?
3. An English Socialist, he set up a community in the United States called 'New Harmony'. It failed but would prove to be an important milestone in practical socialism. Who was this Englishman?
4. In which European City did a banker family, known as the Hopes, come to the forefront?
5. This man took power in France after the 1830 Revolution. Who was he?
6. From which Royal House/Family line did the man mentioned in Question 5 emerge from?
7. This Royalist and staunch Conservative was Prime Minister of France between 1839 to 1848. His opposition to concessions with the radical left would eventually lead to his downfall. Who was he?
8. What came in to being in France in 1848?
9. Of which art form was the politically influential Alphonse de Lamartine a master?
10. This man championed cooperative workshops in his book

*L'Organisation du travail.* However, the creation of National Workshops in France realized only part of his ideals. Who was this man?

11. What in 19th Century French History is the 'June Days'?
12. He was elected President of France with 5,400,000 votes in 1848. Who was he?
13. In which year in the 1850s was the Empire restored to France?
14. Who was Eugénie of Montijo?
15. This man was commissioned to rebuild Paris. Who was he?

**Answers to European History 19th Century II**

1. Charles X.
2. Pierre Joseph Proudhon.
3. Robert Owen.
4. Amsterdam. Other banker families in Europe at the time were the Rothschilds and the Barings.
5. Louis Phillipe—The Citizen King.
6. The Bourbon-Orléanist House.
7. François Guizot.
8. The Second Republic.
9. Poetry. He was also a Historian and played a significant part in the creation of the Second Republic.
10. Louis Blanc—he would later flee to England.
11. A period during 1848 that saw the closure of the National Workshops, followed by two days of uprising and the brutal suppression of that uprising. A great divide was created between the Socialists and the Republicans.
12. Louis Bonaparte.
13. 1852
14. A Spanish Countess—she was the beautiful wife of Louis Bonaparte.
15. Baron Hausmann.

## 204. European History in the 19th Century III

1. In which Country was the 1825 Decembrist Rebellion crushed?
2. Whose fleet was destroyed at the Battle of Navarino in 1827?
3. This Egyptian leader agreed with British demands to quit Greece in 1828. Who was he?
4. Milos Obrenovic became 'Supreme Chief' of which state in 1830?
5. This Prussian General and Military Strategist died in 1831. Who was he?
6. This civil war broke out in Spain in 1834. Which civil war was it?
7. This German Region was granted a liberal constitution by the English King William IV in 1833. Which region was this?
8. His reign as Emperor of Austria ended with his death in 1835. He was succeeded by his son, Ferdinand II. Who was this man being described here?
9. Who succeeded Alexander I as Tsar of Russia in 1825?
10. A Conference held in London in 1840 closed these two straits to the warships of any nations. Which straits were these?
11. Who was the first King of the newly created independent Greek state?
12. What was the 'Sick Man of Europe'?
13. This 13-year-old became Queen of Spain in 1843. Who was she?
14. In which Country did The Sonderbund War breakout in 1847?
15. The Historian, De Tocqueville once wrote, "Here begins again the French Revolution—this is exactly the same." What was he speaking about?

### Answers to European History in the 19th Century III

1. Russia
2. Turkey's by a British and French fleet acting in agreement with the Russians.
3. Mehmet Ali. Ali would later fight the Turks defeating them in Syria in 1832. Of interest Ali, Wellington and Napoleon were all born in the same year, 1769.
4. Serbia

5. Karl von Clausewitz.
6. The Carlist War.
7. Hanover. The English Kings were also the state heads of Hanover. This constitution would be cancelled by Ernst Augustus in 1837. Ausustus was the new King of Hanover.
8. Francis II. He was also the last Holy Roman Emperor (1798-1806).
9. Nicholas I. Some say however that Alexander never died in 1825 but lived out his last years as a religious hermit in Siberia.
10. The Bosporus and the Dardanelles.
11. Otto I of Bavaria.
12. The Ottoman Empire whose fate kept alive the Eastern Question.
13. Isabella II. Following the military revolt that brought down the government of General Espartero.
14. Switzerland. The Sonderbond was formed in 1844 to protect the Catholic cantons.
15. The Crisis of 1848. Europe's Year of Revolutions.

## 205. European History in the 19th Century IV

(Almost all of these questions deal with the 1848-49 Revolutions).

1. Which Agrarian disaster caused food riots to breakout in Europe in 1846-47?
2. In which country did the first of the 1848 revolutions breakout?
3. Which two men led the Hungarian revolution of 1848?
4. In which type of vehicle did Klemens von Metternich flee to safety from Austria following the student uprising of 1848?
5. In which port city did the patriots Daniele Manin and Niccolo Tommasseo force the Austrian Garrison to capitulate?
6. Which people's revolution was the poet Jan Kollár associated with?
7. This man is credited with leading the forces that restored Austrian control over much of Italy. Who was he?
8. This country's army entered Rome in July 1849 forcing the Italian liberals to flee. Name the country?
9. This man became Austrian Emperor in December 1848, after his uncle Ferdinand was persuaded to abdicate?

10. Which Balkan people sided with the Austrians to defeat the Hungarians?
11. In which German City was an unsuccessful Parliament consisting largely of intellectuals and notables established?
12. This Editor of the Rhine Gazette would learn much from the class struggles of the 1848 revolution. Who was he?
13. In which Army was Marshal Windischgraetz a leading figure?
14. He refused the crown of a unified German Empire claiming that he did not want a crown of rubbish made up of clay and mud. Who was he?
15. This country came to Austria's assistance and helped defeat the Hungarians at the Battle of Vilagos. Their reason for assistance is they wanted a free hand in dealing with the Turks in the East. Name this Country?

### Answers to European History in the 19th Century IV

1. The Irish Potato Disease of 1845-46. This spread to Europe causing a shortage of wheat, price doubling, and food riots to breakout in France, Germany, Belgium, and Italy.
2. Italy in January 1848.
3. Louis Kossuth and Ferenc Deák.
4. A laundry van.
5. Venice
6. The Czech Revolution.
7. Field Marshal Joseph Radetzky.
8. France
9. Francis Joseph. He would rule until well into the First World War.
10. The Croats.
11. Frankfurt
12. Karl Marx.
13. The Austrian Army. He restored Vienna to the Monarchy.
14. King Frederick Wilhem IV. His decision set back an early attempt at German unification. The King was a believer in the divine right of kings and felt that such a position could not be handed to someone by the public.
15. Russia

## 206. European History in the $19^{th}$ Century V

1. This man planned to unite Italy into a confederation under the pope. His group of followers were sometimes dubbed the 'neo-Guelphs'. However, his plan ultimately failed as the pope did not want to alienate the Habsburg rulers. Which man is being described here?
2. Which two Northern Italian Kingdoms did Sardinia-Piedmont hope to join with to form a kingdom of Northern Italy?
3. Which house ruled Sardinia-Piedmont at the time of Italian unification?
4. Who was the King of Sardinia-Piedmont at the time of unification?
5. This man guided the Sardinia-Piedmont directed unification drive. He was Prime Minister of the Kingdom for most of the period between 1852 and 1861. Who was he?
6. An assassination attempt on Napoleon III by this Italian refugee temporarily set back French support for Italian unification. Who was this refugee?
7. His opposition to the unification process in Italy earned this pope the nickname 'Pio No No'. What was his more formal name?
8. France's war with this Country in 1859 opened up the prospects for Italian unification. Which Country was this?
9. This was the most important battle of the war mentioned in Question 8. What was the name of this Battle?
10. Which International Organization was born from the war mentioned in Questions 8 and 9?
11. Piedmont had already won Lombardy through The Treaty of Villafranca. She would later gain Parma, Modena, and Tuscany. In exchange, France would win control of Savoy and this port City. Which city is this?
12. This man was King of the Two Sicilies in 1860. Who was he?
13. Which Royal House did the King mentioned in Question 12 represent?
14. Which European political figure once worked as a candlemaker in New York City?
15. What was the Italian term for the unification drive of the $19^{th}$ Century?

### Answers to European History in the 19th Century V

1. Vincenzo Gioberti.
2. Lombardy and Venetia.
3. The House of Savoy.
4. Victor Emmanuel II. His nickname was 'il re galantuomo' (or the Cavalier King).
5. Camillo Cavour.
6. Felice Orsini. He tried to assassinate Napoleon III and his wife when they were on their way to the opera in Paris.
7. Pope Pius IX.
8. Austria
9. Battle of Solferino.
10. The International Red Cross which was founded by Swiss native, Henri Dunant, after he saw the plight of the wounded from the Battle of Solferino
11. Nice
12. Francis II.
13. The House of Bourbon.
14. Giuseppe Garibaldi.
15. The Risorgimento.

## 207. European History in the 19th Century VI

1. What were Giuseppe Garibaldi's troops nicknamed?
2. Why was Piedmont at first reluctant to aid Garibaldi?
3. This City would serve as the first Capital of Italy. Which City was this?
4. Italy formed an alliance with this military power in 1866. Which power was this?
5. This port City fell into Italian hands after The Treaty of Vienna. Which city was this?
6. One of the last pieces of the puzzle; Rome would fall into Italian hands in which year?
7. Which type (or class) of Prussian family did Bismarck emerge from?

8. Which man became King of Prussia in 1860?
9. This man became Chief of the Prussian Army in 1857. His military successes drove German unification. Who was he?
10. Against which Country did Prussia go to war against in 1864?
11. Which Territory did Prussia win in the war mentioned in Question 10?
12. Who was Prussia's ally in the war mentioned in Questions 10 and 11?
13. What was another name for The Prussian-Austrian War of 1866?
14. Bismarck was Ambassador to this Eastern Power between 1859 and 1862. Which power was this?
15. This was the greatest Battle of The Austrian-Prussian War. Which battle was this?

**Answers to European History in the 19th Century VI**

1. The redshirts or the 'Thousand'. They would succeed in driving the Bourbons from the Two Sicilies. Power was later handed over to The Piedmontese Army.
2. They did not wish to absorb the economically backward Kingdom of the Two Sicilies. They also feared that the war might escalate toward Rome and this would bring in Foreign intervention (either answer will do).
3. Turin
4. Prussia
5. Venice. Italy won Venice despite suffering setbacks against the Austrians in the fighting at the time (Battles of Custozza and Lissa). It was her alliance with Prussia that would win the rights for Italy at the negotiating table.
6. 1870
7. Junkers Class. These families had ruled the villages and countryside of Prussia since the Middle Ages.
8. Wilhelm I at the age of 64.
9. Field-Marshal Helmuth von Moltke.
10. Denmark

11. Schleswig and Holstein.
12. Austria. Bismarck manipulated the Austrians into siding with him on behalf of the German. Confederation.
13. The Seven Weeks War.
14. Russia
15. The Battle of Sadowa fought in Bohemia and won by the Prussians.

## 208. European History in the 19th Century VII

1. Which Confederation did Bismarck form with the new states that fell under Prussian control after the war with Austria in 1866?
2. What was the name of the Parliament for this new Confederation?
3. Which river divided this Confederation from the rest of Germany along a North-South Axis?
4. Which country's demand did Bismarck dismiss as an 'innkeeper's bill'?
5. The Throne of which Country became vacant in 1868?
6. This telegram, which asked Prussia to humiliate herself by withdrawing her candidacy from the throne of the country mentioned in Question 5, would provide the impetus leading to the War of 1870. What was this telegram called?
7. What was France's biggest weakness in The War of 1870?
8. This French Hero of the War of 1859 was driven out of Alsace by the Prussians. Who was he?
9. The French failed to relieve this City during the war, which turned out to be a crucial failure. Which city was this?
10. What was the deciding battle of the War?
11. After the establishment of the Third Republic, this Politician flew out of Paris by balloon to rally support in the Provinces against Prussia. Who was he?
12. Which Treaty ended The Franco-Prussian War?
13. In which building was the Second Reich proclaimed?
14. Which King of Bavaria had to be bought onto the side of German unification only by a series of promises, one of which was the Bavarian Brewing Industry would be protected by a reduced duty?

15. This Territory was ceded to Germany at the end of The Franco-Prussian War by France. Which Territory was this?

**Answers to European History in the 19th Century VII**

1. The North German Confederation. Twenty-five million Germans were now ruled from Berlin.
2. The Reichstag.
3. The River Main.
4. French demand for Territory to compensate them for remaining neutral during the Prussian-Austrian War and to placate security threats that France felt had increased as a result of growing Hohenzollern power.
5. Spain, causing a succession crisis.
6. The Ems Telegram.
7. She had no allies—Bismarck had seen to this through the use of skillful diplomacy beforehand. Also from a war perspective, France did not have the military generals to match the calibre of Prussia.
8. Patrice MacMahon, a Frenchman of Irish descent.
9. Metz
10. The Battle of Sedan. The Prussians defeated the French and Napoleon III himself fell into Prussian hands.
11. Léon Gambetta.
12. The Treaty of Frankfurt.
13. In the Palace of Versailles, specifically, The Hall of Mirrors.
14. Louis II (Ludwig II).
15. Alsace-Lorraine. The Mayor of Strasbourg died of shock on hearing of the peace plan with Prussia and her allies.

## 209. European History in the 19th Century VIII

1. This Government was set up in Paris in 1871 in opposition to the National Government?
2. Who benefited from The Italian Law of Guarantees?

3. Against which Organization was Bismarck's Kulturkampf policy directed?
4. Germany, Russia, and Austria established an alliance in 1872. What was this alliance called?
5. This man became King of Spain in 1874. He would rule until 1885. Who was he?
6. Which people suffered a massacre at the hands of the Turks in 1876?
7. This Country declared war against Turkey in 1877 in support of a Balkan insurrection against the Turks. Which country was this?
8. This Law aimed at the left was introduced in Germany in 1878. Which Law was this?
9. The Treaty of Berlin signed at the Berlin Congress in 1878, undid some of the concessions of this earlier Treaty signed less than a year before. What was this earlier Treaty?
10. This Liberal Pope sought to heal the rift between The Vatican and The French Third Republic through his Bull, the Immortale Dei of 1885. Who was this pope?
11. The Triple Alliance signed in 1882 involved which three powers?
12. Which mile limit was agreed on in 1882 at The Hague Convention as the limit for territorial water?
13. This man was the First President of The French Third Republic. His term lasted between 1871-1873. He was a respectable Historian. Who was he?
14. This General failed in a coup d'etat in Paris in 1887. Who was he?
15. Who dismissed Bismarck as Chancellor in 1890?

## Answers to European History in the 19th Century VIII

1. The Paris Commune—it ruled for two months.
2. The Pope—he was allowed possession of The Vatican.
3. The Catholic Church. Kuturkampf stood for the 'struggle of civilizations'. It would prove to be a failure on Bismarck's behalf.
4. The Three-Emperors League.
5. Alfonso XII.

6. The Bulgarians.
7. Russia. Russia would invade Bulgaria and Romania.
8. The Anti-Socialist Law.
9. The Treaty of San Stefano. The Berlin Treaty undid some of the agreements of San Stefano as the latter was too favourable to Russia.
10. Leo XIII.
11. Germany, Austria, and Italy.
12. Three miles.
13. Adolphe Thiers.
14. Georges Boulanger.
15. Kaiser Wilhem II. Punch Magazine lampooned this in a cartoon entitled 'Dropping the Pilot'.

## 210. European History in the 19th Century IX

1. Which Empire was the subject of the Compromise of 1867?
2. Which Treaty ended The Crimean War?
3. According to this Treaty, the Kingdoms of Wallachia and Moldavia would be combined to form which country?
4. Why was Count Badeni dismissed as Prime Minister of Austria in 1897?
5. What was The Bach System?
6. France formed an alliance with this Country in 1893. Name this Country?
7. Which Country had politicians named 'Hohenlohe and Caprivi'?
8. Who masterminded the building of The Suez Canal in 1881?
9. This journalist led the campaign against Captain Alfred Dreyfus in the media. Who was he?
10. Who was the real traitor in The Dreyfus Affair?
11. This writer leapt to Dreyfus's defence with his work *J'accuse*. Who was he?
12. Over which island did Greece and Turkey go to war in 1897?
13. Which Turkish organization, hoping to win liberal reform in their country, was formed in Geneva in 1891?

14. What relation was Kaiser Wilhem II to Queen Victoria?
15. What was the aim of the International Conference held in the Hague in 1899?

## Answers to European History in the 19th Century IX

1. The Austro-Hungarian Empire. It was given three governments: A Central Government (Emperor and 3 ministers—for Foreign Affairs, Armed Forces and Finance), an Austrian Government (with the Emperor as Constitutional Monarch created by the February Patent of 1861) and a Kingdom of Hungary (with the Emperor again serving as the Constitutional Monarch).
2. The Treaty of Paris, signed in 1856.
3. Romania. Beginning of the breakup of the Ottoman Empire.
4. For agreeing to recognize Czech as an official language. This created intense resistance by the German population prompting the Emperor to dismiss Badeni.
5. A policy of Germanizing the Austro-Hungarian Empire in the 1850's. Alaxander Bach, the Minister of the Interior was entrusted with the policy—hence the name.
6. Russia
7. Germany. They were chancellors after Bismarck.
8. Ferdinand de Lesseps.
9. Edouard Drumont.
10. Another Army Officer, Esterhazy. Documents forged to put Dreyfus's guilt beyond doubt were manufactured by Colonel Henry.
11. Emile Zola. He was sentenced to prison for his work, fled to England and returned to a hero's welcome in France after Dreyfus had been cleared.
12. Crete
13. The Young Turk Movement.
14. He was her grandson through her daughter, Victoria.
15. To find a means to solve international conflicts peacefully.

## 211. The Industrial Revolution I

1. Which type of Industry did the factories of the Industrial Revolution replace?
2. Between which two cities did the first railway open up to carry passengers?
3. In which decade of the $19^{th}$ Century were the first ocean cables laid down?
4. This German businessman had the first streetcar running in Berlin in 1881. Who was he?
5. A rebellion by this group of people in Northern England in 1811, resulted in the destruction of Industrial Machinery. Who were they?
6. This world famous German Industrial Works opened in 1810 in Essen. What was it?
7. What is the Frenchman François Appert associated with?
8. He built the first practical steam locomotive at Killingworth Colliery near Newcastle in 1814. Who was he?
9. What did John Macadam use that revolutionized his method of constructing roads?
10. This was the first steamship to cross the Atlantic. Which steamship was this?
11. What is Charles Macintosh associated with?
12. How did John Walker revolutionize the Match Industry in 1827?
13. What is the electrician Joseph Swan associated with?
14. Which Technology field are L.J.M. Daguerre and J.N. Niepce associated with?
15. This American invented the Reaping Machine in 1834. Who was he?

### Answers to The Industrial Revolution I

1. The Cottage or Domestic Industry.
2. Stockton and Darlington.
3. The 1850's under the direction of Lord Kelvin. The firework display designed to celebrate this feat set the New York City Hall on fire.
4. Werner Siemens of Siemens Corporation fame.

5. The Luddites, led by Ned Ludd.
6. The Krupp Works.
7. The canning of food.
8. George Stephenson. His engine 'The Rocket' would win a prize of 500 pounds in 1829 at The Rainhill Trials.
9. Crushed stones.
10. The Savannah. It crossed the Atlantic in 26 days in 1818.
11. The invention of a waterproof fabric (later used in raincoats) in 1823.
12. He introduced Sulfur friction matches.
13. The invention of the carbon filament used in lighting and heating.
14. Photography. They were the leading pioneers in the Technology.
15. Cyrus Hall McCormick.

## 212. The Industrial Revolution II

1. Which type of device did the 'SS Great Britain' use in 1843 to cross the Atlantic?
2. Which type of crane did William Armstrong patent in 1845?
3. Who devised the continuous switch sewing machine in 1851?
4. What invention is E.G. Otis associated with?
5. What happened in Titusville, PA in 1859?
6. How many barrels did R.J. Gattling have on the gun he invented in 1862?
7. Who opened his first home for destitute children in Stepney, London in 1866?
8. Who was Karl Marx's main opponent in The First International?
9. Where was The First International formed?
10. In the Second International, which movements stood in opposition to Orthodox Marxism? Hint: Its leaders were Eduard Bernstein and August Bebel.
11. What did the Gunsmith Firm E. Remington start producing in 1873?
12. Which transportation vehicle did A.A. Pope begin manufacturing in the U.S. in 1878?

13. Who invented the pneumatic tire?
14. In which American City was the first entirely steel-framed building erected in 1890?
15. Who invented the punch card system?

**Answers to The Industrial Revolution II**

1. The Propeller. It was the first propeller-driven ship to cross the Atlantic.
2. The hydraulic crane.
3. Isaac Singer.
4. The first safety elevator (1857).
5. The first oil well was drilled there.
6. Ten
7. Dr. T.J. Barnardo.
8. Mikhail Bakunin, Leader of the Anarchists.
9. In London in 1868.
10. Revisionism. Philosophy argued that working class prosperity had increased. Workers revolution had been postponed and that the labour movement should look into gaining concessions with respect to suffrage and working conditions from Liberal Politicians holding power.
11. Typewriters
12. The bicycle
13. J.B. Dunlop in 1888.
14. Chicago
15. H. Hollerith in 1889.

## 213. The Industrial Revolution III

With which Invention are the following inventors most associated?

1. Cecil Booth.
2. Ferdinand Carré.
3. Jacob Schick.

4. James Dewar.
5. Emile Berliner.
6. John Kay.
7. Richard Trevithick.

Who invented the following?

8. Barbed Wire.
9. Polaroid Camera.
10. Wireless
11. Fountain Pen.
12. Tank
13. Spinning Jenny.
14. Zip Fastener.
15. Cylinder Lock.

## Answers to The Industrial Revolution III

1. Vacuum cleaner in 1901.
2. Refrigerator in 1858.
3. Electric shaver in 1928.
4. Vacuum flask in 1885.
5. Gramophone in 1887.
6. Flying Shuttle in 1733.
7. Steam locomotive in 1804.
8. Joseph Glidden in 1873.
9. Edwin Land in 1947.
10. Guglielmo Marconi in 1895.
11. Lewis Waterman in 1884.
12. Ernest Swinton in 1914.
13. James Hargreaves in 1764.
14. Whitcomb Judson in 1892.
15. Linus Yale Jr. in 1865.

# 214. U.S. History in the 19th Century I

1. What was the name of the slave woman who Thomas Jefferson was alleged to have had an affair with?
2. This man was Chief Justice presiding over the Marbury Madison decision. Who was he?
3. Which Policy Manifesto was announced in a message to Congress by the President on December 2, 1823?
4. By which factor did the Louisiana purchase increase the size of the U.S.?
5. What was the cost to the U.S. of The Louisiana Purchase?
6. Who was Secretary of State under Thomas Jefferson?
7. In the Jefferson Administration, there were five Cabinet Positions, these were: Secretary of State, Secretary of the Treasury, Secretary of War, Attorney General and a fifth position. What was this fifth position?
8. Which Indian Group was defeated by General William Harrison at The Battle of Tippecanoe in 1811?
9. Which Act introduced by Jefferson prohibited trade with England to retaliate against the latter's Policy of Impressment?
10. Which Party was James Monroe a member of?
11. Who was the leader of the 'War Hawks' in Congress from 1810 onwards?
12. Against which two British ships did the U.S. Frigate Constitution score her greatest victories?
13. What was the single main strategy followed by the U.S. in the early part of The War of 1812 to force a change in British Maritime Policy?
14. The defense of which fort inspired the writing of the 'Star-Spangled Banner'?
15. Which Naval Victory by the U.S. in The War of 1812 forced the British to turn back to Canada?

### Answers to U.S. History in the 19th Century I

1. Sally Hemings. Claims were brought to light by Jefferson's Federalist opponents in the 1804 election, but did not impact the election results.
2. John Marshall.
3. The Monroe Doctrine. European Nations were warned not to interfere in Western Hemisphere politics.
4. It doubled the size by adding 827,000sq. mi of territory.
5. $15 million
6. James Madison, later President Madison.
7. Secretary of the Navy.
8. The Shawnee Indians; Their leader was Tecumseh.
9. The Nonintercourse Act. It replaced the Embargo Act.
10. The Democratic-Republican Party.
11. Henry Clay of Kentucky.
12. The Guerriére and The Java.
13. The Invasion of Canada—it failed.
14. Fort McHenry.
15. The Battle of Plattsburg Bay on Lake Champlain.

## 215. U.S. History in the 19th Century II

1. Which Treaty ended The War of 1812?
2. Which Battle was fought after this war had ended?
3. In which year did the U.S. purchase Florida from Spain?
4. According to the Missouri Compromise (1820), Missouri would be admitted to the Union, but slavery would be barred in territory of The Louisiana Purchase north of this line of latitude. What was the line of latitude?
5. Which reform did John Quincy Adams argue was needed for the Civil Service?
6. Congress adopted a resolution for the annexation of this region in 1845. Which region was this?
7. In which City was a Women's Rights Convention held in 1848?

8. This Treaty settled a border dispute with Canada over Maine. It was signed in the early 1840's. What was this Treaty called?
9. Which 19th Century President strengthened his power base by the use of a kitchen cabinet of close advisors, as well as the practice of rewarding government positions to party supporters?
10. What was the patronage appointment policy described in Question 9 known as?
11. It opened in 1825 to link the Atlantic Ocean to the Hudson River. What is being described here?
12. The suspension by many U.S. banks of specie (payment by coinage) caused a financial crisis in the late 1830's. What was this crisis known as?
13. Which Party was Martin Van Buren a member of?
14. How long did William Harrison's Presidency last?
15. Which Federal Financial Institution was dismantled by Andrew Jackson?

**Answers to U.S. History in the 19th Century II**

1. The Treaty of Ghent.
2. Battle of New Orleans (January 1815). Combatants were unaware the treaty had been signed.
3. In 1819 by President James Monroe for a cost of $5 million.
4. 36 Degrees 30 Minutes North.
5. He felt that it had to be professional. Free of patronage and not aligned to any particular political party. His support for such a policy as President created much opposition.
6. Texas
7. Seneca Falls, NY.
8. The Webster-Ashburton Treaty. The U.S. mastermind behind the treaty was the Secretary of State, Daniel Webster.
9. Andrew Jackson.
10. The Spoils System.
11. The Erie Canal. It opened up a fast route to the West.
12. The Panic of 1837. It caused a depression that lasted until 1840.

13. The Democratic Party.
14. One month. He died of pneumonia.
15. The National Bank in favour of State Banks.

## 216. U.S. History in the 19th Century III

1. What was 'The Trail of Tears'?
2. Who led a slave rebellion in Southampton, Virginia that resulted in the death of 55 whites?
3. What was the name of the Abolitionist Journal edited by William Lloyd Garrison?
4. Which party were Henry Clay and Daniel Webster both members of?
5. How many children did John Tyler have?
6. Who led the American Party that settled Texas at the invitation of the Mexicans?
7. Which Mexican President announced a unified constitution in 1836 for all Mexicans including Texas?
8. Who led the Americans at The Battle of the Alamo?
9. At which Battle did Sam Houston and his men gain revenge for The Alamo?
10. Which trail linked Independence, Missouri with the Old Spanish trail to Los Angeles?
11. With whose Presidency is the term Manifest Destiny most associated?
12. Who first coined the term 'Manifest Destiny'?
13. Which parallel was established as the border between Canada and the U.S. in 1846?
14. Between which two years was the Mexican-American War fought?
15. He defeated the Mexicans at Vera Cruz and took Mexico City. Who was he?

**Answers to U.S. History in the 19$^{th}$ Century III**

1. The U.S. Policy of forcefully migrating Native Americans from the Southeast to lands across the Mississippi.
2. Nat Turner. His rebellion followed two earlier ones, both of which were unsuccessful. The first was led by Gabriel Posser in 1800 and took place in Richmond Virginia, the second led by Denmark Vesey occurred in Charleston in 1822.
3. The Liberator.
4. The Whigs.
5. Fourteen (the most by any President). Eight sons and six daughters from two marriages (to Letitia Christian and Julia Gardiner).
6. Stephen Austin.
7. President Santa Anna.
8. Colonel William Travis (187 Americans faced 3000 Mexicans at the Battle).
9. The Battle of San Jacinto which was fought in April 1836 and lasted 18 minutes. Nine Americans died. Mexican losses were in the hundreds.
10. The Sante Fe Trail.
11. James K. Polk's Presidency.
12. The Newspaper Editor, John O'Sullivan, to justify the occupation of Texas and Oregon.
13. The 49$^{th}$ Parallel by The Oregon Treaty of 1846.
14. 1846-1848.
15. General Winfield Scott.

## 217. U.S. History in the 19$^{th}$ Century IV

1. Which Treaty ended The Mexican-American War?
2. The U.S. won territory in the Mexican-American War. This territory forms part of which modern American States?
3. Under which Compromise was California admitted as a Free State, while no restrictions on slavery were placed on New Mexico, Utah, and Texas?

4. This Act passed in May 1854 almost killed the Democratic Party in the North. Which Act was this?
5. From which three political groups was the Republican Party created?
6. Which President dispatched Matthew Perry to Japan?
7. Who was the winner of the 1852 Presidential Election?
8. Associate Roger Taney with Dredd Scott?
9. Who said, "I am certain that the crimes of this guilty land will never be purged away by blood"?
10. Who was the 'scalawags'?
11. Who did Andrew Johnson try to dismiss as Secretary of War that led to his Impeachment as President?
12. What was the purpose of the 1867 Southern Homestead Act?
13. What group first met in Nashville's Maxwell House in April 1867?
14. Who led the Indians at The Battle of Little Bighorn (two names)?
15. Over which tribe was Chief Joseph the leader of?

**Answers to U.S. History in the 19th Century IV**

1. The Treaty of Guadalupe Hidalgo.
2. Arizona, California, Colorado, Nevada, New Mexico, Texas, Utah, and Wyoming.
3. The Compromise of 1850.
4. The Kansas-Nebraska Act. It called for 'popular sovereignty' in the territories and would eventually provide the foundation for clashes between pro- and anti-slavery groups in these territories.
5. Northern Democrats, Whigs, and Freesoilers.
6. Millard Fillmore.
7. Franklin Pierce.
8. Taney was The Supreme Court Justice who wrote the Majority Decision in the infamous Dredd Scott v Sandford Court Case. Taney ruled that blacks, whether free or not, had no standing before the court. Scott, although living on free soil, was not a citizen but a property of his owner.
9. John Brown.

10. Southern-born White Republicans. They were hated by other Southerners as traitors and were often associated with the exploitation of illiterate blacks.
11. Edwin M. Stanton.
12. To open up the South to blacks and whites loyal to the Union.
13. The Klu Klux Klan.
14. Sitting Bull and Crazy Horse.
15. The Nez Perce.

## 218. U.S. History in the 19th Century V

1. Who was known as 'Long Hair'?
2. This man was elected President in 1868. Who was he?
3. To the closest million, how much did Russia sell Alaska to the U.S. for in 1867?
4. Where did the East and West rails link up at on May 10, 1869?
5. This man built a ferry business into a steamship empire, then expanded into railroads. Who was he?
6. Rutherford Hayes became President in 1876 in an election which has often been seen as fraudulent. Who was his losing opponent?
7. By 1879, this company controlled over 90% of the U.S.'s refining capacity. Which company was this?
8. He is estimated to have stolen over $30 million from The New York Treasury. Known also as 'The Boss', he was sentenced to 12 years in prison. He escaped, was caught, and re-admitted to prison where he died. Who is being described here?
9. The consequence of The Anarchist Bomb in this famous riot weakened The Knights of Labor. What was this riot known as?
10. Against which company did the American Railway Union strike against in 1894?
11. This party had a platform that advocated national ownership of railways, telegraph, and telecommunication systems. It was formed in 1892 in St Louis. What was this Party?
12. Who said, "You shall not crucify mankind on a Cross of Gold?"
13. This battleship arrived in Havana in 1898 to protect American interests. Which battleship was this?

14. Which of the following territories did the U.S. not win in the Spanish American War: Puerto Rica, Philippines, Cuba, Guam, or Wake Island?
15. What number President was Grover Cleveland?

**Answers to U.S. History in the 19th Century V**

1. General George Custer. He was called this by the Sioux.
2. Ulysses S. Grant.
3. $7.2 million.
4. Promontory Point, Utah.
5. Cornelius Vanderbilt.
6. The Democrat Samuel Tilden.
7. Standard Oil.
8. William Tweed of Tammany Hall Fame.
9. The Haymarket Square Riot.
10. The Pullman Car Company.
11. The Populist Party. It was very strong in the Farm Belt states.
12. Wiliam Jennings Bryan. He led the Democrats, at age 36 (the youngest Presidential Nominee ever) in the 1896 Presidential Election, but was defeated by William McKinley.
13. The Maine.
14. All of these territories were won by the U.S. in the Spanish American War.
15. Twenty-two and twenty-four.

## 219. World History 1900-1914 I

1. Which American became Governor General of the Philippines in 1901?
2. This Treaty signed in 1902 ended The Boer War. Which Treaty was this?
3. Britain signed a Treaty with this world power in 1902. Which world power was this?
4. Who succeeded King Umberto I of Italy after the King was assassinated by an anarchist in 1900?

5. What reached Port Arthur in 1901?
6. What Agreement was reached between England and France in 1903?
7. The frontier of which American state was settled in 1903?
8. Who organized the U.S. Steel Corporation in 1901?
9. She founded the National Women's Social and Political Union in 1903. Who was she?
10. Which war broke out in February 1904?
11. Which German Corporation was created by Carl Duisberg in 1904?
12. This French Labour Leader issued the socialist newspaper *L'Humanité* in Paris in 1904. Who was he?
13. He was elected President of the U.S. in 1904. Who was he?
14. Which crisis was caused by the Kaiser's visit in 1905?
15. What was the nickname of William Haywood's International Workers of the World?

**Answers to World History 1900-1914 I**

1. W.H. Taft.
2. The Treaty of Vereeniging.
3. Japan. Treaty recognized the independence of China and Korea.
4. His son, Victor Emmanuel III.
5. The Trans-Siberian Railroad.
6. The Entente Cordiale.
7. Alaska
8. J.P. Morgan.
9. Emmeline Pankhurst.
10. The Russo-Japanese War. Japan besieged Price Arthur and occupied Seoul.
11. I.G. Farben.
12. Jean Jaurès.
13. Theodore Roosevelt.
14. The Tangier Crisis.
15. Wobblies

# 220. World History 1900-1914 II

1. Which Country did U.S. Troops occupy in 1906 following a reconciliation period after a liberal revolt?
2. Which European Country gained independence in 1905?
3. Which two countries signed The Treaty of Bjorko for mutual help in Europe?
4. Which Country was forced to cede the Sinai Peninsula to Egypt in 1906?
5. This ship was launched in 1906. It displaced 17,900 tons and had a speed of 21 knots. What was it called?
6. Upton Sinclair's Novel *The Jungle* encouraged this Act. What was the name of this Act?
7. England and France agreed upon the independence of this Southwest Asian Country in 1907. Which Country was this?
8. Which European power completed the occupation of Sumatra in 1907 by defeating the Achinese tribe?
9. This future Soviet Leader captured 375,000 rubles in 1907 from a transport of the State Bank in Tiflis. Who was he?
10. This Territory became the 46th State of The Union in 1907. Which Territory was this?
11. What was restricted by the U.S. in 1907?
12. Who did Tsar Nicholas II meet with in Reval in 1908?
13. Which Country won the right to occupy Bosnia and Herzegovina in 1908?
14. How did J.P. Morgan stop the run on Banks caused by The Panic of 1907?
15. Over which Country did Manuel II become King of in 1908?

### Answers to World History 1900-1914 II

1. Cuba. They would remain as occupiers until 1909.
2. Norway. Prince Charles of Denmark would be elected as King Haakon VII of Norway.
3. Russia and Germany.

4. Turkey under British pressure.
5. The HMS Dreadnought.
6. The U.S. Pure Food and Drugs Act.
7. Siam
8. The Dutch.
9. Josef Stalin.
10. Oklahoma
11. Immigration to the country.
12. The English King Edward VII.
13. Austria. In an agreement signed in September 1908 with Russia.
14. He imported $100 million worth of gold from Europe.
15. Portugal. He would rule until 1910 when he would be deposed by a revolution that allowed Portugal to become a Republic. Manuel II would consequently seek refuge in Britain.

## 221. World History 1900-1914 III

1. This sultan was deposed by the Young Turks in 1909 and replaced by his brother Mohammed V who would be ruler until 1918. Who was this deposed sultan?
2. In which Country did Aristride Briand become Premier in 1909?
3. Civil War broke out in this Central American Country in 1909. It would last up to 1911. Which country was this?
4. Who succeeded King Leopold II as King of Belgium?
5. This oil company was formed during prior to 1910 to exploit opportunities in the Middle East. Which oil company was this?
6. Japan annexed this Country in 1910. Name this Country?
7. Which small Balkan Nation was proclaimed a Kingdom in 1910 under Nicholas I?
8. What was 'The Mann Act'?
9. This man was named Premier of Greece in 1910. Who was he?
10. This infamous wife poisoner was executed in 1910. Who was he?
11. What was the name of the German gunboat that arrived in Agadir in 1911 to create an international crisis?
12. What were the two main Libyan regions won by Italy in her war against Turkey in 1911?

13. Who introduced the National Health Insurance Bill in the British Parliament in 1911?
14. The famous "Place in the Sun" speech referred to which Country?
15. The Premier Boutros Ghali was executed in 1910. From which Country did he come from?

**Answers to World History 1900-1914 III**

1. Sultan Abdul Hamid II.
2. France
3. Honduras
4. Albert I in 1909. Albert would rule until 1934.
5. The Anglo-Persian Oil Company.
6. Korea
7. Montenegro
8. An Act passed by Congress in 1910 that prohibited the transport of women across state lines for immoral purposes.
9. Eleuthérios Venizélos.
10. H.H. Crippen.
11. The Panther.
12. Tripoli and Cyrenaica.
13. David Lloyd George.
14. Germany. It was given by Kaiser Wilhelm II in Hamburg in 1911.
15. Egypt

## 222. World History 1900-1914 IV

1. These two regions became States of the Union in 1912. Which two regions were these?
2. The Turks closed these straits to shipping in 1912. Name these straits?
3. An alliance between these three countries was renewed in 1912. Which three countries were these?
4. Over which Country did Tewfik Pasha become Grand Vizier in 1912?

5. Which railroad into the Middle East did the Germans help build?
6. Italy and France signed which Treaty in 1912?
7. Which series of European wars were fought between 1912 and 1913?
8. Which European Country was partitioned at the end of these wars?
9. The Northern and Southern parts of this African Country were united in 1914. Which Country was this?
10. The 'Zabern Affair' in Alsace-Lorraine strained relationships between which two countries?
11. This French President visited Britain in 1913. Who was he?
12. Which American Financial institution was established in 1913?
13. Which Treaty ended the Russo-Japanese War?
14. This American won the Nobel Peace Prize in 1912 for his work on International Arbitration. Who was he?
15. This Country became a Dominion of the British Empire in 1907. Name the Country?

**Answers to World History 1900-1914 IV**

1. Arizona and New Mexico.
2. The Dardanelles.
3. Austria, Germany, and Italy.
4. Persia
5. The Baghdad Railroad.
6. The Treaty of Lausanne.
7. The Balkan Wars—consisted of Two Wars.
8. Macedonia
9. Nigeria
10. Germany and France.
11. Raymond Poincaré.
12. The U.S. Federal Reserve System.
13. The Treaty of Portsmouth signed in 1905.
14. Elihu Root.
15. New Zealand.

# 223. The Russian Revolution I

1. The date, January 22, 1905 is known by what other name?
2. What happened on this day?
3. This famous Manifesto urging change in Russia followed in the same year. What was it called?
4. A mutiny broke out on this ship in 1905. Which ship was this?
5. By which name was the Liberal Russian Constitutional Democratic Party known as?
6. What was called in 1906?
7. This Russian Prime Minister, known for his Agrarian reforms, was assassinated in 1911. Who was he?
8. Leon Trotsky became editor of this newspaper in 1908. Which paper was this?
9. Lenin took his name from this event. What was it?
10. This Party had five Congresses between 1898 and 1907. Which party was this?
11. Into which two groups did the party described in Question 10 split up into?
12. Which disease did Rasputin claim he could cure Tsar Nicholas II's son of?
13. What did Rasputin die of?
14. Who led the conspirators that eventually killed Rasputin?
15. To what was St. Petersburg renamed in 1914?

### Answers to the Russian Revolution

1. Bloody Sunday.
2. Russian Government Troops fired on a march of industrial workers in St. Petersburg. Over 5000 were shot at. The event would serve as a prelude to The Russian Revolution and provided the world with a bitter view of the Russian Empire and the suffering of the populace.
3. The October Manifesto.
4. The Potemkin. It was later the subject of a Sergei Eisenstein movie.

5. The Kadet Party.
6. The First Duma.
7. Pyotr Stolypin.
8. *Pravda* (the paper was based in Vienna).
9. The Lena Goldfield massacre of April 4, 1912. One hundred and seventy Tsarist troops were shot dead by Russian government troops.
10. The Russian Social Democratic Party.
11. The Bolsheviks and The Mensheviks.
12. Hemophilia
13. Drowning. Despite being poisoned, beaten and shot. It was from submersion in the Moika Canal of the Neva River.
14. Both Prince Felix Youssoupov (husband of the Tsar's niece) and Grand Duke Dimitri Pavlovich (Tsar's cousin). Give yourself one point if you got at least one of these correct.
15. Petrograd

## 224. Russian Revolution II

1. How many Dumas had been called in Russia by 1912?
2. Who did Tsar Nicholas II abdicate in favour of on March 15, 1917?
3. Who was placed in charge of the Provisional Government by the individual referred to in Question 2?
4. What was Lenin's real name?
5. This 'Theses' was issued by Lenin soon after his return to Russia in 1917. What was this called?
6. Through which station did Lenin re-enter Russia?
7. The July disturbances allowed this man to become dictator. Who was he?
8. The broadcasting of this Order decreased the Russian troops morale to fight in World War I. What order was this?
9. Russia was still using this Calendar at the time of the Revolution. Which Calendar was this?
10. Lenin constantly argued that the Russian people needed these demands to be met. What demands were they?

11. This Cossack Chief tried to overthrow the Russian Government in September 1917 but failed. Who was he?
12. The Bolsheviks seized power in Russia over this period. Give the month/s and year?
13. This Treaty ending Russian involvement in World War I would be signed in March 1918. What was it called?
14. According to the Treaty, these five European states had to be cleared of Russian troops. Name three of these states?
15. Which organization was created by the Bolsheviks in December 1917 to fight against counter-revolution?

**Answers to the Russian Revolution II**

1. Four Dumas—1906, 1907 (2) and 1912.
2. The Grand Duke Mikhail Alexandrovich Romanov, the third son of Tsar Alexander III. He would be the last Emperor of Russia.
3. Prince Lvov.
4. Vladimir Ilyich Ulyanov.
5. The April Theses. It outlined the strategy that should be followed to bring about revolutionary change in Russia.
6. Finland Station.
7. Alexander Kerensky.
8. Order No. 1 of the Petrograd Soviet which denounced and called for an end to Russian involvement in the war.
9. The Julian Calendar. Its inaccuracy caused discrepancies as to which dates important events occurred during the Revolution.
10. Peace, land, and bread.
11. General Lavr Kornilov.
12. October/November 1917.
13. The Treaty of Brest-Litovsk.
14. The Ukraine, Turkey, Estonia, Latvia, and Finland.
15. The Cheka.

## 225. The First World War—Events of 1914

1. Who assassinated Archduke Francis Ferdinand and his wife Sophie in Sarajevo on June 28, 1914?
2. Which Country did Austria attack soon after this assassination?
3. What was the name of the attack strategy followed by the Germans at the outbreak of the war?
4. A victory at which Battle saved France from being overrun by Germany?
5. Who were Germany and Austro-Hungary's main allies in the war?
6. Which city did the Germans take on August 20, 1914?
7. To the nearest million, how many civilians would die during the course of World War I?
8. Which country's forces was driven back at the Battles of the Frontiers?
9. Name one of the two countries that provided troops to face the Germans at the ill-fated Battle of Mons?
10. What do Historians call the period between September 15th and November 24th when troops from both sides attempted to outflank and envelope the other?
11. Name one of the two Generals who led Germany to victory over the Russians at Tannenberg in 1914?
12. What further Russian loss followed The Battle of Tannenberg?
13. Which two powers clashed at The Battle of Rava Ruska between September 3rd and September 11th 1914?
14. Who were the victorious forces at the Battle of Jadar River?
15. Where did German submarines attack the British Grand Fleet on October 18, 1914?

### Answers to the First World War—Events of 1914

1. Gavrilo Princip. A Serb and member of the underground Black Hand organization. Princip would die in 1918 in an Austrian prison.
2. Serbia

3. The Schlieffen Plan.
4. The Battle of the Marne.
5. Turkey and Bulgaria. Together they formed the Central Powers.
6. Brussels
7. Seven million including 1.5 million Armenians killed in a massacre by the Turks. Eight million soldiers would die in the war and a further 21 million would be wounded.
8. The French.
9. Britain and Belgium. Troops of the two countries failed to stem the German advance.
10. The Race to the Sea.
11. Generals Paul von Hindenburg and Erich Ludendorff.
12. The First Battle of the Masurian Lakes.
13. Russia and Austro-Hungary. The Russians were victorious winning control of most of Galicia. However the losses on both sides totaled 500,000.
14. The Serbs. They beat the Austro-Hungarian forces, however they could not withstand a later Austrian offensive which would result in Belgrade falling into enemy hands on December 2, 1914.
15. At Scapa Flow.

## 226. The First World War—Events of 1915

1. Why did the Turks deport the Armenian population to Syria and Palestine? An event that resulted in the death of a million Armenians.
2. This battle, which is associated with the name of a beverage, was fought during the first three months of 1915. It resulted in a loss of 300,000 French and German troops. Which battle was this?
3. At which battle did the Germans first use poisonous gas?
4. The Allies suffered a loss of 250,000 casualties and six battleships in this campaign which lasted between February 1915 and January 1916 in the Dardanelles. Which campaign was this?
5. This British Nurse was executed by the Germans on October 7th as a spy. Who was she?
6. These vehicles of war were used to bomb Britain from January 19th onwards. What were these vehicles of war?

7. What was innovative about the Fokker warplane of 1915?
8. Which Country entered the war on May 23, 1915 on the Allied side?
9. This British Liner was sunk without warning by the Germans on May 7, 1915. 1198 people died including 128 Americans. What was the name of the Liner?
10. What did the British start using in 1915 as an anti-submarine weapon?
11. This heavy German cruiser was sunk off Dogger Bank on Jan 24, 1915. What was its name?
12. Which two powers faced off at Kut in 1915?
13. This man was appointed British Commander-in-Chief in 1915. Who was he?
14. What was destroyed on July 2,1915 by a bomb planted by Erich Muenter a German instructor at Cornell?
15. How many battles did the Italians and the Austrian-Germans fight over the Isonzo line in 1915?

**Answer to The First World War—Events of 1915**

1. Several reasons, the most important of which was the Turks wanted to stop the secret recruitment of Armenians by the Russians to fight against the Turks.
2. The First Battle of Champagne.
3. The Second Battle of Ypres (April 22nd to May 25th).
4. The Gallipoli Campaign.
5. Edith Cavell.
6. Dirigibles
7. It was the first to have its machine gun synchronized with its propeller.
8. Italy
9. The Lusitania.
10. The depth charge.
11. The Blücher.
12. The British and the Turks in the campaign for Mesopotamia.
13. Douglas Haig

14. The U.S. Senate Reception Room. Muenter then shot J.Pierpont Morgan a day later before committing suicide on July $6^{th}$.
15. Four (another Five battles would be fought on this front in 1916).

## 227. The First World War—Events of 1916

1. This failed German assault and siege of the French Fortress on the Meuse River cost the French and the Germans 550,000 and 450,000 casualties respectively. Which battle is being described?
2. Who succeeded Francis Joseph as Austrian Emperor in 1918?
3. This man became British Prime Minister in 1916. Who was he?
4. At the start of 1916 who was Commander-in-Chief of the French Forces?
5. A failed five-month British and French attack on this River would begin in June 1916. It would cost 1.25 million casualties. Which River was this?
6. Who led the Arabs in their War of Independence that began in 1916?
7. What name was given to the Russian Summer Offensive in 1916 that lasted between June $4^{th}$ and September $20^{th}$?
8. What were the two first names of Middle Eastern Hero, Lawrence of Arabia?
9. Who commandeered the British Fleet at the Battle of Jutland?
10. What was significant about the Battle of Jutland from a British standpoint?
11. On whose side did Romania enter the war on August the $27^{th}$?
12. This Irish Republican leader was executed on August $3^{rd}$ for trying to secure German support for the Easter uprising. Who was he?
13. The Trench War on the Western Front has often been described as this type of war. Clue: Begins with a letter 'A'. What type of war was it?
14. Which Country was the first to use tanks in 1916?
15. Which famous British military figure died in 1916, when the cruiser he was travelling on (the Hampshire) was hit by a mine?

**Answers to The First World War—Events of 1916**

1. The Battle of Verdun (Feb 21st to Dec 18th).
2. His grandnephew, Charles (Carl) I. Carl would rule until 1918.
3. David Lloyd George.
4. Joseph Joffre.
5. The Somme.
6. Hussein Ibn Ali, Sharif of Mecca.
7. The Brusilov Offensive named after the Russian general Alexei Brusilov. It was successful against the Austrians, but was beaten back by German counter-attacks at the cost of 1 million casualties on each side.
8. Thomas Edward.
9. Admiral John Jellicoe.
10. Although technically a stalemate, the Germans were forced to break off and head for home. They never again dared to attack the British at sea for the remainder of the war staying put at their bases.
11. The Allied side. The Rumanians started by attacking Austro-Hungarian positions in Transylvania. They were however beaten back by a German counteroffensive.
12. Roger Casement.
13. A War of Attrition.
14. The British.
15. Field Marshal Horatio Kitchener, Hero of the Sudan and influential figure during the Anglo-Boer War. His face is best associated with the ' Country Needs You' recruitment drive on the Home Front.

## 228. History of the First World War—Events of 1917

1. How many miles of territory did the Allies gain at Passchendaele?
2. By which other name is The Battle of Passchendaele known as?
3. This failed offensive in 1917 triggered a mass mutiny in the French Army. What was the Offensive?
4. Troops from which Country took Vimy Ridge on April 9,1917?

5. True or False: The British attack on Palestine began with an unsuccessful attack on Giza in 1917?
6. The British attack at Cambrai was directed against this German line. What was this line called?
7. Which Country underwent a War of Independence from Russia between 1917 and 1920?
8. Which side was victorious at The Battle of Caporetto?
9. She was executed on October 15,1917 as a German spy by the French. Who was she?
10. Which Southern European Country entered the war in June 27th on the side of the Allies?
11. This man headed the American Forces in Europe. Who was he?
12. This man took over command of the British troops in Palestine in 1917. Who was he?
13. What changed with respect to the British Royal Family in 1917?
14. This Pope issued a Peace Note in 1917. Who was he?
15. Which war figure numbered 4 million in 1917?

**Answers to the History of the First World War—Events of 1917**

1. A mere 5 miles. At the cost of over 300,000 casualties, mainly British.
2. The Third Battle of Ypres.
3. The Nivelle Offensive (April 16th to the 20th).
4. Canada
5. False. The attack was on Gaza. Giza is in Egypt.
6. The Hindenburg Line. The British Third Army with 200 tanks succeeded partially in their task. Their breakthrough was not large, but they were able to hold it.
7. Finland
8. The Germans and Austrians. They finally broke through the Italian line at the Isonzo River.
9. Mata Hari (aka Margaretha Geertruide Zelle—the Dutch dancer).
10. Greece. Their troops first saw action at Salonika.
11. General John 'Black Jack' Pershing.

12. General Allenby.
13. Their German names and German titles were renounced.
14. Pope Benedict XV.
15. The amount of British merchant shipping (in tons) lost in the year. Most of it due to German U-boat attacks.

## 229. History of the First World War—Events of 1918

1. Which Country launched the Lys Offensive between April 9th and April 29th?
2. Whose troops took the Village of Cantigny on May 29th?
3. What was the last major battle in the Middle East portion of the war?
4. Which country's troops took Beirut on October 5th?
5. How many allied airplanes did the 'Red Baron', Manfred von Richthofen, shoot down?
6. Who eventually shot him down?
7. What time and date was the World War I armistice declared?
8. This man became the first President of the New Czechoslovak republic in 1918. Who was he?
9. This Party won the Irish Elections in 1918. Who were they?
10. Which Battle resulted in the final defeat of the Bulgarians?
11. What was the last Battle of the Italian-Austrian front?
12. What was the last German offensive of the war?
13. From which river did the German forces fall back as a result of the Allied offensive from September 26th onward till the war's end?
14. Which two Allied countries launched the successful St. Mihiel Offensive?
15. Which Baltic Country started an Independence War in 1918 which would win them independence a year later?

**Answers to the History of the First World War—Events of 1918**

1. Germany. It was the second of five failed German offensives launched in 1918.
2. The Americans.
3. The Battle of Megiddo. The British under Allenby defeated the Turks at Jaffa and later took Damascus, Homs and Aleppo. The Turks were forced into an armistice on October 30th.
4. The French.
5. Eighty Allied Planes.
6. The Canadian Pilot, Roy Brown, during aerial combat over The Somme.
7. At 11:00 am on November 11th, 1918.
8. Tomás Masaryk.
9. Sinn Fein.
10. The Battle of Vardar. Bulgarians were forced into an armistice on September 29th.
11. The Battle of Vittorio Veneto. Three hundred thousand Austrians were taken prisoner.
12. The Second Battle of the Marne; it of course failed.
13. The Meuse River.
14. The Americans and the French.
15. Estonia with British help.

## 230. The Treaties at the end of World War I

1. What did the 14th of Woodrow Wilson's Fourteen Points call for?
2. What was renounced in the 1st of these Fourteen Points?
3. Who represented France at The Treaty of Versailles?
4. The Allies signed The Treaty of Neuilly with which former World War I enemy?
5. Which Polish City became a Free port as a result of The Treaty of Versailles?
6. For how long would the left bank of the Rhine be occupied according to the Versailles provisions?

7. With which defeated parties were the following treaties signed: a) Saint-Germain-en-Laye; b) Trianon; c) Sèvres?
8. What percentage of her population would the Germans lose at Versailles?
9. How large was the German Airforce permitted to be after Versailles?
10. Which Country would gain Eupen-Malmedy?
11. This penalty has often been considered to be the toughest of all the punishments given to the Germans at Versailles. What was this penalty?
12. Versailles forbade this Union. What was it?
13. To which size (in men) was the German army limited?
14. This clause blamed Germany for World War I. What was it more commonly known as?
15. To which Country did the Kaiser Wilhelm II eventually flee to and die in?

**Answers to The Treaties at the end of World War I**

1. The formation of a general organization to guarantee the political independence of all states.
2. Secret Diplomacy.
3. Georges Clémenceau.
4. Bulgaria
5. Danzig
6. Fifteen years. The French regarded the Rhine as France's ideal boundary with Germany.
7. a) Austria b) Hungary c) Turkey. Give yourself 1 point if you got 2 or more of these correct.
8. Ten Percent and 1/7th of her territory.
9. Not large at all. In actual fact, Germany was banned from having an airforce at all. Submarines, tanks, warships, and Heavy artillery were not permitted as well for the Germans.
10. Belgium
11. The Forced payment of Reparations to the Allies.
12. The Unification of Germany and Austria (aka Anschluss).

13. One hundred thousand men.
14. The War-Guilt clause.
15. The Netherlands.

## 231. Between the World Wars (I)

1. She was the first woman elected to the British Parliament. Who was she?
2. Name two of the three countries that formed the Little Entente in 1920?
3. Which Amendment gave woman the right to vote in the U.S.?
4. From which city were The League of Nations Headquarters moved in 1920?
5. Who won the Nobel Peace Prize in 1919?
6. Who staged a monarchist coup that would ultimately fail in Berlin in 1920?
7. Where in 1921 was a disarmament Conference held?
8. This man was elected German Minister for Reconstruction in 1921. Who was he? Hint: He would be made Germany's Foreign Minister a year later.
9. Who was inaugurated as the 29$^{th}$ US President in 1921?
10. This socialist's sentence was commuted to 10 years by the President being described in Question 9. Who was the Socialist?
11. Who succeeded David Lloyd George as Prime Minister in 1922?
12. Which two countries signed The Treaty of Rapallo in 1922?
13. Which Country faced the resignation of its President Pilsudski in 1922?
14. Who proclaimed a Turkish Republic in 1922?
15. Who was re-elected German President in 1922?

### Answers Between the World Wars (I)

1. Lady Nancy Astor, who was actually of American birth. She succeeded her husband as Conservative MP for Plymouth.
2. Czechoslovakia, Yugoslavia, and Romania.

3. The 19th Amendment.
4. Paris
5. Woodrow Wilson.
6. Wolfgang Kapp.
7. Washington
8. Walter Rathenau.
9. Warren Harding (Hey! What do you know, five questions in a row whose answers end with the letter 'W').
10. Eugene Debs.
11. A. Bonar Law (he was the first British Prime Minister of Colonial (Canadian) origin).
12. The USSR and Germany.
13. Poland
14. Mustapha Kemal (aka Atatürk).
15. Friederich Ebert.

## 232. Between the World Wars (II)

1. To which Eastern European country's throne did Alexander I ascend to in 1923?
2. Hearings for this oil scandal were heard in Washington DC in 1923. What was the scandal?
3. What dropped to a rate of 4 million to the U.S. Dollar in 1923?
4. In 1923, this man took power as a Dictator in Spain. Who was this man?
5. Which Country was struck by an Earthquake in 1923 that left 120,000 dead?
6. Sixty-five percent of the population voted for this man in Italy in 1924. Who was he?
7. He was the First Labour Prime Minister of England. He came to power in 1924 after the resignation of Stanley Baldwin. Who was he?
8. This Leader of the Italian Socialists was murdered in 1924 by the Fascist Quadristi. Who was he?
9. This report removed German reparations from the world of political influence. What was this report called?

10. What is the claim to fame of American Nellie Tayloe Ross?
11. Which Scandinavian Country annexed Spitsbergen in 1925?
12. This conference held in 1925 produced several treaties that emphasized international cooperation. They were thought to be a triumph of Austin Chamberlain (Britain), Aristide Briand (France), and Gustav Stresemann (Germany). With the coming of Hitler in the 1930s many of these treaties would be violated. Where was the original conference held?
13. By which name is the German Federal Republic that existed between 1918 and 1933 also known as?
14. Which Country suffered from a very significant General strike in 1926?
15. What was 'Balilla'?

**Answers to Between the World Wars II**

1. Yugoslavia
2. The Teapot Dome Oil Scandal.
3. The German Mark.
4. Miguel Primo Riviera.
5. Japan (around the Tokyo-Yokohama area).
6. Benito Mussolini. Of course the elections were held using Fascist methods. All Non-Fascist parties had been dissolved in 1923.
7. Ramsay MacDonald.
8. Giacomo Matteoti.
9. The Dawes Report after Charles Dawes. Later, the U.S. Vice President under Calvin Coolidge.
10. She was the first woman to become Governor (in 1925 in Wyoming).
11. Norway
12. Locarno
13. The Weimar Republic.
14. Britain
15. An Italian Fascist Youth movement that begun in 1926.

## 233. Between the World Wars (III)

1. Which American statesman suggested a pact in 1927 for the renunciation of war?
2. Which Country suffered from an 'economic' Black Friday in 1927?
3. These two Anarchists were executed in 1927 in the U.S. Who were they?
4. Italy signed a 20-year Treaty of Friendship with this African Country in 1928. Which country was this?
5. This country's economy collapsed in 1928 due to an over-production of coffee beans. Which country was this?
6. In Britain, this age limit was reduced from 30 to 21 in 1928. What was it?
7. What did 1929's Lateran Treaty establish?
8. What day in 1929 was Black Friday?
9. This man was elected Premier of France in 1929. Who was he?
10. Which important Treaty was signed in Washington in 1929?
11. Name four of the five countries who signed a Treaty for naval disarmament in 1930?
12. This 'international' language grew in popularity in the 1920s. In 1928, there were 1776 groups around the world. Which language is this?
13. In which Country were Catholic Fascist Heimwehr units established in 1930?
14. What did France begin building in 1930?
15. Which Democrat did Herbert Hoover defeat to win the 1928 Election?

### Answers to Between the World Wars (III)

1. F.B. Kellog. His brainchild would come alive as the Kellog-Briand Pact of 1928 that was signed by 65 countries.
2. Germany
3. Nicola Sacco and Bartolomeo Vanzetti. FBI files released years later showed that Saco was probably guilty and Vanzetti probably

innocent of holding up the payroll of the shoe factory in Braintree, Mass that left two men dead.

4. Ethiopia (needless to say this would not last very long).
5. Brazil
6. The minimum age for women's suffrage.
7. An independent Vatican City. In the same year, the Pope Pius XI could leave the Vatican for the first time.
8. October 28,1929. U.S. Securities lost $28 billion dollars in value.
9. Aristide Briand.
10. The Inter-American Treaty of Arbitration.
11. Britain, US, France, Japan, and Italy.
12. Esperanto
13. Austria
14. The Maginot Line.
15. Al Smith by 444 electoral votes to 87.

## 234. Between the World Wars (IV)

1. Six gangsters were gunned down in this famous 1929 hit. What was this called?
2. This King left Spain and went into hiding in 1931. Who was he?
3. Issued in 1931, this Statute defined dominion status within the British Empire. What was it?
4. Which Party won 558 seats in the British election in 1931?
5. Who suggested, in 1931, a one-year moratorium for the payment of war debts and reparations?
6. The Stimson Doctrine protested this country's aggression. What was the Country?
7. He was elected Irish President in 1932. Who was he?
8. A march of 17,000 ex-servicemen in Washington took place in 1932. What did the ex-serviceman want?
9. The Fascist Government in Italy began drainage of these swamps southeast of Rome in 1932. Work would be completed in 1934. What were the swamps called?

10. What did Germany claim it could abolish with its 1933 issued Four-Year Plan?
11. Sixty thousand of these professionals left Germany between 1933 and 1939. Who were these professionals?
12. She became the First Woman to hold a cabinet position in the U.S. when she was made Secretary of Labor in the Roosevelt Administration. Who was she?
13. The first U.S. Aircraft carrier was launched in 1933. What was it called?
14. The TVA was launched in 1933. What did it stand for?
15. This Act was made law in 1933. It was designed to help American Farmers. What was it called?

**Answers Between the World Wars (IV)**

1. The St. Valentine's Day Massacre.
2. King Alfonso XIII.
3. The Statute of Westminster.
4. The Coalition or National Government.
5. U.S. President Herbert Hoover. Also in 1931, the German Danatbank went bankrupt leading to the bankruptcy of all German banks.
6. Japan, who were being very aggressive in Manchuria.
7. Eamon de Valera.
8. A passage of law permitting cashing of their bonus certificate. The Bill was defeated in the Senate. The Government then offered to pay for the troops passage home. U.S. troops under General Douglas MacArthur were called in to drive out the last 2,000 ex-sevicemen.
9. The Pontine Marshes.
10. Unemployment
11. Artists ie. actors, painters, musicians etc.
12. Frances Perkins.
13. The Ranger.
14. Tennessee Valley Authority.
15. The Far Credit Act.

# 235. Between the World Wars (V)

1. What did the 1934 U.S Gold Reserve Act authorize the President to do?
2. This man became Austrian Chancellor in 1934 after the assassination of Engelbert Dolfuss by the Nazis. Who was the new Chancellor?
3. This Western European Country was severely hit by a General strike in 1934. Which Country was this?
4. What major initiative was introduced in Britain's 1934 Road Traffic Act?
5. This region was incorporated into Germany in 1935 after a pro-German result in a plebiscite. Which Region was this?
6. This man was elected French Premier in 1935. Who was he?
7. Italy invaded this Country in 1935. What was the Country?
8. In which Southeast Asian Country did Rama III become King in 1935?
9. It can be abbreviated with the acronym 'SSA'. It was signed into law by President Roosevelt in 1935. What is being described here?
10. What major change to its Armed forces did Germany introduce in 1935 to repudiate The Treaty of Versailles?
11. The Germans occupied this region in 1936. Which Region was this?
12. Germany, Italy, and Hungary created this Pact in 1936. What was it called?
13. Who did King Edward VIII abdicate on December 11, 1936 to marry?
14. Germany began building this line in 1936. What was it called?
15. The Japanese sank this U.S. gunboat in Chinese waters in 1937. What was the name of the gunboat?

### Answers Between the World Wars (V)

1. To revalue the dollar.
2. Kurt von Schuschnigg. He would later become dictator in Austria as head of the Fatherland Front.

3. France
4. Driving Tests.
5. Saarland
6. Pierre Laval.
7. Abyssinia. The League Council would declare Italy an aggressor and impose sanctions.
8. Siam (Thailand). He would be assassinated in 1946.
9. The Social Security Act.
10. The Introduction of Compulsory Military Service.
11. The Rhineland. Also in 1936, elections in Germany gave Hitler 99% of the vote.
12. The Rome Pact. Agreement between Germany and Italy would later develop into the Rome-Berlin Axis.
13. Mrs. Wallis Simpson, later the Duchess of Windsor.
14. The Siegfried Line.
15. The 'Panay'.

## 236. Between the World Wars (VI)

1. What has been described as the leading cause of the Spanish Civil War (1936-1939)?
2. Which Pro-Republican armed group beat an Italian force at Guadalajara in 1937?
3. Who were the eventual victors in the Spanish Civil War?
4. What did Lord Halifax's visit to Berlin in 1937 mark?
5. These people left the Czech Parliament in 1937 after rioting broke out in Czechoslovakia. Who were these people?
6. Name two of the three locations that Neville Chamberlain met Hitler at in 1938?
7. On which date in 1938 did Germany occupy Sudetenland?
8. What did the initials 'HUAC' stand for?
9. He was installed as the puppet president of Czechoslovakia in 1938. Who was he?
10. What was proclaimed on March 13,1938?
11. With which Country did England sign a Treaty of mutual assistance in 1939?

12. Germany broke her naval pact with this European Country in 1939. Which country was this?
13. Italy joined this Pact in 1937 and Hungary in 1939. In the same years, each of the countries left the League of Nations respectively. What was this Pact called?
14. Who did Vyacheslav Molotov replace as USSR Commissar of Foreign Affairs?
15. What title did Hitler give himself in 1938?

**Answers to Between the World Wars (VI)**

1. Increasing resentment of the Army towards the socialist and anti-clerical tendencies of President Azana's Popular Front Republican Government?
2. The International Brigade.
3. The Fascists under General Franco.
4. The beginning of The Policy of Appeasement.
5. The Sudeten Germans.
6. Berchtesgarden, Godesberg, and Munich.
7. October 10, 1938.
8. House Un-American Activities Committee. It was formed in 1938 and headed by the Democrat, Martin Dies.
9. Emil Hacha, after the resignation of President Benes.
10. Anschluss—Germany and Austria united. The Nazi, Arthur Seyss-Inquart was chosen as Chancellor of Austria two days before the Anschluss. A plebiscite on April 10th showed that 99.75% of the Austrian population supported Anschluss. (I often wonder who the other 0.25% were).
11. Poland
12. Great Britain.
13. The Anti-Comintern Pact.
14. Maxim Litvinov. Litvinov would later become the ambassador to the U.S.
15. War Minister; a hint of what was to come.

# 237. 1945-1949 (I)

1. Into how many different Regions was Germany divided by the Allies at the end of World War II?
2. In which Country was Klement Gottwald elected Premier in 1946?
3. In which City/Town did Winston Churchill give his 'Iron Curtain' speech?
4. Which two parties merged in East Germany in 1946?
5. Formed in 1945, it is known as the World Bank. What is its official name?
6. Who was the First United Nations Secretary-General?
7. What did President Truman create in 1946 to regulate the Nuclear Industry?
8. In which City did the Swedish diplomat, Raoul Wallenberg, who saved countless Jewish lives during the holocaust, disappear in?
9. This energy producing industry in Britain was nationalized in 1947. Which industry was this?
10. What is the more common name for The European Recovery Program?
11. This 1947 Act was passed over President Truman's veto. It restricted the rights of labor unions. What was this act called?
12. In 1947, the U.S. withdrew as mediator in this Country. Which Country was this?
13. This Slovakian War Leader was executed in 1947. Who was he?
14. Which Country was involved in a Civil war from 1944 to 1949 that involved such groups as EKKA, EAM/ELAS?
15. Who did American troops prevent from grabbing the Port of Trieste from Italy in 1947?

## Answers to 1945-1949 (I)

1. Four regions to be controlled by France, the UK, the U.S.A., and the USSR.
2. Czechoslovakia. Gottwald would eventually become President through a communist coup d'etat in 1948.

3. Fulton, Missouri in 1946. (At Westminster College on March 5, 1946).
4. The East German Social Democrats and The Communists.
5. The International Bank for Reconstruction and Development.
6. Trygve Lie of Norway.
7. The Atomic Energy Commission.
8. Budapest. He is thought to have been abducted by the Russians for reasons which even today are still unclear.
9. The Coal Industry.
10. The Marshall Plan.
11. The Taft-Hartley Act.
12. China
13. President Tiso.
14. Greece. The war was essentially a fight between the Communists and Monarchist Partisans for control of the Country.
15. The Yugoslavs. People of Trieste would later vote by plebiscite in 1949 to join Italy.

## 238. 1945-1949 (II)

1. In which Country did Mátyas Rákosi become Premier in 1947?
2. What was 'Bizonia'? Hint: It is not a 'Sci-Fi' word.
3. This doctrine was issued by the U.S. in 1947 in response to Soviet expansion what was it called?
4. Who were the four main candidates in the 1948 U.S. Election?
5. What was the main goal of The Hague Congress of 1948 that was chaired by Winston Churchill?
6. This Dutch Queen abdicated in 1948 and was succeeded by her daughter, Juliana. Who was she?
7. What did the British Citizenship Act of 1948 grant?
8. This man became U.S. Secretary of State on January 7,1949. He succeeded George Marshall. Who was he?
9. Who told the U.S. House of Representatives Un-American Activities Committee on August 2,1948 that 10 years earlier Algar Hiss, had given him secret State Department Documents to pass on to the Soviets?

10. What officially ended on May 12,1949?
11. President of the Parliamentary Council, this man proclaimed the formation of the Federal Republic of Germany in 1949. Who was he?
12. Which Treaty was signed by 12 Western Nations on April 4, 1949?
13. This man, the first U.S. Secretary of Defense, resigned in March 1949. He would later commit suicide on May 22nd of the same year. Who was he?
14. Omar Bradley was appointed by President Truman to this position in 1949. It had only recently been established by law. What was the position?
15. This man wrote an article entitled *'The Sources of Soviet Conduct'*, in 1947. It would form the basis for Truman's Policy of Containment. Who was this Writer?

**Answers to 1945-1949 (II)**

1. Hungary. He was backed of course by the Soviet troops occupying Hungary.
2. The name given to the combined British and American zones in Germany which were merged on January 1,1947?
3. The Truman Doctrine. It was adopted in response to the Communist insurrections in Greece and Turkey. U.S. offered to support countries threatened by communist insurgencies.
4. Harry Truman, Thomas Dewey, Henry Wallace (the darling of the leftist Democrats), and Strom Thurmond, (who gained Southern support). Truman won with 24.1 million votes to Dewey's 22 million.
5. To Promote European Unity.
6. Queen Wilhelmina.
7. British passports to all citizens of the Commonwealth Citizens.
8. Dean Acheson.
9. Whittaker Chambers. He would be indicted on December 15, 1948 on two counts of perjury for lying about his connection to a Soviet spy ring.

10. The Berlin Blockade by the Soviets. It had lasted for over a year. The airlift into West Berlin, however would only end on September 30,1949, after more than 275,000 flights had been made into West Berlin.
11. Konrad Adenauer.
12. The North Atlantic Treaty which led to the creation of NATO.
13. James Forrestal.
14. Chairman of the Joint Chief of Staff.
15. George Kennan. The article was titled by 'X' and appeared in the magazine Foreign Affairs.

## 239. The 1950s (I)

1. Which two countries in Europe proclaimed the Oder-Niesse as the Frontier in 1950?
2. This British Prime Minister visited Washington in 1950. Who was he?
3. This Act was passed in 1950, despite a Presidential veto, it called for severe restrictions against Communists, especially in highly sensitive areas, registration of communist organizations, and the banning of individuals who have belonged to Totalitarian organizations from entering the U.S. Which Act was this?
4. This man was found guilty in 1950 of betraying British Atomic Secrets. Who was he?
5. Never too late, this Country joined the Council of Europe in 1950. Which Country was this?
6. President Truman survived an assassination attempt in 1950, led by these Nationalists. For what Territory were these nationalists trying to win independence?
7. This man became Prime Minister of Iran in 1951. Who was he?
8. This couple was sentenced to death in 1951 for espionage against the U.S. Who were they?
9. This Amendment to the U.S. Constitution limited the President to two terms served. What was the number of this Amendment?
10. This U.S. diplomat and businessman was elected Head of the Mutual

Security Agency in 1951. Its duty was to supply aid to foreign countries. Who was he?

11. What breakthrough in the television market in the U.S. occurred in 1951?
12. Kim Philby, Donald Maclean, Guy Burgess, and Anthony Blunt were all members of which Soviet Spy Ring?
13. In which Country did General Mohammed Naguib seize power in 1952 and establish a Government?
14. Which Three countries met in Honolulu in 1952 as part of the Pacific Council?
15. During August 1952, 16,000 people escaped from this European City. Which city was this?

**Answers to the 1950s (I)**

1. Poland and East Germany.
2. Clement Attlee.
3. The McCarran Act.
4. Klaus Fuchs.
5. West Germany,
6. Puerto Rica. In this attempt on Truman's life, one of the nationalists was killed, the other sentenced to death. His sentence was later commuted to life.
7. Mohammed Mossadegh. He would later nationalize the Anglo-Iranian Oil Company. His Government would be ousted by supporters of Mohammed Reza Shah Pahlavi with U.S. and British support.
8. Julius and Ethel Rosenberg.
9. The $22^{nd}$ Amendment.
10. Averell Harriman.
11. Colour Television was introduced.
12. The Cambridge Five.
13. Egypt
14. The U.S., Australia, and New Zealand.
15. East Berlin. They escaped to West Berlin.

# 240. The 1950s (II)

1. Philip Murray and William Green died in 1952. Both individuals were leaders of what grouping of the U.S. populace?
2. In which year was Elizabeth II crowned Queen of England?
3. This Country detonated its first atomic bomb on October 3, 1952. Which Country was this?
4. From what did Josef Stalin die of on March 5, 1953?
5. Who headed the Collective Leadership that succeeded Stalin?
6. This Yugoslav leader visited London in 1953. Who was he?
7. The USSR condemned this man who was head of the Soviet Secret Police (NKVD) to death in 1953. Who was he?
8. This Central European Nation staged a large protest over occupation in 1953. Which Nation was this?
9. What hearings began in 1953 when Senator Joe McCarthy began criticizing the level of security at Fort Monmouth, NJ?
10. The U.S. signed a Defence Agreement with this Asian power in 1954. What was this power?
11. The U.S. and Canada agreed to build radar-warning stations across Northern Canada. This was to be called the 'DEW Line'. What did 'DEW' stand for?
12. Formed in 1954, what does 'SEATO' stand for?
13. The first Nuclear-powered submarine was launched at Groton, Conn on January 21, 1954. What was it called?
14. On April 7th, President Eisenhower, presented this Theory. It described a view of the possible progress of Communism. What was this Theory called?
15. After a U.S. sponsored invasion from Honduras in 1954, President Jacobo Arbenz fled his country. Which Country did he leave?

### Answers The 1950s (II)

1. Labour
2. 1953. She was proclaimed queen in 1952 after her father George VI died of cancer. Elizabeth heard the news when she was on a Safari in Africa.

3. Britain
4. A Cerebral hemorrhage.
5. Georgi Malenkov.
6. Josep Broz Tito. A man of whom Stalin once said that all he had to do was 'shake his little finger and Tito would disappear'. It was not that simple; Tito would survive until 1980.
7. Lavrenty Beria. It is believed that Beria was actually executed several months before the conviction.
8. Austria
9. The Army-McCarthy Hearings. They would end in 1954 and would lead to the ultimate fall of Joe McCarthy.
10. Japan
11. Distant Early Warning. It gave warning of approaching aircraft or missiles over the Arctic.
12. The Southeast Asian Treaty Organization.
13. The Nautilus.
14. The Domino Theory.
15. Guatemala

## 241. The 1950s (III)

1. The USSR decreed an end of war with this Country in 1955. Which Country was this?
2. Who succeeded Winston Churchill as Prime Minister of the UK in 1955?
3. These two trade Unions in the U.S. merged in 1955. What were they?
4. West Germany joined this organization in 1955. Which organization was this?
5. This reconnaissance aircraft made its first flight on August 4, 1955. What was it?
6. This alliance was born on May 15, 1955. What was it?
7. This rebellious Cypriot Archbishop was transported to the Seychelles in 1956. Who was he?
8. What kind of Republic did Pakistan become in 1956?

9. At which Congress did Nikita Kruschev denounce the 'Cult of Personality' surrounding Stalin?
10. This Polish Leader called for the Soviets to withdraw from Hungary in 1956. Who was this Leader?
11. What prompted the Egyptians to nationalize the Suez Canal in 1956?
12. This Hungarian Leader announced the abolition of One-Party Government in Hungary on October 30th. On the same day, Hungarian rebels stormed the Communist Party Headquarters in Pest and executed the defenders. Who was this Hungarian leader?
13. Which area of the globe did the Eisenhower Doctrine target?
14. Ramon Magsaysay died in an aircraft collision on March 17, 1957. Which Country was this anti-Communist the President of?
15. Which British Prime Minister did Eisenhower meet with in March 1957 to mend issues following The Suez Canal Crisis?

**Answer to The 1950s (III)**

1. Germany
2. Anthony Eden.
3. The A.F.L. and the C.I.O.
4. NATO
5. The U2.
6. The Warsaw Pact.
7. Archbishop Markarios.
8. An Islamic Republic.
9. The 20th Congress of the Communist Party of the Soviet Union—beginning the policy of 'De-Stalinization'.
10. Wladyslaw Gomulka.
11. The withdrawal by the U.S. of a loan to Egypt for construction of the Aswan High Dam.
12. Imre Nagy. The Soviets would take Budapest on November 7th, violating a self-conduct agreement, Nagy would be kidnapped with close associates on November 23, 1956. He would be executed in 1958.

13. The Middle East. Eisenhower asked Congress for approval of actions to aid countries in the Middle East threatened by Communist Aggression.
14. The Philippines.
15. Harold Macmillan.

## 242. The 1950s (IV)

1. Britain became the third Country to explode this bomb. The British explosion occurred on May 15, 1957. Which bomb was this?
2. West Germany issued the Hallerstein Doctrine in 1955 (December 9th). What did the Doctrine espouse?
3. Malenkov and Molotov were removed from office in the Soviet Union on June 29, 1957. Both were members of which so-called group?
4. In 1958, the U.S. agreed to supply IRBMs to Britain. What does 'IRBM' stand for?
5. What incident brought General De Gaulle back to power as Premier in 1958?
6. The long-range shelling of Quemoy and Matsu in 1958 caused a diplomatic crisis between which two countries?
7. This Caribbean Union came into being in 1958. What was it called?
8. Which Republic was born in France in 1958?
9. Where in South America was Richard Nixon attacked by anti-American demonstrators on May 13, 1958?
10. What free trade grouping was born on January 1, 1958?
11. This Cuban leader fled to the Dominican Republic after being ousted by Fidel Castro. Who was this leader?
12. To which Country did the Dalai Lama flee to in 1959 from Tibet?
13. This West Berlin Mayor was honoured in New York in 1959 as a symbol of resistance to the Soviet Union. Who was this Mayor?
14. What was the name of the debate held between Kruschev and Nixon on the benefits of Soviet and American life? The debate occurred on July 24, 1959.
15. Who replaced John Foster Dulles as Secretary of State in 1959?

### Answers to The 1950s (IV)

1. The Hydrogen Bomb. Britain was now a member of the Fusion Club.
2. The West German Government would not maintain diplomatic relations with countries that recognized East Germany.
3. The 'Anti-Party Group'. The event represented a triumph for Kruschev and the Central Committee of the Communist Party.
4. Intermediate-range Ballistic Missiles.
5. The Algerian Crisis.
6. The U.S. and China.
7. The West Indian Federation.
8. The Fifth Republic.
9. Caracas
10. The European Common Market.
11. Fulgencio Batista.
12. India
13. Willy Brandt.
14. The Kitchen Debate.
15. Christian Hertner.

## 243. The 1960s (I)

1. What was the name of the U.S. Reconnaissance Pilot who was shot down over the USSR in 1960?
2. Where in 1960 did Kruschev, De Gaulle, Macmillan, and Eisenhower meet only to see their talks fail?
3. On February 26, 1960, Princess Margaret of the UK got engaged to this man. Who was this man?
4. This Mediterranean Country became a Republic on August 16, 1960. Which Country was this?
5. This convicted rapist was executed at San Quentin prison after 12 years of futile appeals. Who was he?
6. She was the first woman to be elected Prime Minister in the world. It happened in Ceylon in 1960. Who was this woman?

7. To the closest 10,000, by how much did Kennedy defeat Nixon in the popular vote in the 1960 Presidential Election?
8. Who was the British Labour Party Leader c. Nov 1960?
9. In 1960, Soviet Premier Kruschev promised $250 million dollars in aid to this Indonesian President. Who was the Indonesian President?
10. With which Country did the U.S. break off all diplomatic relations on January 3, 1961?
11. By an executive order from President Kennedy which Organization was established on March 1, 1961?
12. Where did Cuban exiles stage a disastrous landing in 1961?
13. Which border was closed on August 12, 1961?
14. Who succeeded Dag Hammerskjöld as UN Secretary General?
15. Which British Politician elected as an MP for Bristol Southeast was also known as Viscount Stansgate?

**Answers to The 1960's (I)**

1. Francis Gary Powers. He would later be found guilty of spying by a Soviet court.
2. Paris
3. Anthony Armstrong-Jones.
4. Cyprus. Its first President was Archbishop Markarios. The Turkish Cypriot Dr. Kutchuk would be chosen as Vice President.
5. Caryl Chessman.
6. Mrs. Sirimavo Bandaranaike.
7. 120,000
8. Hugh Gaitskell.
9. President Sukarno.
10. Cuba
11. The Peace Corps.
12. On the Bay of Pigs on the Cuban South Coast.
13. The East-West Berlin border. Beginning of the building of the Berlin Wall.
14. U Thant of Burma.
15. Anthony Wedgewood Benn.

# 244. The 1960s (II)

1. This American who had been elected speaker of the House for 10 terms died in 1961. He was succeeded by John McCormack. Who was this American?
2. What was the claim to fame of the French Soldier Raoul Salan?
3. This Russian ballet star defected on June 16, 1961. Who was he?
4. What was the name of the convicted Soviet Spy who was traded for the U-2 pilot shot down in May 1960?
5. Kruschev threatened to withdraw his missile base in Cuba if the U.S. removed bases from this Country. Name this Country?
6. Who was the U.S.'s Ambassador to the UN at the time of the Cuban Missile Crisis?
7. In exchange for withdrawing U.S. Missiles from Cuba, what did the U.S. promise the USSR (2 items)?
8. The U.S. planned on supplying Britain with ABM's in 1962 but this was later cancelled. What does 'ABM' stand for?
9. Which European Country suffered bomb attacks at the hands of the OAS?
10. In November 1962, China won a border dispute with this Country. Which Country was this?
11. Who said in 1962, "We must learn from capitalist countries to imitate what is . . . good and profitable?"
12. In West Germany, three editors of which magazine were charged with treason in October 1962?
13. A robbery on which British train route netted 2.5 million pounds?
14. Which three powers signed a Nuclear Testing Ban in 1963?
15. How did Charles de Gaulle 'slap Britain in the face' in 1963?

### Answers to The 1960s (II)

1. Sam Rayburn.
2. An ex-general, Salan, was involved in a scheme in 1961 to execute President Charles de Gaulle.
3. Rudolf Nureyev.
4. Rudolf Abel. He was traded for Francis Gary Powers.

5. Turkey
6. Adlai Stevenson.
7. To lift the blockade of Cuba and that the U.S. would not invade Cuba.
8. Aircraft-launched Ballistic Missile.
9. France. The OAS opposed French policy in Algeria.
10. India
11. Nikita Krushchev.
12. Der Spiegel
13. The Glasgow-London Line.
14. The U.S., the USSR, and the UK.
15. By preventing British entry into the EEC.

## 245. The 1960s (III)

1. This man was elected Labour Leader in February 1963. Who was he?
2. This jail in the U.S. closed in 1963. Which jail was this?
3. This Minister of War in Britain was charged with impropriety in his acquaintanceship with 21-year-old Christine Keeler. Who was this Minister of War?
4. Who replaced Konrad Adenauer as Chancellor of West Germany?
5. This much-loved Liberal Pope died in 1963. He was succeeded by Pope Paul VI. Which Pope is being described here?
6. Who said, "ich bin ein Berliner?"
7. Which Governor of Texas was in the same car as Kennedy when the President was shot?
8. What pro-Castro group did Lee Harvey Oswald Chair?
9. This American won the Nobel Peace Prize in 1964. Who was he?
10. Who resigned as British Prime Minister in 1964?
11. Planes from this Country attacked Cyprus in 1964?
12. Who succeeded King Paul I of Greece?
13. Which two alternative youth culture groups caused great disturbances in British sea resorts in 1964?
14. Who ran as Lyndon Johnson's running mate in his successful 1964 election campaign?

15. Which Country exploded her first Atomic Bomb in 1964?

**Answers to The 1960s (III)**

1. Harold Wilson.
2. Alcatraz
3. John Profumo.
4. Ludwig Erhard.
5. Pope John XIII.
6. President John F. Kennedy on June 26, 1963.
7. John Connally. Connally himself was wounded.
8. Fair Play for Cuba.
9. Martin Luther King.
10. Alec Douglas-Home.
11. Turkey. United Nations Peace Troops were forced to take over in Cyprus.
12. His son, Constantine II.
13. The Mods and the Rockers.
14. Hubert Humphrey of Minnesota.
15. China

## 246. The 1960s (IV)

1. Which type of Society did LBJ promise upon being sworn in as President on January 20, 1965?
2. Which Anniversary of the signing of the Magna Carta was celebrated in Britain in 1965?
3. This Health bill first proposed by President Kennedy in 1960 became law in 1965. Which bill was this?
4. The U.S. Marines arrived in this Country, new Cuba, to assist the new government against Leftist insurgents. Which Country was this?
5. This man was elected Tory leader in Britain in 1965. Who was he?
6. West Germany sent their first ambassador to this Middle Eastern country in 1965. Name the country?

7. Who did Charles De Gaulle defeat to win the 1965 French Presidential Election?
8. This man returned to Saigon as U.S. Ambassador on July 8, 1965. Who was he?
9. Who succeeded Krushchev as Premier of the Soviet Union?
10. Ian Brady and Myra Hindley earned this nickname. What was it?
11. Which Country requested the removal of NATO Troops in 1966?
12. Which Group demonstrated in China against Western influence in 1966?
13. In 1966, Pope Paul VI met this Soviet Foreign Minister. Who was he?
14. This man succeeded McGeorge Bundy as National Security Advisor in 1966. Who was this man?
15. A Grand Coalition of these two parties took power in Germany in 1966. Which two parties were they?

## Answers to The 1960s (IV)

1. A Great Society.
2. The 750th Anniversary. In the same year, Runnymede Field was dedicated to the late President John F. Kennedy.
3. The Medicare Bill.
4. The Dominican Republic.
5. Edward Heath.
6. Israel
7. François Mitterand.
8. Henry Cabot Lodge.
9. Alexei Kosygin.
10. The Moors Murderers.
11. France
12. The Red Guard.
13. Andrei Gromyko.
14. Walt Rostow.
15. The Christian Democrats and the Social Democrats.

# 247. The 1960s (V)

1. On August 11, 1966 Indonesia signed a peace-deal ending three years of bush war with this Southeast Country. Which Country was this?
2. This man killed 12 people at The University of Texas in Austin, before being shot dead by a policeman. Who was this man?
3. This U.S. built fighter plane, used by the German Air Force in the 1960s, was noted for its many crashes. What was the plane?
4. Army colonels took power in which Country in 1967?
5. What did Jack Ruby die of?
6. This American Nazi Leader was shot dead in Arlington, Va in 1967. Who was he?
7. This daughter of Stalin fled to the West in 1967. What was her name?
8. In 1967, the Queen met these estranged relatives in public. Who were they?
9. This European enclave voted overwhelmingly to stay with Britain in September 1967. Name this enclave?
10. Che Guevara was shot dead in the jungle of this South American Country. Which Country is this?
11. Who wrote a book about mankind called *The Naked Ape*?
12. British troops left this port in Southern Yemen in 1967, after 128 years of colonial rule. Name this port?
13. This Liberal Leader took power in Czechoslovakia in January 1968. Who was he?
14. This American 'spy ship' was seized by the North Koreans in 1968. What was this ship's name?
15. Who was the U.S. Secretary of State in January 1968?

### Answers to The 1960s (V)

1. Malaysia
2. Charles Whitman.
3. The Starfighter.

4. Greece
5. A blood clot to the lung. He was suffering from cancer.
6. Lincoln Rockwell.
7. Svetlana Alliluyeva (give yourself one point if you just got Svetlana).
8. The Duke and Duchess of Windsor.
9. Gibraltar
10. Bolivia
11. Desmond Morris.
12. Aden
13. Alexander Dubcek.
14. Pueblo
15. Dean Rusk.

## 248. The 1960s (VI)

1. This man was sworn in as Canadian Prime Minister in 1968. Who was he?
2. Richard Nixon won the 1968 election with the narrowest margin since which earlier Presidential Election?
3. This English politician spoke about a 'river of blood'. Who was this politician?
4. Which City was the site of student uprising and demonstrations in May 1968?
5. In which month in 1968 did Russian tanks roll into Prague to crush the uprising?
6. Which two Senators were Hubert Humphrey's rivals for the Democratic nomination in 1968?
7. This student publicly burnt himself to death to protest Soviet occupation of his country. Who was he?
8. Into which city were 600 British troops dispatched to in 1969 to quell violence?
9. What was the name of the woman passenger whose body was found in a car driven by Edward Kennedy that plunged into a pond at Chappaquiddick?
10. This man was elected French President in 1969. Who was he?

11. This U.S. Supreme Court of Justice resigned in 1969 following disclosure of some questionable dealings with convicted financiers. Who was he?
12. Who did General Franco of Spain nominate as his successor in 1969?
13. These two countries clashed over a disputed island in middle of the frozen Ussuri River in 1969. Which two countries were they?
14. This riot in New York City marked the beginning of the Gay Rights movement. What was this riot called?
15. This group was found not guilty in 1969 for violating the Civil Rights Act with respect to demonstrations at the Democratic Convention in 1968. Who were they?

## Answers to The 1960s (VI)

1. Pierre Eliot Trudeau.
2. The 1912 Election.
3. Enoch Powell. Speaking about Britain's Immigration Policy.
4. Paris
5. August
6. George McGovern and Eugene McCarthy.
7. Jan Palach in 1969.
8. Belfast
9. Mary Jo Kopechne.
10. Georges Pompidou.
11. Abe Fortas
12. Prince Juan Carlos.
13. The Soviet Union and China.
14. Stonewall
15. The Chicago Eight.

## 249. African History (Prior to the 20th Century) I

1. This Conference took place between November 1884 and February 1885. It was called to ease tension between the European powers over the partition of Africa. Which Conference was this?
2. This European power set up a permanent settlement in the Cape of Good Hope in 1652. Which Power was this?
3. Ships from this Country bombarded Algiers, Tunis, and Tripoli in 1688. Name this Country?
4. This West African people set up a kingdom under Tutu with its capital at Kumasi after it had thrown off the yoke of the Denkera. Which people are being described here?
5. Omani forces took possession of this East African Port from the Portuguese in 1698. Name this Port?
6. By 1710 Tripolitania had become independent from this Middle Eastern Country. Name this Country?
7. Which Title was given to Hussein ben Ali who ruled Tunis from 1705 to 1710?
8. These tall people began moving into Kenya and Tanzania c. 1700 displacing the Bantu. Who were they?
9. This Tribe began a series of invasions in West Africa between 1750 and 1799 which would allow them to take the Central Niger Valley. Who were they?
10. This Bantu tribe drove south to reach the Keiskama River. Who were the Tribe?
11. The French lost bases to this Country in Senegal during the Seven Year War. Name this Country?
12. This European population migrated northward in Southern Africa crossing the Orange River in 1760. Who were they?
13. From which Country was Ali Bey driven out of temporarily in 1766?
14. Name one of the two indigenous groups that were first encountered by whites in South Africa?
15. Mikael Sehul was decisively defeated in 1784, leaving his country

in a state of anarchy. The period of 'princes would follow there'. Name this Country where Mikael Sehul ruled?

**Answers to African History (Prior to the 20th Century) I**

1. The Berlin Conference; it was called by Bismarck.
2. The Netherlands (Dutch).
3. France
4. The Ashanti.
5. Mombasa
6. Turkey
7. He was the Bey of Tunis.
8. The Masai.
9. The Tuaregs.
10. The Xhosa.
11. Britain. The French would win back these bases from Britain after the American Revolution.
12. The Boers.
13. Egypt
14. The Khoisa and the San or the Hottentots and Bushmen.
15. Ethiopia

## 250. African History (Prior to the 20th Century) II

1. The Ashanti Forces under King Osei Bonsu took control of this Coast in 1806. Name the Coast?
2. This leader broke Mameluke power in Egypt in 1811. Who was he?
3. An American invasion force under this man entered Algiers on May 3, 1814 to force the release of American prisoners and end piracy. Who was this man?
4. Which Zulu Leader was victorious at The Battle of Gqoki Hill in 1818?
5. Which name did the Zulus give to the soldiers who fought in their highly disciplined regiment formations?

6. What was the 'Mfecane'?
7. The first of these West African wars were fought between 1724-1726. Name these series of wars?
8. In which Country did Abd-el-Kadr lead a war of resistance against the French?
9. Which migration began in Southern Africa in 1836?
10. This Zulu Leader ordered the massacre of a Boer Party led by Piet Retief in 1838. Who was the Zulu leader?
11. Why did the Kingdom of Dahomey go into decline after 1840?
12. The British occupied and annexed this future Province of South Africa in 1843. Name this Province?
13. The Eighth War between the British and Xhosas on the Eastern front of the Cape Colony ended in 1853. By which other name were these wars known as?
14. This General and Statesman, who helped mastermind The Boer Victory over the Zulus at Blood River died in 1853. An important city in South Africa was named after him. Who was this man?
15. Al-Hajj Umar led a jihad of these West African people. His forces would eventually take the Bambara Kingdom. Which people did this man lead?

## Answers to African History (Prior to the 20th Century) II

1. The Gold Coast.
2. Mohammed Ali.
3. Stephen Decatur.
4. Shaka. He defeated the forces of Zwide of Ndwandwe.
5. Impis
6. A period called the Crushing when Shaka's Zulu forces destroyed, attacked and absorbed many of its rivals, killing between 1-2 million people and laying the foundation for the Zulu Empire.
7. The British-Ashanti Wars.
8. Algeria
9. The Great Trek. The movement of Boers northwards from the Cape Colony to the High Veld.

10. Dingane
11. Its fortune was based on the slave trade that was effectively ended.
12. Natal
13. The 'Kaffir' Wars.
14. Andries Pretorius. The City of course is Pretoria ('my birthplace').
15. The Fulani.

## 251. African History (Prior to the $20^{th}$ Century) III

1. This Republic was established in the Transvaal in 1854. Name this Republic?
2. This Basuto Leader led his people to victory over both the Boers and British at different times. Who was this man?
3. Which Country penetrated the Cameroons in 1860?
4. Belgium penetrated this Region of Africa between 1877 and 1885. Which Region was this?
5. At which Battle did a Zulu force of 20,000 defeat a British force of 1800 soldiers and colonials, leaving 1400 British and colonials dead for the loss of 2,000 Zulus?
6. Which war was broke out in Southern Africa in December 1880?
7. Who led the Sudanese-Dervish forces that defeated the Egyptians in 1881?
8. This man led The Royal Niger Company forces that conquered the Islamic State of Nupe in 1896 and helped ensure British domination of Nigeria towards the end of the $19^{th}$ Century. Who was this man?
9. After bombarding Tamatave and Majunga in 1883, the French won protectorship over this island Country. Name the Country?
10. Which City was besieged by Mahdist Forces between February 1884 and January 1885?
11. Which Region in East Africa did Britain make a protectorate in 1887 in order to stifle German encroachment?
12. In which Modern West African Country did France lose their protectorate in 1894 at the end of the Second Mandingo-French War?

13. At which Battle in 1896 were the Italians defeated by the Abyssinians forcing their withdrawal from the Country?
14. Who led the British forces to victory in the Second Sudanese-Egyptian-British War?
15. Name two of the three cities that were besieged by the Boers in the first year of the Second Anglo-Boer War?

**Answers to African History (Prior to the 20th Century) III**

1. The South African Republic by Marthinus Pretorius the eldest son of Andries Pretorius.
2. King Mosheshu. Founder of the nation of Basutoland—later Lesotho.
3. Germany
4. The Congo.
5. Battle of Isandhlwana; fought January 22,1879. The Zulus were led by Cetshwayo. After some early success, the Zulus however would be defeated by the British at Ulundi, ending their war against the British.
6. The First Anglo-Boer War. The Boers would defeat the British at Laing's Nek and Majuba Hill and force the British via The Treaty of Pretoria to recognize the independent Transvaal Republic.
7. The Mahdi (aka Muhammad Ahmad).
8. Sir George Goldie.
9. Madagascar
10. Khartoum. The British Forces at Khartoum were led by General Charles Gordon who was killed along with his remaining regiment.
11. Kenya
12. The Ivory Coast. The French would however prevail defeating the Ivory Coast Forces in the Third Mandingo-French War in 1898.
13. The Battle of Adowa.
14. General Horatio Kitchener. His biggest victory occurred at Omdurman where Kitchener's Forces defeated the Dervish Army of 40,000 to 50,000 men. The Dervish suffered a loss of 20,000 compared to British-Egyptian losses of less than 500.
15. Mafeking, Kimberley, and Ladysmith.

# 252. Modern African History I

What are the modern names of these African Countries/Territories?

1. Portuguese West Africa.
2. Bechuanaland
3. German East Africa.
4. Dahomey
5. Northern Rhodesia.
6. French Guinea.
7. German South West Africa.
8. Gold Coast.
9. Upper Volta.
10. Nyasaland
11. Rio De Oro.
12. French Somaliland.
13. Southern Rhodesia.
14. British East Africa.
15. Spanish Guinea.

## Answers to Modern African History I

1. Angola
2. Botswana
3. Tanzania
4. Benin
5. Zambia
6. Guinea
7. Namibia
8. Ghana
9. Burkina Faso.
10. Malawi
11. Western Sahara.
12. Djibouti
13. Zimbabwe

14. Kenya
15. Equatorial Guinea

## 253. Modern African History II

1. This Conference was held in 1906 to settle the differences between France and Germany that had occurred from the First Moroccan Crisis. Name this Conference?
2. This Province attempted to achieve independence from the Congo (Zaire) in the 1960s. Which Province was this?
3. Who was the Leader of this breakaway province?
4. During the crisis caused by this breakaway, whose Government in the Congo was overthrown?
5. The ANC issued this Charter in South Africa in 1956. The Charter emphasized non-racialism as opposed to racial exclusivity. What was the name of the Charter?
6. What was the name of the military wing of the ANC?
7. In which Country did the MPLA seize power in 1975?
8. Jonas Savimbi headed which organization?
9. In which Country did Hissene Habre rule?
10. Niger and Mali were both included in which Region governed by the French c. 1912?
11. This man became Prime Minister of Zimbabwe in 1980. Who was he?
12. Which Party did he lead to power?
13. Who was his chief African rival in Zimbabwe?
14. This man's idealism, outlined in the Arusha Declaration, greatly effected Tanzania. Who was this man?
15. This secret body emerged in 1918 to promote Afrikaner power in South Africa. What was this called?

### Answers to Modern African History II

1. The Algeciras Conference.
2. Katanga (now Shaba).

3. Moïse Tshombe.
4. Patrice Lumumba's. He would be assassinated in 1961.
5. The Freedom Charter.
6. The Umkhonto we Sizwe.
7. Angola
8. UNITA also in Angola. They are the rivals to the MPLA.
9. Chad
10. French West Africa.
11. Robert Mugabe.
12. ZANU-PF.
13. Joshua Nkomo Head of ZAPU.
14. Julius Nyerere. He believed in an African-based socialism.
15. The Broederbond (Brother Bond).

## 254. Modern African History III

1. In which Country did FRELIMO win power in 1975?
2. Which Region attempted to break away from Nigeria between 1967 and 1970?
3. What was/is the most predominant Ethnic Group in this region?
4. Who led the Federal Government in Nigeria that fought to prevent this breakaway?
5. This Party took power in South Africa in 1948. Which Party was this?
6. This African Leader led a coup that overthrew President Dacko in the Central African Republic in 1966. In 1976, he renamed the Country 'The Central African Empire'. Who was this African Leader?
7. Who did Idi Amin (Dada) seize power from in January 1971?
8. In which year was Nelson Mandela sentenced to life imprison?
9. In which Country did Hastings Kamazu Banda rule for over 30 years?
10. Put these Five South African Prime Ministers in chronological order (earliest to latest) that they held power in South Africa: Daniel Malan, Jan Smuts, John Vorster, Pieter Willem Botha, and Johannes Strijdom?

11. After which event did the African National Congress move to armed insurrection against the South African Government?
12. Where did the Germans put down a Herero-Hottentot insurrection in 1904?
13. This man led a non-violent campaign in South Africa against discrimination between 1906 and 1913. Who was this man?
14. This man emerged as The Power in Ethiopia after the Civil War in 1916-1917 between the Muslims and the Coptic Christians. Who was this man?
15. In which Country did Mohammed Siad Barre hold power?

## Answers to Modern African History III

1. Mozambique
2. Biafra
3. The Ibo.
4. Yakubu Gowon.
5. The National Party.
6. Jean Bedel Bokassa. He saw himself as a modern day Napoleon. He would eventually be overthrown in 1979.
7. Milton Obote. Like Bokassa, Amin would also lose power in 1979; a bad year for dictators.
8. 1964. He would be released on April 11, 1990 and in 1994 would become South Africa's first Black President.
9. Malawi
10. Smuts, Malan, Strijdom, Vorster, and Botha.
11. The Sharpeville Massacre of 1960.
12. German South West Africa (Namibia).
13. Mohandes "Mahatma" Gandhi.
14. Ras Tafari (later Haile Selassi I).
15. Somalia (1969-1991). After his death, the country deteriorated into the 'chaos of the warlords'.

## 255. Modern African History IV

1. In which North African Country was The Rif War fought between 1921 and 1926?
2. This man co-founded SWAPO to fight for independence. He became the first President of Namibia in March 1990. Who was this man?
3. This Boer General became Prime Minister of South Africa between 1924 and 1929. Who was this General?
4. This Zulu Leader of Inkatha was born in 1928. Who is he?
5. The Mau Mau uprising took place in this Country. Which country was this?
6. Which Party did Jomo Kenyatta lead to power in 1964?
7. Who succeeded Kenyatta as President in 1978?
8. What does 'ELF' stand for?
9. This Leader of Mozambique died in a suspicious aircraft crash in 1986. Which Leader was this?
10. Born in 1942, this man, who was later assassinated, was the General Secretary of the South African Communist Party. Who was he?
11. In which Country was Kwame Nkrumah Prime Minister between 1952 and 1957?
12. Which Guinean Leader gave Nkrumah the status of Co-Head of State after Nkrumah had been overthrown?
13. Which Mineral has been the principal driver of the Zambian economy?
14. Which Country enacted The Suppression of Communism Act in 1950? The basis of its Police State.
15. What was the largest tribal group within the Mau Mau Organization?

### Answers to Modern African History IV

1. Morocco. It was the Moroccan War of Independence that Abd el-Krim led against the Spanish and French Forces. The Moroccans would be defeated in the war but not after some successes such as The Battle of Anual.

2. Sam Nujoma.
3. James Hertzog.
4. Mangosuthu Gatsha Buthelezi.
5. Kenya
6. The Kenyan African National Union.
7. Daniel Arap Moi.
8. Eritrean Liberation Front.
9. Samora Machel.
10. Chris Hani.
11. Ghana
12. Sekou Toure.
13. Copper
14. South Africa.
15. The Kikuyu.

## 256. Modern African History V

1. The United Nations issued its first condemnation of this policy in 1952. Which Policy was this?
2. In Sudan, which two population groups have fought the country's Civil War since the mid 1950s?
3. Which Party would take power in Algeria in 1962?
4. Who was the first Premier of the independent Algeria?
5. A revolt by which people was put down by the French Army in Algeria in January-February 1960?
6. Which Tribe failed in its attempt between 1962 and 1963 to seize power in Rwanda?
7. Amilcar Cabral led a revolt in Guinea-Bissau against which Colonial Power?
8. Against which dominant minority did Black Africans rebel in Zanzibar?
9. This Head of the ANC won the Nobel Prize for Peace in 1960. Who was he?
10. Which West African Country had leaders such as Mobido Keita and Moussa Traore?

11. In which Country did Haile Mariam Mengistu seize power in a coup d'etat in 1974?
12. Chad fought a war with this Country between 1975 and 1987. Which Country was this?
13. He was the last Leader of the White Government in Rhodesia. Who was this man?
14. This man seized power in Ghana in 1981 and ruled as a Dictator. Who was/is he?
15. Yuweri Musaveni took power in this Country in 1986. Which Country was this?

**Answers to Modern African History V**

1. Apartheid
2. The Muslim dominated North which has traditionally held power against the Christian and Anamist South.
3. The FLN.
4. Ahmed Ben Bella.
5. A revolt by French Colonists.
6. The Tutsis.
7. Portugal. Cabral's group was known as 'PAIGC' or 'African Party' for the Independence of Guinea and Cape Verde.
8. The Arabs.
9. Albert Luthuli.
10. Mali
11. Ethiopia
12. Libya
13. Ian Smith
14. Jerry Rawlings.
15. Uganda

## 257. Latin American History I

1. This Peruvian civilization was famous for its large designs in the sand using pebbles. The largest design is a bird that is 275m long. Who were these people?

2. This Inca ruler was kidnapped by the men of Francisco Pizarro. He was later garroted. His death would speed up the downfall of the Inca. Who was this man?
3. Many people believe that this civilization was behind the legends of Eldorado. Beginning with a letter 'C', these people lived in the Colombian Highlands until they were destroyed by the Spanish in the 16th Century. Who were these people?
4. The Tihuanaco civilization lasted between 800 BC and 1200 AD, its main city was situated near this famous South American Lake in Bolivia. Which Lake was this?
5. This vegetable had been cultivated by the Andean Indians since c. 200 AD. Which vegetable was this?
6. For which god did the Aztecs mistake Hernando Cortes?
7. This civilizations' Golden Era lasted from AD 250 to AD 900. They lived in Southern Mexico, Guatemala and parts of Belize. Who were they?
8. Who was the Aztec Chief God and God of Matter?
9. Fifteen thousand men were sacrificed to this Aztec Sun God. Who was he?
10. What is the modern name of the City 'Tenochtitlan'?
11. This Ancient Middle American culture dominated the coastal plains between 1200 BC to 400 BC. Their name is the Nahuatl Indian word for 'inhabitant of rubber country'. Who were they?
12. This warrior culture was based at the City of Tollan. They ruled Central Mexico between 900 to 1200 AD. Their civilization seems to have been created from several ethnic groups. Who were they?
13. What was Tlachtli?
14. This South American civilization called gold 'the sweat of the sun' and silver as the 'tears of the moon'. Who were they?
15. This 'last'outpost of the Mayan civilization was built in the Yucatan Peninsula. The city had two wells, also known as 'cenotes'. The citizens drank from one well and used the other for sacrifice. Name this city?

**Answers to Latin American History I**

1. The Nazca.
2. Atahualpa
3. The Chibcha.
4. Lake Titicaca.
5. The potato.
6. Quetzcoatl
7. The Mayans. They were also brilliant astronomers and Mathematicians.
8. Tezcatlipoca
9. Huitzilopochtli
10. Mexico City. It was founded by the Aztecs in AD 1200.
11. The Olmec.
12. The Toltec.
13. An Aztec game with similarities to volleyball and basketball.
14. The Incas.
15. Chichén Itzá.

## 258. Latin American History II

1. Over control of which Country did the Dutch and Portuguese fight in the 1640's—1650's?
2. Which native population did Columbus discover in Jamaica?
3. Which Treaty signed in 1494 divided South America between the Portuguese and the Spanish?
4. Who were the Paulistas?
5. Which City had by the mid 18th Century, become the most important non-South American Western Hemisphere city for the Spanish?
6. This Chilean Capital was founded in 1541. Which City was this?
7. The states of Nambicuara, Piro and Guarani in Central South America were controlled by which Missionary Group until 1767?
8. This European Power sacked Rio de Janeiro during the War of the Spanish Succession. Who were they?

9. By 1538, Spanish control had been established in this Northern South American Country. Which Country was this?
10. A stable government was set up by Francisco de Toledo in this Region of South America that includes the cities of Callao and Cuzco. What was this Region?
11. This Dominican Friar, who championed the humane treatment of Native Americans, set up a colony at Cumaná (off the coast of modern Venezuela); unfortunately it failed. Who was this man?
12. The city of Córdoba was established by the Spanish in 1573. In which modern Country does it reside?
13. Which Mineral is associated with the South American mine at Potosí? Founded in 1545.
14. What were Spain's possessions in Central America collectively known as in c. 1812?
15. The Dominican Republic and Haiti share which island in the Caribbean?

**Answers to Latin American History II**

1. Brazil. The Portuguese would eventually win.
2. The Arawaks.
3. The Treaty of Torsdesillas. As Portuguese settlement spread west the Portuguese would gain a larger share of South America than the Treaty originally intended. The Treaty of Madrid and San Idefonso (1777) updated The Treaty of Torsdesillas.
4. Portuguese slave traders.
5. Havana. The Spanish would lose it to the British in 1762, but regained control of it by ceding Florida.
6. Santiago
7. The Jesuits
8. The French.
9. Colombia
10. Peru
11. Bartolomé de Las Casas.
12. Argentina

13. Silver
14. Vice-Royalty of New Spain. Spanish possessions in the Americas were divided into four Regions: Vice-Royalty of New Spain (Central America), Vice-Royalty of New Granada (Northern South America), Vice-Royalty of Peru (Western South America) and the United Provinces of La Plata (Argentina and Uruguay).
15. Hispaniola

## 259. Latin American History III

1. In which Country did Miguel Hidalgo lead an unsuccessful revolt in 1810-1811?
2. Name the individual who routed the Spanish in 1819 at The Battle of Boyacá and found the Republic of Gran Colombia?
3. Which Portuguese Royal Family fled to Brazil in 1807 under British escort?
4. Which Country did Juan Manuel Rosas rule as a Dictator between 1929-1852?
5. Mexican conservatives tried to make this man Emperor in 1863, it failed, and he would later be executed in 1867. Who was this 'unlucky Emperor'?
6. Which Country fought a war against Argentina, Uruguay, and Brazil between 1864 to 1870?
7. This man, with an Irish surname, played an important part in The Chilean Revolution. He would become the country's 'Supreme Dictator' between 1817 to 1823. Who was this man?
8. In South America, who were the Mestizos?
9. Who led the Revolutionary Forces to victory over the Spanish in Argentina?
10. This type of seabird dropping that is used as fertilizer was a major source of revenue for Peru, however it was exhausted within 20 years. What was this product?
11. This Amazonian city prospered because of the rubber boom (1890-1920). Its opera house was completed in 1896. Which City was this?
12. Which three countries fought The War of the Pacific between 1879-1883?

13. This man ruled Mexico as a Dictator after a period as an elected President between 1833 and 1836. Who was this man?
14. This Country succeeded in winning independence from Colombia in 1903. Which Country was this?
15. The Liberal Guzman Blanco is associated with which Country?

**Answers to Latin American History III**

1. Mexico
2. Simón Bolivar.
3. The Braganzas.
4. Argentina
5. Maximilian I.
6. Paraguay. Known as The War of the Triple Alliance. It cost Paraguay 60% of its population.
7. Bernardo O' Higgins.
8. A class of mixed Indian and European people in South America. They had more rights under the Spanish and Portuguese administration than the mulattos (African-European) and zambos (African-Indian), but not as much rights as the peninsulares (Spanish born whites) or reinóis (Portuguese born whites).
9. Jose de San Martín. He also took Peru, but gave control to Bolivar.
10. Guano
11. Manaus
12. Chile, Bolivia, and Peru.
13. Antonio de Santa Anna.
14. Panama
15. Venezuela. He was President between 1870 and 1888 and introduced many social and political reforms.

## 260. Latin American History IV

1. Which two South American countries fought The Chaco War between 1932 and 1935?

2. In which Country did Getúlio Vargas lead a revolution in 1930?
3. In 1921 Guatemala, Honduras and El Salvador formed which republic?
4. This Mexican leader's regime fell in 1911. It had lasted for 34 years. Which Leader was this?
5. Which product did Cuba mostly rely on the United States to import c. 1920?
6. He was elected President of Argentina in 1946. Who was he?
7. In which year did Fidel Castro seize power in Cuba?
8. The 'Dirty Wars' were fought in which Country?
9. What does 'CARIFTA' stand for?
10. What war did Honduras and El Salvador fight in 1969?
11. This Costa Rican Leader, who helped steer his country through much of the turmoil of the region, won the Nobel Prize in 1987. Who was this Leader?
12. With which Caribbean Country was the Politician Eric Williams associated?
13. This pro-American Dictator was the strongman in Paraguay between 1954 and 1989. Who was this man?
14. In which Country were the Tonton Macoute a civilian militia?
15. Which Party did Raúl Alfonsín lead to power in Argentina in the early 1980's?

### Answers to Latin American History IV

1. Bolivia and Paraguay.
2. Brazil
3. The Republic of Central America.
4. Porfirio Diaz.
5. Sugar
6. Juan Perón.
7. 1959
8. Argentina between 1976-1982.
9. The Caribbean Free Trade Association; it was formed in 1968.
10. The Soccer or Football War. During this war, the Acajutla Oil Refinery was destroyed by the Honduran Air Force.

11. Arias Sánchez.
12. Trinidad and Tobago. He took the country into the Federation of the West Indies in 1958.
13. Alfredo Stroessner.
14. Haiti under the regime of François 'Papa Doc' Duvalier.
15. The Radical Union Party.

## 261. Canadian History I

1. Who was the winning General at the Battle of the Plains of Abraham on September 13, 1759?
2. Humphrey Gilbert proclaimed this future Canadian province for England in 1583. Which Province was this?
3. This Native tribe was Explorer Samuel De Champlain's greatest enemy. Who were they?
4. Jean de Brébeuf and Gabriel Lalement were both tortured to death. What were their professions?
5. This Company was born on May 2, 1670. Which Company was this?
6. French Settlers in the Maritime Region were known by this name. What was/is the name?
7. The British seized this fortress on July 26, 1758. Which Fortress is this?
8. This former Governor of Newfoundland was executed in 1757. Who was he?
9. This Native Chief continued waging war in Britain even after The Treaty of Paris had given Britain control of Canada. He would eventually try and take Detroit. Who was he?
10. Who suffered a defeat in Quebec City on December 31, 1775?
11. John Julian was the chief of a native population who were a strong presence in Nova Scotia. Which people were they ?
12. This Town became Capital of Upper Canada on August 26, 1793. Which Town was this?
13. Lord Selkirk was granted 300,000 km of land around this river west of Lake Superior. Which River was this?

14. Which Province was once known as Lower Canada?
15. This woman warned the British ahead of time of an American attack in 1813. Who was this woman?

**Answers to Canadian History I**

1. James Wolfe.
2. Newfoundland
3. The Iroquois.
4. They were both Jesuit Priests. It happened during the time when the Iroquois destroyed the Huron Nation and overran the Jesuit Mission.
5. Hudson's Bay Trading Company.
6. Acadians
7. Louisbourg; it had fallen before in 1745.
8. John Byng. Although he had won local respect in Newfoundland for trying to stop a monopolistic trade policy in St. John's, his failure to attack French ships off the British-held island of Minorca to relieve the British Fort St. Phillip bought about his court martial and execution.
9. Chief Pontiac.
10. The Americans under the leadership of Richard Montgomery and Benedict Arnold. Championing the defence of Quebec City was the Governor Guy Carleton.
11. The Micmac.
12. York (Toronto).
13. The Red River. It was intended that he would establish a colony there of Scottish crofters.
14. Quebec
15. Laura Secord.

## 262. Canadian History II

1. In 1829, the Welland Canal was completed linking these two Great Lakes. Name these Lakes?

2. Who was the First Prime Minister of Canada?
3. In which Year did The Canadian Confederation come to be?
4. This Métis Leader rebelled and captured Fort Garry (now Winnipeg) in 1869. Who was this Leader?
5. What was the earlier name of the Royal Canadian Mountain Police?
6. During the Prime Ministership of Sir Wilfrid Laurier (1896 to 1911), Canada entered a period of prosperity. What name was given to this Period?
7. Which school crisis faced both Prime Ministers, Sir Mackenzie Bowell and his successor Sir Charles Tupper?
8. She led the fight for women's voting rights in Alberta. Who was she?
9. He was Canada's Prime Minister during the Depression years 1930-1935. Who was he?
10. In 1905, two Provinces were created in Canada. Name them?
11. With which Country did Prime Minister John Diefenbaker insist on maintaining relations after 1962?
12. Which important judiciary change occurred in Canada during the Prime Ministership of Louis St. Laurent?
13. This man led Newfoundland into The Canadian Confederation in 1949. Who was he?
14. This city hosted Expo '67. Which City was this?
15. For what did Lester Pearson win the 1957 Nobel Peace Prize?

**Answers to Canadian History II**

1. Lakes Erie and Ontario.
2. Sir John A. MacDonald.
3. 1867 on July 1st.
4. Louis Riel. Riel's actions forced the Federal Government to create the Province of Manitoba
5. The North West Mounted Police. Its creation was the work of legislation introduced by Canada's second Prime Minister, Alexander Mackenzie.
6. The Sunshine Years.
7. The Closing of French schools in Manitoba. Tupper introduced a bill to protect separate French schools in Manitoba

8. Nelly McClung. Women would win the right to vote federally in 1918 after the passing of The Women's Franchise Act supported by the Prime Minister Sir Robert Borden.
9. Richard Bennett.
10. Saskatchewan and Alberta.
11. Cuba, despite the Cuban Missile Crisis.
12. The Canadian Supreme Court became the final court of appeal. There was no recourse judicially to any courts in Britain anymore.
13. Joseph 'Joey' Smallwood.
14. Montreal
15. For his work in organizing the UN Emergency Force during the Suez Canal Crisis (Pearson is one of the fathers of UN peacekeeping).

## 263. Modern Black American History I

1. Which Institution did George Washington Carver champion to provide education for disadvantaged black farmers?
2. What was the claim to fame of Hiram Revels and Blanche Kelso Bruce?
3. The Supreme Court decision in this case argued that 'separate but equal' facilities were constitutional. Which Case was this?
4. He was the leading advocate of Gradualism. Who was this man?
5. This book was published in 1935 to debunk army tests which claimed to prove that Blacks were mentally inferior. What was the book?
6. What was the first and last names of the individual who sued because his daughter could not go to an all white school?
7. Which lawyer represented the man mentioned in Question 6 in his case?
8. He led the National Urban League during the 1960's. Who was this man?
9. Martin Luther King founded the SCLC. What does the acronym mean?
10. In response to whose arrest did Martin Luther King organize the 381 day Montgomery bus boycott?

11. Ezell Blair, David Richmond, Joseph McNeil, and Franklyn McCain organized a sit-in at this store's lunch counter in Greensboro, NC. Which Store was this?
12. In which year did Martin Luther King lead his memorable march on Washington?
13. In March 1965, 600 Blacks marched from this Town to Montgomery. They were met with a violent reaction organized by Sheriff Jim Clark. Which City were they marching from?
14. This Field Secretary of the NAACP in Mississippi was shot in the back as he walked home. Who was this man?
15. How did Autherine Lucy earn a position in Civil Rights History?

**Answers to Modern Black American History I**

1. Tuskegee Institute in Alabama.
2. They were both elected to the Senate from Mississippi during the period of Reconstruction.
3. Plessy v Ferguson (1896). Decision laid the basis for the 'Jim Crow' Laws.
4. Brooker T. Washington.
5. *Negro Intelligence* by Otto Klineberg.
6. Oliver Brown. The Supreme Court would eventually decide in Brown v. Board of Education of Topeka that 'separate but equal' was unconstitutional.
7. Thurgood Marshall.
8. Whitney Young Jr.
9. Southern Christian Leadership Conference.
10. Rosa Lee Parkes, who had refused to give up her seat to a white as was required to by the law in Alabama.
11. Woolworth's
12. 1963 on the 28th of August.
13. Selma. The event became known as 'Bloody Sunday'.
14. Medger Wiley Evers.
15. Lucy was the first black student to be admitted to the University of Alabama.

# 264. Modern Black American History II

1. Complete this George Wallace quote: "Segregation now! Segregation tomorrow! . . ."
2. These types of tests were banned federally in 1965. This would help Black Americans to vote. What were these tests?
3. What was Malcolm X's earlier name?
4. These two men founded The Black Panthers. Who were they?
5. What was the motto of The Black Panthers?
6. Who took over the Leadership of the SCLC after Martin Luther King's death?
7. In which City was Malcolm X assassinated?
8. Another march on Washington occurred soon after Martin Luther King's Death. It would end in a Solidarity rally and it involved 50,000 people. What was this march called?
9. The banning of this tax made it also easier for Blacks to vote in the South. What were these taxes?
10. This man is alleged to have coined the phrase ' Black Power'. His policy of building alliance with radical whites led to his resignation from the Black Panthers. Who was he?
11. This Detroit born diplomat helped organize the cease-fire that ended The Arab-Israel War of the late 1940's. He was awarded the Peace Prize in 1950. Who was this man?
12. This man was one of the Founders of the NAACP. He studied at both Harvard and Berlin Universities. He died in Ghana in 1963. Who was this man?
13. Why did Louis Farrakhan split from the Nation of Islam?
14. Which City was Andrew Young the Mayor of?
15. Jesse Jackson organized Operation PUSH in 1971. What does/did PUSH stand for?

### Answers to Modern Black American History II

1. "Segregation forever!"
2. Literacy tests.

3. Malcolm Little.
4. Huey P. Newton and Bobby Seale.
5. Power flows from the Barrel of a Gun.
6. The Reverend Ralph D. Abernathy.
7. New York City in the Audubon Ball Room.
8. The Poor People's March.
9. Poll Taxes.
10. Stokely Carmichael.
11. Ralph Bunche.
12. William du Bois.
13. He did not agree with the decision by Elijah Mohammed's son to allow Whites to join the organization. Farrakhan would split off and form the Final Call to the Nation of Islam.
14. Atlanta
15. People United to Save Humanity.

## 265. Russian History I

1. The period between 859-1253 AD is known by which name in Russian History?
2. This Prince converted the Russian people to Christianity. Who was he?
3. This man ruled Russia between 1598 and 1605. He tried very much to westernize the country, but failed because of church opposition. Who was this man?
4. This Russian Leader defeated the Swedes at Neva in 1240. Who was this Leader?
5. Tartars from this Region burnt Moscow in 1571. Which Region was this?
6. Which Tsar was responsible for the Terror of the Oprichnina?
7. Fedor I helped lay the foundation for this North Russian Port City. Which City was this?
8. This power West of Russia occupied Moscow between 1610 and 1612. Who were they?
9. Who was the first Romanov Tsar of Russia?

10. Muscovy joined with this power in 1654 to form a Union. What was the other Power?
11. The Russian Capital moved to this City in 1713. Which City was this?
12. Peter the Great assumed this title in 1721. What was this title?
13. All the ruling Romanov Tsarinas have had either one of the following first names: Catherine, Anna and which other name?
14. This Palace was completed in 1796. Which Palace was this?
15. What could non-nobles no longer purchase from 1746 onwards?

**Answers to Russian History I**

1. Period of Kievan Rus.
2. Grand Prince Vladimir.
3. Boris Godunov.
4. Alexander Nevsky.
5. Crimea
6. Ivan the Terrible.
7. Archangelsk
8. The Poles (Poland).
9. Mikhael Fedorovich in 1613.
10. The Ukraine.
11. St. Petersburg.
12. Emperor
13. Elizabeth
14. The Alexander Palace.
15. Serfs

## 266. Russian History II

1. This Leader was deported in 1926. Who was he?
2. In which Town were the Tsar and his family executed?
3. This General set up a regime in Crimea from March to November 1920. Who was this General?
4. Lenin introduced this Policy in March 1921 to weaken the peasant

revolts that had broken out against the Bolsheviks all over the country. What was this Policy called?

5. Which two colours fought the Russian Civil War?
6. At which Naval base did a revolt breakout in March 1921?
7. Which position did Josef Stalin achieve in April 1922?
8. This one-time ally of Stalin was ousted from the Politburo in 1929. He would die in the purges in 1938. Who was he?
9. Which Plan was adopted in 1928?
10. Which two individuals ruled Russia in a triumvirate together with Stalin after the death of Lenin?
11. This man's death began the Great Terror of the Purges. Who was he?
12. Which Region became an autonomous Jewish state in 1934?
13. Which type of farming system was favoured by Stalin and Co. in the Five-Year Plans?
14. What term did Stalin use to label all peasants who opposed his agricultural reforms?
15. This man was the Chief Prosecutor during the Great purges. Who was he?

**Answers to Russian History II**

1. Leon Trotsky.
2. Ekaterinburg
3. General Wrangel.
4. The NEP or New Economic Policy. It was a mixture of socialism and capitalism.
5. The Whites and the Reds.
6. Kronstadt. It was put down by both Trotsky and Tukhachevsky.
7. He became Secretary General of the Communist Party.
8. Nikolai Bukharin.
9. The First Five-Year Plan.
10. Zinoviev and Kamenev.
11. Sergei Kirov.
12. Birobidzhan

13. Collective Farms.
14. Kulaks
15. Andrey Vyshinsky.

## 267. Indian History I

1. This civilization dominated the Northern Indian sub-continent c. 2700 BC. Which civilization was this?
2. These people expanded into the Ganga Valley c. 1000 BC. Who were these people?
3. This man established the first Indian Empire in 322 BC. Who was this man?
4. Aryabhatta was born in 476 AD, with what scientific discipline is he most associated with?
5. Which Dynasty did Chandragupta I establish in 320 AD?
6. The Chola King Erata conquered this Island in 145 BC. Which Island was this?
7. Of 544 BC, 527 BC, and 521 BC, when did the Buddha reach Nirvana?
8. This King defeated Kalinga in a bloody war that led to 100,000 deaths in 261 BC. Later on, he would renounce war and devote himself to peace. Who was this King?
9. These people invaded India in 1221. Who were these people?
10. Name the Dynasty that was set up by Qutbuddin in 1206?
11. This man invaded India in 1398. Who was he?
12. Who was the first ruler of the Mughal Dynasty?
13. In 1564, Akbar abolished the poll tax on people of this religion. What was this religion?
14. When Akbar defeated Rana Pratap at The Battle of Haldighat, which Region fell under Mughal control in 1576?
15. Who succeeded Akbar to the Mughal throne?

### Answers to Indian History I

1. The Harappa Civilization.

2. The Aryans.
3. Chandragupta Maurya.
4. Astronomy
5. The Gupta Dynasty.
6. Ceylon or Sri Lanka.
7. 544 BC.
8. Ashoka. He would denounce hunting and become a strict vegetarian. He was also dubbed the Devanama Piyadasi or 'beloved of the gods'.
9. The Mongols under Genghis Khan.
10. The Slave Dynasty.
11. Timur
12. Babur
13. Hinduism
14. Bengal
15. Jahangir

## 268. Indian History II

1. A Charter was given to this Company in 1600. Which Company was this?
2. With which religion is the Guru, Arjan associated with?
3. This European power opened a factory in Pulicat in 1609. Who were they?
4. Shah Abbas besieged and took Qandahar in 1622. From which Country was the Shah from?
5. Shah Jahan built this monument in 1631 in honour of his dead wife. What is the name of this monument?
6. This Mughal Leader captured Bidar and Kalyani in 1657. Who was he?
7. This City, now the Capital of India's Film Industry, was ceded to the English in 1661. Name this City?
8. These people raided Malwa in 1699, captured Salsette and Bassrein in 1739 and invaded Bengal in 1742. Who were they?
9. Nadir Shah captured this Indian City in 1739. Name this city?
10. Who did the British defeat at the Battle of Wandiwash in 1760?

11. This series of wars were fought between 1767-1769,1780-1784, 1790-1792, and 1799. What were they called?
12. This man, who became Governor-General in August 1823, declared war on Burma on the 24th February 1824. Who was this man?
13. This murderous cult was suppressed between 1829 and 1837. Who were they?
14. This practice was outlawed in 1829. It involved the suicide of a new widow. What was it called?
15. Which event forced the British Crown to take over direct control of the Indian Government in 1858?

**Answers to Indian History II**

1. The English East India Company.
2. Sikhism. He was executed in 1606.
3. The Dutch.
4. Persia
5. The Taj Mahal. His dead wife's name was Mumtaz Mahal.
6. Aurangezeb
7. Bombay (Mumbai).
8. The Marathas.
9. Delhi
10. The French.
11. The Mysore Wars.
12. Lord Amherst. Britain was worried about Burmese advancement into Indian Territory following recent gains by the Burmese in Assam.
13. The Thuggee—from whose name the word 'Thug' is derived.
14. Sati
15. The Indian/Sepoy Mutiny of 1857.

## 269. Indian History III

1. From which City was the Imperial Capital moved to Delhi in 1912?

2. Which area did the British annex after defeating the Sikhs in 1849?
3. This Organization had its first meeting in 1885. Which Organization was this?
4. Put these Acts in the order they occurred (earliest to latest): Indian Navy Act, Defence of India Act, Newspaper Act, and Vernacular Press Act?
5. Rioting broke out between these two groups in 1823. Which two groups were they?
6. This movement led by Gandhi was called off in 1934. Which movement was this?
7. In which Year did India win independence?
8. These two Leaders met in 1944, but failed to reach an agreement over Pakistan. Who were they?
9. India nationalized this Organization in January 1948. Which Organization was this?
10. India concluded a treaty with this Country in 1954. A year later, the two countries would be at war. Which Country is this?
11. An act regarding this caste in India came into being in 1955. Which Act was this?
12. This Portuguese Colony was liberated on December 19, 1961. Which Colony was this?
13. Who succeeded Jawaharlal Nehru as Prime Minister in 1964?
14. This female politician was expelled from the Congress Party for indiscipline. Who was she?
15. Morarji Desai resigned from which political party?

**Answers to Indian History III**

1. Calcutta
2. Punjab
3. The Indian National Congress.
4. Vernacular Press Act (1878), Newspaper Act (1908), Defence of India Act (1915), and Indian Navy Act (1927)
5. The Hindus and the Muslims.
6. Civil Disobedient Movement.

7. 1947 (15th August).
8. Mahatma Gandhi and Muhammad Ali Jinnah.
9. The Indian Reserve Bank.
10. China
11. Untouchability Act.
12. Goa
13. Lal Bahadur Shastri.
14. Indira Gandhi.
15. The Janata Party.

## 270. History of the Far East I

1. This Dynasty ruled China from the 16th to the 11th Century BC. Which Dynasty was this?
2. This 4000 mile network connected the Far East to Europe between 500 BC and 1500 AD. Which Network was this?
3. Put these three dynasties in order (earliest to latest): Ch'in, Zhou and Han?
4. This Emperor built the Great Wall of China. Who was he?
5. How many Kingdoms dominated China from AD 220-280?
6. This religion reached China in 50 AD. Which Religion was this?
7. What did Cai Lun invent in 150 AD?
8. Rebellions by this sect weakened the Chinese Empire between the 2nd and 3rd Century AD. What was this sect called?
9. Along which axis did China begin to divide politically between the 4th and 6th Century AD?
10. Wen Di reunited China in the 580s Over which dynasty was he the First Emperor?
11. Political and social reform known as Taika took place in this Country between 646-700 AD. Which Country was this?
12. The Angkorian Dynasty ruled over this Country from 802. Which Country was this?
13. This City became Capital of Japan in 794 AD. Which City was this?
14. This Clan would start to win control of the Japanese Emperors around 858 AD. Which Clan was this?

15. It sounds like a fruit drink and it collapsed around 907 AD. What is being described?

**Answers to the History of the Far East I**

1. The Shang Dynasty.
2. The Silk Road/Route.
3. Zhou (1066 BC to 771 BC), Ch'in (771 BC to 206BC), Han (206 BC to 26 AD).
4. Shi Huangdi. The wall is 5,000km long.
5. Three. The Wei, Shu and Wu—during the early part of the Period of Disunity.
6. Buddhism. It would be banned in China in 845 AD.
7. Paper
8. The Yellow Turban Sect.
9. The North-South Axis.
10. The Sui Dynasty.
11. Japan
12. Cambodia or Khmer—founder was Jayawarman II.
13. Kyoto (aka Heian-kyo), marked the beginning of Heian period in Japanese history that lasted until 1185. Japan gained more independence from China during this period.
14. The Fujiwara.
15. The Tang Dynasty.

## 271. History of the Far East II

1. Lady Mursaki Shikibu wrote a famous Novel between 1008-1020. What was this Novel called?
2. A mechanical clock was built in Kaifeng c. 1090. What drove this clock?
3. Which Temple in Southeast Asia was built by Suryawarman II between 1113-1150?
4. Emperors from which Dynasty began re-building the Great Wall of China to protect the Country against Northern invaders in 1488?

5. The Chinese capital moved to Beijing in 1421. Which City had it existed in before then?
6. With which Country is King Trailok associated?
7. These people were driven out of China in 1368. Who were they?
8. The Onin War in Japan ended the authority of this shogunate in Japan. What was the shogunate?
9. Which Country beat off the Japanese invaders between 1592 and 1598?
10. With which type of art form is the reign of the Chinese Emperor Wan Li most associated?
11. Which period began in Japan with the capture of the capital city by Oda Nobunaga in the 16th Century?
12. The Tokugawa Period in Japanese history which began with the victory of Tokugawa Ieyasu over his rivals at The Battle of Sekigahara has another name that is associated with the old name of Tokyo. What is this Period also called?
13. The Japanese persecuted people of this religion between 1612 and 1639. Which Religion was this?
14. What is another name for the Manchu Dynasty that took over China in 1644?
15. This Island became Chinese Territory in 1683. Which Island was this?

**Answers to the History of the Far East II**

1. *Tale of Genji*
2. Water
3. The Temple of Angkor Wat.
4. Ming
5. Nanking or Nanjing.
6. Thailand
7. The Mongols.
8. The Ashikaga Shogunate.
9. Korea
10. Pottery (Porcelain making).

11. Period of National Unification.
12. The Edo Period.
13. Christianity
14. The Quing Dynasty.
15. Formosa (Taiwan).

## 272. The 1970s (I)

1. The hermit nation of Albania concluded a Trade Agreement with this other Communist Country in 1970. Which Country was this?
2. This British Conservative Leader won an election in 1970. Who was he?
3. Which Country hosted Expo '70?
4. What did the Yugoslav President, Tito, announce in 1970 that he would be succeeded with?
5. An assassination attempt was made on Pope Paul VI when he was visiting this Asian Country. Which Country was this?
6. Which Revolutionary Group did Abimael Guzmán Reynoso find in Peru in 1970?
7. President Nixon appointed this man to the Supreme Court in 1970. Who was this man?
8. How many students were killed in the Kent State Massacre?
9. Two hundred and thirty one million of these were in use globally in 1970. What is being mentioned here?
10. Which sports team from the U.S. did Mainland, China host in 1971?
11. This European Country granted women the right to vote in 1971. Which Country was this?
12. This British Corporation known for the quality of its product declared bankruptcy in 1971. Which Corporation was this?
13. Why did tension worsen in Northern Ireland in 1971?
14. This man succeeded Walter Ulbricht as Head of the East Germany Communist Party. Who was this man?
15. What was Richard Nixon's most drastic action ordered in 1971 to curb inflation?

**Answers to The 1970s (I)**

1. China. For a long time China supplied Albania with bicycles.
2. Edward Heath.
3. Japan, the city of Osaka.
4. A collective leadership with a rotating presidency.
5. The Philippines.
6. The Shining Path. It was a Maoist-orientated group that would grow in strength in the 1980s.
7. Harry Blackmun who would be influential in the Roe v Wade decision.
8. Four
9. T.V. Sets.
10. The U.S. Table Tennis Team. "No! It didn't include Forrest Gump."
11. Switzerland
12. Rolls-Royce Ltd.
13. Britain introduced policies of preventive detention and internment without trial.
14. Erich Honecker.
15. A 90-day freeze on wages and prices.

## 273. The 1970s (II)

1. The U.S. Supreme Court ruled in 1971 that this activity may be ordered to achieve racial desegregation. What was this activity?
2. In which prison were 10 guards and 32 prisoners killed when police stormed it following a five-day siege?
3. This Country was involved in a War of Independence and was also hit by a cyclone in 1971 that killed 220,000 people. Which Country was this?
4. This Island was returned to Japan by the U.S. in 1972. Which Island was this?
5. What did 'CREEP' stand for?
6. Who was the Judge in the Watergate affair?
7. This Democrat resigned from the 1972 ticket with George

McGovern and was replaced by Sargent Shriver. Who was he?

8. This man concocted the Howard Hughes "Biography" in 1972. Who was he?
9. Paul Henri Spaak died in 1972. He was one of the original founders of the Common Market. Which Country was he from?
10. In which Country did Norman E. Kirk lead the Labour Party to victory over the National Party in 1972?
11. This Country rejected entry into the Common Market in 1972. Which Country was this?
12. How many Israeli athletes were killed by terrorists in the Munich Olympic Games in 1972?
13. Which currency was devalued for the second time in two years in 1973?
14. This Greek Premier announced the abolition of the monarchy in 1973. A few months later he, himself was removed in a bloodless coup. Who is being described here?
15. These two defendants of the 'Pentagon Papers' were freed in 1973. Who were they?

**Answer to The 1970s (II)**

1. Busing
2. Attica
3. Bangladesh
4. Okinawa
5. Committee to Reelect the President
6. John J. Sirica
7. Senator Thomas Eagleton. He was shown to have had a history of mental depression. The change in running mates did not help. Nixon and Agnew still won 49 out of the 50 states. However, the Democrats won majorities in both Houses of Congress in 1972.
8. Clifford Irving.
9. Belgium. He was a Premier of the country at one time.
10. New Zealand.
11. Norway

12. Eleven
13. The U.S. Dollar.
14. George Papadopolous.
15. Daniel Ellsberg and Anthony Russo.

## 274. The 1970s (III)

1. Who did Richard Nixon name to replace Archibald Cox as the Watergate Prosecutor?
2. What position did Gerald Ford hold in politics before he was appointed to replace Spiro T. Agnew, as Vice President?
3. Who chaired the Senate Watergate Committee?
4. Which South Dakota Town was occupied by militant Indians in 1973?
5. Name two of three Countries that joined the EEC in 1973?
6. This Chilean Leader was ousted by a military junta in 1973. Who was this Leader?
7. This man succeeded Willy Brandt after Brandt was forced to resign as German Chancellor. Who was this man?
8. Which Organization kidnapped Patty Hearst in 1974?
9. In which two Southern European Countries were dictatorships deposed in 1974?
10. This man agreed to pay $432,787.13 in back taxes in 1974. Name this person?
11. This measure was adapted in the U.S. to save fuel in 1974, but the law was later repealed. What is being described here?
12. This American General was appointed Supreme Commander of The North Atlantic Treaty Organization in 1974. Who was he?
13. American Telephone & Telegraph, the U.S.'s largest private employer banned discrimination against this segment of the population. Which segment is this?
14. Who succeeded Juan Perón as President of Argentina in 1974?
15. Who succeeded Golda Meir as Head of the Israeli Cabinet when she stepped down in 1974?

**Answers to The 1970s (III)**

1. Leon Jaworski.
2. He was Leader of the Republicans in the House of Representatives.
3. Senator Sam J. Ervin, Jr.
4. Wounded Knee. The militants would hold out for 70 days.
5. The United Kingdom, Ireland, and Denmark.
6. Salvador Allende Gossens.
7. Helmut Schmidt. Brandt resigned after one of his close aides was shown to be an East German spy.
8. The Symbionese Liberation Army.
9. Portugal and Greece.
10. Richard Nixon.
11. Year round Daylight Savings Time. A measure that was necessitated by gasoline shortages caused by the Arab Oil Boycott.
12. General Alexander Haig.
13. Homosexuals.
14. His wife, María Estela. She would be overthrown in a coup d'etat in 1976. Lt. General Jorge Videl would then become President of Argentina's Military Junta.
15. Yitzhak Rabin.

## 275. The 1970s (IV)

1. Due to the crisis in Cyprus, the US cut off aid to this country in 1975. Name the country?
2. These three figures were sentenced to two-and-a-half to eight years in prison for their role in the Watergate cover-up. Name two of them?
3. This Saudi King was assassinated by his nephew in 1975. Who was he?
4. Name the two women who tried to assassinate Gerald Ford in 1975?
5. The Cape Verde and São Tome and Principe Nations gained independence from which European colonial power in 1975?

6. This Russian Physicist won the Nobel Peace Prize in 1975. Who was he?
7. This City appealed to the U.S. Federal Government in 1975 in order to avoid a default. Which city was this?
8. Where did the leaders of 35 nations sign a charter for the Conference on Security and Cooperation in 1975?
9. This Justice retired after 36.5 years on The U.S. Supreme Court. Who was he?
10. This South American Country nationalized its oil industry in 1976. Which Country was this?
11. In which Middle Eastern Country did Elias Sarkis become President in 1976?
12. Who succeeded Harold Wilson in 1976 as Prime Minister of the U.K.?
13. In which Township south of Johannesburg did rioting breakout in 1976?
14. These two men met in the first ever vice-presidential debate. Who were they?
15. He won approval for a second term as Secretary General of the United Nations. Who was he?

**Answers to The 1970s (IV)**

1. Turkey. The Turks had invaded Cyprus the year before.
2. John N. Mitchell, John D. Erlichman, and H.R. Haldeman.
3. King Faisal. The nephew was beheaded. Khalid, the brother of Faisal would succeed him.
4. Sara Jane Moore and Lynette"Squeaky" Fromme (a Manson disciple).
5. Portugal. Other colonies that gained independence from Portugal in 1975 were Angola and Mozambique. Portuguese-Guinea would gain independence a year before to become Guinea-Bissau.
6. Andrei Sakharov. He developed the Soviet Union's Hydrogen Bomb.
7. New York.
8. Helsinki. The Helsinki Accord.

9. Justice William O. Douglas. He was replaced by John Paul Stevens.
10. Venezuela
11. Lebanon
12. James Callaghan.
13. Soweto
14. Walter Mondale and Robert Dole.
15. Kurt Waldheim.

## 276. The 1970s (V)

1. In 1976, the Seychelles Islands declared their independence from which colonial power?
2. This Homeland Republic was created in South Africa in 1976. It was the first of its kind. Which Republic was it?
3. Which area voted to become the 27th Province of Indonesia in 1976?
4. Who did Jimmy Carter pardon en masse in 1977?
5. What did Jimmy Carter say could bring on a "national catastrophe" that had to be responded to with the "moral equivalent of war"?
6. To which position was the Communist Party chief Leonid Brezhnev elected to in 1977?
7. This Watergate felon was released in 1977 after serving 52.5 months in prison (longer than any other Watergate conspirator). Who was he?
8. This Organization won the Nobel Peace Prize in 1977. Which Organization was this?
9. The Socialist Government of which Portuguese Prime Minister collapsed in 1977?
10. How did Brigadier General Omar Torrijos make it into the world news in 1977?
11. In which Country did the 10-day old Minority Government of Premier Bulent Ecevit collapse to be replaced by another short-lived government under Suleyman Demirel?
12. He was elected Mayor of Paris in 1977. A surprise as leftists controlled three-quarters of the municipalities of the large cities in France. Who was he?

13. The U.S. established relations with this Country in 1978. Which Country was this?
14. Which important symbol did the U.S. return to Hungary in 1978 after it had been in American hands for 32 years?
15. Which type of gun did the Son of Sam, David R. Berkowitz, use to kill his victims?

**Answers to the 1970s (V)**

1. The United Kingdom.
2. Transkei
3. Portuguese Timor.
4. All American draft evaders of the Vietnam War Era.
5. The Energy Crisis. The U.S. Department of Energy would be established in 1977.
6. President of the Soviet Union. He was the first leader to combine these two positions.
7. G. Gordon Liddy.
8. Amnesty International.
9. Mario Soares' Government
10. Torrijos was the Panamanian Chief of Government who signed the new Canal Treaties with Jimmy Carter.
11. Turkey in 1977.
12. Jacques Chirac, now of course the President of France.
13. People's Republic of China.
14. The Crown of St. Stephen.
15. A .44 caliber.

## 277. The 1970s (VI)

1. In which Country was Spyros Kyprianou elected President in 1978?
2. With which Asian Communist Country did the Soviet Union sign a 25-year Treaty of Friendship and Cooperation in 1978?
3. Which South American Country had its 200th coup in 158 years of independence in 1978?

4. Hourari Boumédienne died in 1978. Which country was he a ruler?
5. What was the claim to fame of Brig. General Margaret A. Brewer?
6. Who shared the Nobel Peace Prize in 1978?
7. This former Prime Minister of Minister of Pakistan was hanged by the Military Government of General Zia. Who was he?
8. This group seized power in Nicaragua in 1979. Who were they?
9. What was the name of The Arms Limitation Treaty signed between the Soviet Union and the U.S. in 1979?
10. This former English Liberal Leader was acquitted in 1979 of conspiring to murder the homosexual Norman Scott. Who was he?
11. This Scandal brought down and forced the resignation of John Voster as President of South Africa. What was this Scandal called?
12. Who won an election in 1979, thanks partially to the "Winter of Discontent?"
13. This U.S. Embassy in North Africa was attacked by a mob in 1979. Where was the Embassy located?
14. This cousin of the queen was murdered by the IRA in 1979. Who was he?
15. In which did Country Babrak Karmal become Head of State?

## Answers to The 1970s (VI)

1. Cyprus
2. Vietnam
3. Bolivia
4. Algeria between 1965 to 1978.
5. She was the first female general in The U.S. Marine Corps.
6. Israeli Prime Minister Menachem Begin and Egyptian President Anwar Sadat.
7. Zulfikar Ali Bhutto.
8. The Sandanistas.
9. The SALT-2 Arms Limitation Treaty.
10. Jeremy Thorpe.

11. Muldergate
12. Margaret Thatcher. The Winter of Discontent, as well as the rejection of the Labour Party's devolution plans for Scotland and Wales helped Thatcher ride in to power.
13. Tripoli in Libya.
14. Earl Mountbatten.
15. Afghanistan following the Soviet Invasion.

## 278. History of the Far East III

1. This Manchu Emperor expelled the Junkar people from Tibet. He also enthroned the 7[th] Dalai Lama in 1720. Despite this, he was known for his enlightenment. Who is being described here?
2. Missionaries from this sect introduced Christianity to Korea. What is the name of this sect?
3. Thailand was invaded by this neighbouring Country in 1767. Which Country was this?
4. Which natural disaster hit Japan in 1783?
5. This 'high' lying Country was invaded by China in 1792. Which Country was this?
6. Which Colony was formed by Stamford Raffles in 1819?
7. This Southeast Asian Country was united by Emperor Gia-Long between 1802-1820. Which Country was this?
8. The Russians visited this city, a future target of an atomic bomb attack, in 1804. Name the city?
9. China and Britain fought this War between 1839 to 1842. What was this War called?
10. People from this Island revolted against Dutch rule between 1825 to 1830. Which Island was this?
11. This rebellion caused millions of death in China between 1850 to 1864. Which Rebellion was this?
12. Japan signed The Treaty of Kanagawa with this other Pacific power. Which Country was this?
13. This individual crushed all attempts at reform in China in 1898. Who was she?

14. France proclaimed this Southeast Asian Country as a protectorate in 1899. Which Country was this?
15. Which Country had its first General Election in 1890?

**Answers to the History of the Far East III**

1. Kangxi
2. The Jesuits—specifically Chinese Jesuits.
3. Burma
4. A severe famine—it lasted until 1788.
5. Nepal
6. Singapore
7. Vietnam
8. Nagasaki
9. The Opium War. China lost the war and was forced to open several ports to British trading.
10. Java
11. Taiping Rebellion.
12. The United States.
13. The Dowager Empress, Cixi.
14. Laos
15. Japan—under the new Meiji Constitution.

## 279. History of the Far East IV

1. What was the name of the anti-foreigner rebellion that broke out in China in 1900?
2. Russia annexed this Region Northeast of China proper in 1900. Which Region was this?
3. Whose Navy did the Japanese defeat in the Tsushima Strait in 1905?
4. This man became President of China in 1912 after the overthrow of the Imperial Government. Who was this man?
5. This Party took power in China in 1924. Which Party was this?
6. China recognized this Country to its north as independent in 1913. Which Country was this?

7. In which Year did Mao Zedong seize power in China?
8. Which Nationalist Leader was his chief rival?
9. The majority of the China's population belongs to this ethnic group. Which group is this?
10. From which two Provinces did The Long March take place?
11. This man became Premier and Foreign Minister of China with the establishment of the People's Republic of China. Who was this man?
12. The period between 1958 and 1960 in China is known by what phrase?
13. This Gang collapsed in 1976. What were they called?
14. By 1965, he was the Secretary General of the Central Committee Secretariat. Who was he?
15. Who was Mao Zedong's wife?

**Answers to the History of the Far East IV**

1. The Boxer Rebellion.
2. Manchuria
3. The Russians.
4. Sun-Yat Sen. He ruled the country, but warlords were still influential.
5. The Kuomintang Party.
6. Outer Mongolia.
7. 1949
8. Chiang Kai-Shek.
9. The Han Chinese.
10. From Jiangxi Province to Shaanxi. It was on this march that Mao won Leadership of the Communist Party.
11. Zhou Enlai.
12. The Great Leap Forward.
13. The Gang of Four. They influenced the Cultural Revolution.
14. Deng Xiaoping.
15. Jiang Qing. She played an important role in The Gang of Four and was a leading opponent of Zhou Enlai.

## 280. General Jewish History I

1. This man led the revolt against the Romans between 132 to 135 AD. Who was this man?
2. What great achievement is Rabbi Judah HaNassi associated with?
3. In which Middle Eastern Country was an autonomous Jewish state set up between 513 to 520 AD?
4. According to Heraclius, Jews in this Empire were forced to convert. What was this Empire?
5. Thanks to this King, Jews were able to move into the Rhine Area c. 800. Who was this King?
6. In which Century did Yiddish start to emerge as a language in its earliest form?
7. This Jewish Scholar established a school that would become renowned. It was based in Troyes, France. Who was this Jewish Scholar?
8. This event that occurred between 1095-1099 was very destructive for the Jewish people. What event was this?
9. This accusation first occurred in Norwich, England in 1144. What was this accusation?
10. Who wrote *The Guide to the Perplexed*?
11. This book was burnt in Paris in 1240. Which book was this?
12. Jews were expelled from this Country in 1306. Which Country was this?
13. This horrendous event in Jewish history began in 1478. Which event was this?
14. This German launched a virulent attack on Jews in 1543. His writings are taken by some to be the beginning of modern anti-semitism. Who was he?
15. In which city was the first Jewish 'ghetto' set up?

### Answers to General Jewish History I

1. Bar Kochba. The rebellion was eventually suppressed with sages such as Rabbi Akiva being put to death.

2. The final editing of *The Mishnah*. The book outlines the obligations of Jews in all aspects of life.
3. Babylon
4. The Byzantine Empire.
5. Charlemagne
6. The 11th Century c. 1050. It was a mixture of old French and old Italian dialects spoken by the local Jewish communities with medieval German thrown in as well.
7. Rashi, Shlomo Ben Yitzchak.
8. The Period of the First Crusade.
9. A Blood Libel Accusation. Jews were wrongly accused of killing a Christian child and using the blood in a religious ritual.
10. Maimonides. Campaigns were waged against the book and it would be banned.
11. The Talmud. Twenty-four cartloads of the book were burnt based on the charge by Nicholas Donin, a Jewish convert that it contained heretical ideas. The accusations had prompted a papal investigation.
12. France. They had already been expelled from England in 1290.
13. The Spanish Inquisition.
14. Martin Luther.
15. In Venice in 1516.

## 281. General Jewish History II

1. In which Eastern European Country was the Council of the Four Lands formed in 1581?
2. Which language was created by Jews exiled from Spain?
3. He was the Founder of the Hassidic movement c. 1740. Who was he?
4. In which Eastern European Region did Jews suffer the Chmelnitski Pogroms?
5. He was the false Messiah of 1665-1666. Who was he?
6. Jews from this Country on the Red Sea were temporarily expelled between 1676 to 1680 and exiled to a place called 'Mawaza'. Which Country were the Jews from?

7. In which German city did the First Modern Day Jewish schools open in 1778?
8. This man published his translation of *The Torah* into German in 1783. Who was he?
9. This area for Jewish settlement was created in Russia in 1791. What was it called?
10. In 1844, the Kahal was abolished. What was the Kahal?
11. In which Country did The Jewish Reform Movement begin?
12. Who was Edgardo Mortara?
13. He was the first Jew to sit in the English Parliament. Who was he?
14. Founded in 1897-88, this was the first Jewish Socialist Party in Eastern Europe. What was it?
15. In 1863, Moses Montefiore petitioned the sultan of this North African Country to improve the conditions of the Jews. Which Country was this?

**Answers to General Jewish History II**

1. Poland. It represented the Jewish communities within Poland. It would be abolished in 1746.
2. Latino. The first book in this language was printed in Constantinople in 1510.
3. Ba'al Shem Tov.
4. The Ukraine. Chmelnitski led a revolt against the Polish Crown which resulted in the death of 100,000-200,000 Jews.
5. Shabbetai Zvi.
6. Yemen
7. Berlin
8. Moses Mendelssohn.
9. The Pale.
10. The Community Organization of the Jews in Russia.
11. Germany.
12. He was a 7-year-old Jewish boy who was claimed and taken by the church on the grounds that he had been baptized near death as a baby by his nurse. The episode caused a huge international scandal.

13. Lionel Rothschild. He was elected in 1847, but sat for the first time in 1858 as he did not wish to say the Christian Oath.
14. The Bund.
15. Morocco

## 282. The Arab-Israeli Conflict I

1. At which International Conference after World War I was the Palestine Mandate granted to Britain?
2. This area was separated from Palestine and given to the Emir Abdullah in 1921. What was it named?
3. This declaration promising Palestine as a Jewish homeland was issued in 1917. Which Declaration was this?
4. What did Britain issue on May 17, 1939 to restrict immigration into Palestine?
5. Which Country had a mandate in Syria after the First World War?
6. What was UNSCOP?
7. What was the name of the Arab village that was attacked by the Irgun and Stern Gang on April 9, 1948 in order to end the blockade of Jersulalem and attacks by Arabs on Jewish convoys?
8. Jews from this ship that was denied entry into Palestine by the British were eventually interned in the British-occupied zone of Germany. Which ship was this?
9. This man, the Mufti of Jerusalem, collaborated with Hitler during World War II. Who was he?
10. Of 8, 10 or 12 months how long did the War of Israeli Independence last?
11. According to the United Nations Partition Plan, approved by the UN General Assembly, on November 29, 1947, what was to become of Jerusalem?
12. Which four countries did Israel sign armistices in 1949 with?
13. This man was Israel's Ambassador to the UN at the time of the Suez Canal Crisis. Who was he?
14. Which Gulf did the Egyptians blockade on May 22, 1967 cutting off the Israeli port of Eilat?
15. This party seized power in Syria in 1967. Which Party was this?

### Answers to The Arab-Israeli Conflict

1. The San Remo Conference of 1920.
2. Transjordan. It would gain independence as Jordan in 1946.
3. The Balfour Declaration.
4. A White Paper.
5. France
6. The UN Special Committee on Palestine.
7. Deir Yassin.
8. Exodus 1947.
9. Haj Amin el Husseini.
10. Eight months.
11. It was supposed to be an international zone. The rest of the region of course was split into a proposed Jewish and Arab state (this does not include the East Bank of the Jordan which had already become a separate entity 'Transjordan' earlier).
12. Egypt, Jordan, Lebanon, and Syria with Ralph Bunche, who would later win a Nobel Peace Prize serving as Mediator.
13. Abba Eban.
14. The Gulf of Aquaba.
15. The Ba'ath Party.

## 283. The Arab-Israeli Conflict II

1. This name was given to the guerillas who launched attacks against Israel from border positions in the Arab world, especially Egypt, after 1949. What was the name?
2. The War against Egypt fought in 1956 is known in Israel by another name. What is this other name?
3. This U.S. Ship was mistakenly attacked by the Israelis on June 8, 1967. They thought it was an Egyptian vessel. Which U.S. Ship was this?
4. This UN Resolution called upon Israel to withdraw from territories captured in June 1967. What was this Resolution?
5. Which four territories fell into Israeli hands after The Six Day War?

6. What was estimated at between 1 to 1.5 million after The War of Independence in 1949?
7. What was the name given to the war fought between Israel and Egypt between 1969 to 1970?
8. Who was the Egyptian Leader at the time of The Yom Kippur War?
9. This Israeli General gained much notoriety when he captured the Mitla Pass in 1956. He later fought in the Yom Kippur War. Who was he?
10. Which two forces fought over the Town of Kuneitra?
11. How long did the Arab Oil Boycott against the U.S. that followed the Yom Kippur war go on for?
12. It was reopened on June 5, 1975. What was this?
13. In which Year did Anwar Sadat visit Israel?
14. What was Operation Peace for Galilee?
15. What horrendous event occurred on September 16, 1982?

## Answers to The Arab-Israeli Conflict II

1. Fedayeen
2. The Sinai Campaign.
3. The USS Liberty.
4. Resolution 242.
5. The Golan Heights (taken from Syria), The Gaza Strip (won from Egypt), The West Bank (from Jordan), and the Sinai Peninsula (taken from Egypt).
6. The number of Jewish and Arab refugees. Eight hundred thousand Jews fled the Arab world and between 500,000-650,000 Arabs fled Israel.
7. The War of Attrition.
8. Anwar Sadat.
9. Ariel Sharon.
10. Israel and Syria.
11. Five months.
12. The Suez Canal.

13. 1977. Egypt, Israel, and the U.S. would sign The Camp David Accords on September 17, 1978 and the Egyptian-Israeli Peace Treaty on March 26, 1979.
14. The Israeli invasion of Lebanon in 1982. It was orchestrated to drive the PLO out of Lebanon.
15. The Massacre at the Sabra and Shatilla refugee quarters. Four hundred and sixty people were killed, including 15 women and 20 children by Maronite Christian Phalange Militia. Israel was indirectly responsible for not anticipating the possible Phalange attack.

## 284. The Gulf War

1. Which oil field did Iraq accuse Kuwait of stealing oil from?
2. On which date (day/month/year) did Iraq invade Kuwait?
3. This Kuwaiti Sheik was forced to flee his country. Who was he?
4. What did the Iraqis rename as 'al-Kadhima'?
5. Which province number did Iraq intend Kuwait to become?
6. These two countries announced the deployment of 10,000 troops to the Gulf on September 14-15, 1990. Which two countries were they?
7. What was the name of the Allied Operation to send troops to the Middle East in reaction to the Iraqi Invasion?
8. Talks ended in a stalemate between James Baker and this Iraqi Foreign Minister on January 9, 1991. Who was the Iraqi Foreign Minister?
9. On which (day/month/year) did Operation Desert Storm begin?
10. Where was the first ground battle between the Allies and the Iraqis fought?
11. In which City did an Iraqi Scud missile hit the U.S. barracks killing 28 U.S. soldiers on February 25, 1991?
12. By which non-formal name did the Highway between Iraq and Kuwait become known as toward the end of the war?
13. What was the name of the Battle fought between the U.S. 1st Armoured Division and the Iraqi Republican Guard on February 27, 1991?

14. General Schwarzkopf used a critical 'left hook' maneuver to defeat the Iraqis. What earlier American General had first conceived this maneuver?
15. Who was the U.S. National Security Advisor during the war?

**Answers to The Gulf War**

1. From the Rumaylah Field. Iraq described this as 'economic warfare'.
2. August 2, 1990.
3. Sheik Jaber al-Ahmed al-Sabah.
4. Kuwait City.
5. The 19th province.
6. The United Kingdom and France.
7. Operation Desert Shield.
8. Tariq Aziz.
9. January 17, 1991. At 3:00 a.m. (Baghdad time).
10. Khafji, Saudi Arabia.
11. Dharan, Saudi Arabia.
12. The Highway of Death.
13. The Battle of Medina Ridge.
14. General Grant at the Battle of Vicksburg in 1863.
15. Brent Scowcroft.

## 285. Political Parties

Which Political Party did the following leaders represent in power:

1. Ruud Lubbers.
2. Menachem Begin.
3. Bettino Craxi.
4. Helmut Kohl.
5. Brian Mulroney.
6. Robert Muldoon.
7. Chester A. Arthur.

8. Ian Smith.
9. Carlos Menem.
10. Henry Campbell-Bannerman.
11. Rajiv Gandhi.
12. Garrett Fitzgerald.
13. Olof Palme.
14. Ahmed Sukarno.
15. Noboru Takeshita.

**Answer to Political Parties**

1. Christian Democratic Appeal (The Netherlands).
2. The Likud Coalition (Israel).
3. Italian Socialist Party (PSI).
4. Christian Democrats (Germany).
5. Conservative Party (Canada).
6. National Party (New Zealand).
7. Republican Party.
8. Rhodesian Front.
9. Peronist Party (Argentina).
10. Liberal Party (UK).
11. Congress Party (India).
12. Fine Gael (Ireland).
13. Social Democratic Labour Party (Sweden).
14. Indonesian National Party (PNI).
15. Liberal Democratic Party (Japan).

## 286. General Middle Eastern History

1. Ismail became Shah of which Persian Dynasty in 1501?
2. During his reign from 1520 to 1566, the Ottoman Empire peaked. Who was he?
3. Sultan Mahmud II worked to weaken this group within the Army of the Ottoman Empire. Which Group was this?
4. Sultan Abdul Hamid II undertook the building of this railway

designed to make pilgrimage to Medina easier. What was this Railway called?

5. Which Country expanded into Turkestan between 1860-70?
6. Which Country did the reformer Muhammad Abduh play a leading role in?
7. In which country did Abd al-Qadir lead a revolt against the French between 1832 to 1847?
8. After 1261, the Abbasids continued as Caliphs in this Egyptian City. Which City was this?
9. An alternative name for the Nusaryi Shiites, of which Hafez al-Asad was a member, is what?
10. What was the most common name of Ottoman rulers?
11. A military junta led by this man in Iraq replaced the Monarchy in 1958. Who was this man?
12. This man became King of Morocco in 1961. Who was he?
13. These two countries formed the United Arab Republic in 1958. Which two countries were they?
14. This man replaced the Ayatollah Khomeini as the Spiritual Leader of Iran in 1989. Who was he?
15. This Lebanese President-Elect was killed by a bomb in 1982. Who was he?

### Answers to Middle Eastern History

1. The Safavid Dynasty. He would rule until 1524.
2. Suleiman the Magnificent. He was known to the Turks as Suleiman, the Law-Giver
3. The Janissaries.
4. The Hijaz Railway. It linked Damascus to Medina.
5. Russia
6. Egypt
7. Algeria. It failed and he was forced to surrender in 1847.
8. Cairo. Their dynasty would collapse c. 1517.
9. The Alawi (or Alawites).
10. Mehmed. There were six of them. There were five Murads.

11. Abdul Karem Kassim. He in turn was overthrown in 1963.
12. King Hassan II. He would die in 1999 and would be succeeded by his son, Prince Sidi Muhammad, who would be crowned King Muhammad VI.
13. Egypt and Syria. Syria would pull out in 1961. Egypt would still keep the name until 1971. It then changed to the Arab Republic of Egypt (ARE).
14. The Ayatollah Khamenei.
15. Bashir Gemayel. He was replaced by his older brother, Amin Gemayel, as President. Bashir was 34 at the time of his death.

## 287. Leadership Nationalities

Which countries were the following individuals leaders?

1. Begum Khaleda Zia.
2. Sitiveni Rabuka.
3. Vincent Auriol.
4. Urho Kaleva Kekkonen.
5. Jelle Ziljasta.
6. Canaan Sodindo Banana.
7. Antonio Agostinho Neto.
8. Wilfried Martens.
9. Joe Clark.
10. Albert Reynolds.
11. Hendrik Frensch Verwoerd.
12. Milan Kucan.
13. Michael Norman Manley.
14. Todor Zhivkov.
15. Abdus Salaam Mohammed Arif.

### Answers to Leadership Nationalities

1. Bangladesh
2. Fiji

3. France
4. Finland
5. The Nertherlands
6. Zimbabwe
7. Angola
8. Belgium
9. Canada
10. Ireland
11. South Africa
12. Slovenia
13. Jamaica
14. Bulgaria
15. Iraq

## 288. The 1980s (I)

1. In which mountains did Soviet forces battle Afghani Mujaheddin in 1980?
2. What did President Carter restrict in order to protest against the Soviet invasion of Afghanistan?
3. One hundred and twenty thousand people from this Country were allowed to emigrate to the U.S. in 1980. Which Country was this?
4. In which country did Master Sgt. Samuel Doe seize power?
5. Who broke the five-day seizure of the Iranian Embassy in London?
6. This Secretary of State resigned in protest against the failed American helicopter mission to rescue the hostages in the U.S. Embassy in Iran. Who was he?
7. In which City did worker strikes begin in Poland in 1980?
8. Which Waterway did Iraq hope to gain control of when invading Iran in 1980?
9. In which Central American Country were three American nuns and a lay preacher murdered in 1980?
10. What party did four breakaway members of The British Labour Party create in 1981?

11. This man led The Solidarity Trade Union. Who was he?
12. She became Norway's first female Prime Minister in 1981. Who was she?
13. This hunger striker died in Maze Prison in 1981 after having fasted for 66 days. Who was he?
14. He replaced General Robert Viola as Argentine President in 1981. Who was he?
15. This White House Press Secretary was wounded during John Hinckley's assassination attempt on Ronald Reagan in 1981. Who was he?

**Answer to The 1980s (I)**

1. The Hindu Kush Mountains.
2. Grain sales to the Soviet Union.
3. Cuba
4. Liberia
5. The British Special Air Services (SAS). Two hostages (out of 19) were killed. Three out of the Five terrorists were killed during the course of the events.
6. Cyrus Vance. He was replaced by Edmund Muskie.
7. Gdansk, specifically the Lenin Shipyard.
8. The Shatt al Arab Waterway.
9. El Salvador.
10. The Social Democratic Party.
11. Lech Walesa.
12. Gro Harlem Brundtland.
13. Bobby Sands. He had been elected to the British Parliament to represent Fermanagh and South Tyrone.
14. General Leopoldo Galtieri.
15. Jim Brady.

# 289. The 1980s (II)

1. In which Country was a report released linking 962 people to a secret Masonic lodge known as P2?
2. This man tried to assassinate Pope John Paul II in 1981. Who was he?
3. Senegal and Gambia united to form a Confederation known by which name?
4. Who led the PASOK Party to power in Greece?
5. Argentina invaded but failed to hold onto the Falkland Islands which by June 14, 1982 were back in British hands. What is the Argentinean name for these Islands?
6. Israel returned this Territory to Egypt in accordance with The Camp David Agreement. Which area was this?
7. Who replaced Alexander Haig as Secretary of State?
8. President Reagan extended Soviet Sanctions to West European companies associated with this project in the Soviet Union. What was this project?
9. Israel occupied these two important cities in Southern Lebanon in 1982. Which two cities were they?
10. He became Polish Prime Minister in 1981. Who was he?
11. This man became King of Saudi Arabia in 1982. Who was he?
12. Which Party did Felipe Gonzalez lead to power in Spain in 1982?
13. In which City was Harold Washington elected Mayor in 1983?
14. This Party gained its first seats in the German Parliament in 1983 despite a victory by Helmut Kohl and the Christian Democrats. Which Party was this?
15. How many U.S. Marines were killed in a single suicide Shiite attack during October 1983 (to the nearest 50)?

### Answers to The 1980s (II)

1. Italy. It forced the resignation of Italian Premier Arnoldo Forlani.
2. Mehmet Ali Agca.
3. Senegambia

4. Andreas Papandreou.
5. The Malvinas.
6. The Sinai Peninsula.
7. George Shultz.
8. The Siberian Oil Pipeline.
9. Tyre and Sidon.
10. General Wojciech Jaruzelski. His introduction of Martial Law in Poland in response to Solidarity activity most likely saved the country from a Russian invasion.
11. Prince Fahd.
12. The Socialists.
13. Chicago
14. The Green Party.
15. 242

## 290. The 1980s (III)

1. An airliner belonging to which Country was shot over the Soviet Union in 1983?
2. This Prime Minister of Grenada was killed in a military coup. U.S. troops would then invade the island and institute military rule. Who was this Prime Minister?
3. At which USAF base in the UK did female peace campaigners initiate a permanent picket in 1983?
4. This man succeeded Menachem Begin as Prime Minister of Israel in 1983. Who was he?
5. A Philippine Opposition Leader, this man was shot at Manila Airport after flying home. Who was he?
6. This Nazi war criminal was put on trial in Lyon following extradition from Bolivia. Who was he?
7. This Country became an independent sultanate in 1984 and the 159th member of the United Nations. Which Country was this?
8. Which Temple did Sikh extremists occupy in Amritsar in 1984?
9. In which British City did an IRA bomb kill five people and injure 32 in 1984?

10. To which countries' cabinet were the Rev. Allen Hendrickse and Amichand Rajbansi appointed in 1984?
11. What was the only state won by Walter Mondale in the 1984 Presidential Election?
12. Operation Moses was carried out to bring Jews from this Country to Israel. Which Country was this?
13. This Priest and Solidarity Supporter was beaten to death by the Secret Police in 1984. Who was he?
14. This man succeeded Yuri Andropov as General Secretary of the USSR. Who was he?
15. The UK and China agreed in 1984 that Hong Kong would be handed over to China in which year?

**Answers to The 1980s (III)**

1. South Korea. Two hundred and sixty nine people on board were killed.
2. Maurice Bishop.
3. Greenham Common.
4. Yitzhak Shamir.
5. Benigno Aquino.
6. Klaus Barbie.
7. Brunei
8. The Golden Temple. Two hundred and fifty deaths occurred during the course of events which resulted in its recapture by the Indian Army. Many Sikh members of the Army would mutiny to protest the Government's action.
9. Brighton, during the Conservative Party Conference.
10. The South African Cabinet of President PW Botha. They were the first two non-white men to reach this position.
11. Minnesota, his home State.
12. Ethiopia
13. Father Jerzy Popieluzko.
14. Konstantin Chernenko.
15. 1997

## 291. The 1980s (IV)

1. He was inaugurated as President of Nicaragua in 1985. Who was this dictator?
2. This Albanian Dictator died in 1985. He would be succeeded by Ramiz Alia. Who was this man?
3. From which Country did South Africa withdraw its troops in 1985?
4. A Civilian Government took power in this South American Country in 1985 after 12 years of military rule. Julio Sanguinetti was the new President. Which Country was this?
5. Which Airline had a plane hijacked by Arab terrorists in 1985 that resulted in 39 U.S. passengers being held hostage for 17 days, one of whom was murdered?
6. In which City did Mikhael Gorbachev and Ronald Reagan meet for a two-day summit in 1985?
7. In New Caledonia, independence agitation was directed against this colonial power in 1985. Which power was this?
8. The Anglo-Irish Agreement in 1985 gave this Country a consultative role in Northern Ireland. Which Country was this?
9. Against which Country did President Ronald Reagan announce limited sanctions in 1985?
10. These two countries joined the European Community in 1986. Which two countries were they?
11. Both of these two Libyan cities were bombed by U.S. aircraft following a Libyan missile attack on a U.S. aircraft and a terrorist attack on U.S. Servicemen. Which two cities were they?
12. This person became President of the Philippines in 1986. Who is being described here?
13. In 1986, this Country refused to admit Nuclear weapons into port. Which Country was this?
14. Who did James Wright succeed as Speaker of the House of Representatives in 1986?
15. To which position was Frank Carlucci appointed to in the Reagan Administration in 1986?

**Answers to The 1980s (IV)**

1. Daniel Ortega.
2. Enver Hoxha.
3. Angola
4. Uruguay
5. TWA
6. Geneva
7. France
8. The Republic of Ireland.
9. South Africa.
10. Spain and Portugal.
11. Tripoli and Benghazi.
12. Corazon Aquino.
13. New Zealand.
14. Tip O'Neill
15. National Security Advisor.

## 292. The 1980s (V)

1. In which Country did Joaquim Chissano become President in 1986?
2. This Company overtook Exxon as the largest corporation in the world in 1986. Which Company was this?
3. A government report in 1986 indicated that a hydrogen bomb was accidentally dropped near this City in New Mexico in 1957. Due to a stroke of luck nothing happened. Which City was this?
4. What are the English words for 'glasnost' and 'perestroika'?
5. Troops from this Country entered West Beirut in 1987 to end warfare between the Druze and the Shiite militia. Which Country was this?
6. For whom did the U.S. Senate approve $40 million in aid in 1987?
7. This American Ship was hit by two Iraqi Exocets in 1987. What was the name of this Ship?
8. He landed a Cessna aircraft in Red Square, Moscow in 1987. Who was this man?

9. Why did Ronald Reagan visit Berlin in 1987 (during which he asked Mikhael Gorbachev to tear down the wall)?
10. In which Region of India was Direct Rule imposed in 1987?
11. U.S. Marine Guards at the U.S. Embassy in this City were accused of espionage. Which City was this?
12. E.F. Adams was elected Prime Minister of this Mediterranean Country in 1987. Which Country was this?
13. This Central American Leader was indicted by a U.S. Court on drug smuggling charges in 1988. Who was this man?
14. In which country was Lt. Colonel William Higgins kidnapped by Islamic terrorists in 1988?
15. This U.S. Ship mistakenly shot down an Iranian airliner over the Persian Gulf causing 290 casualties. Name the Ship?

**Answers to The 1980s (V)**

1. Mozambique. Following the death of Samora Machel in a plane accident.
2. General Motors.
3. Albuquerque
4. Openness and reconstruction.
5. Syria
6. Contra Rebels in Nicaragua.
7. The USS Stark.
8. Mathias Rust. A German teenager. He was sentenced to four years, in jail but freed in 1988.
9. To celebrate the 750th Anniversary of the Foundation of the City.
10. Punjab in an effort to weaken Sikh terrorism.
11. Moscow. They were accused of spying for the KGB.
12. Malta. He represented the Nationalist Party.
13. General Manuel Noriega.
14. Lebanon
15. The USS Vincennes.

## 293. The 1980s (VI)

1. This PLO Leader was assassinated by the Israelis in 1988. Who was this man?
2. French Agent Prieur was repatriated by France despite his involvement in the sinking of this Greenpeace Ship. What was the name of this Ship?
3. These two British parties merged in 1988. Which two parties were they?
4. General Ne Win resigned as Ruler of this Country in 1988. He had been in power for 26 years. Which Country was he ruler of?
5. Which three countries agreed in 1988 to a cease-fire in Angola?
6. The INF Treaty signed between the U.S. and the USSR dealt with these types of missiles. Which types of missiles were they?
7. Fighters from this Country were shot down by U.S. planes over The Gulf of Sidra in 1989. Which Country was this?
8. This man succeeded the Emperor Hirohito in Japan. Who was this man?
9. What 'officially' prompted the U.S. to invade Panama in 1989?
10. This American received an Honorary Knighthood from the Queen in 1989. Who was this man?
11. Which takeover in 1989 resulted in the largest entertainment corporation?
12. The candidacy of this man for Secretary of Defense was not approved by the U.S. Congress in 1989. Who was this man?
13. Oliver North was found guilty in 1989 for his role in the Iran-Contra scandal. What was his sentence?
14. Who did Anthony Meyer challenge for the Party Leadership in 1989?
15. He was elected New York's first black Mayor in 1989. Who was this man?

**Answers to The 1980s (VI)**

1. Abu Jihad.
2. The Rainbow Warrior.
3. The Social Democrats and the Liberals to become the Social and Liberal Democrats.
4. Burma
5. South Africa, Angola, and Cuba.
6. Medium-range nuclear missiles.
7. Libya
8. The Crown Prince Akihito.
9. The annulment by General Noriega of the Presidential Elections which the opposition had won.
10. Ronald Reagan.
11. Time Inc.'s takeover of Warner Communications for $13 billion. "A pittance by today's takeovers."
12. John Tower.
13. Three years suspended plus $150,000 in fines.
14. Margaret Thatcher. He failed.
15. David Dinkins.

## 294. The 1990s (I)

1. She was elected Nicaraguan President in 1990 unseating the Sandinistas. Who was this woman?
2. In which Eastern European Country did The Civic Forum win election in 1990?
3. This South African President released Nelson Mandela from prison in 1990. Who was this man?
4. This well-respected Politician resigned as Soviet Foreign Minister in 1990, warning against sinister forces at play in the Soviet Union. Who was this man?
5. She was elected as Ireland's first female President in 1990. Who was this woman?
6. Who stood against Margaret Thatcher in the first round of the Conservative Party Leadership Race?

7. This man was freed in 1990 after 1,596 days as a hostage in Beirut. Who was this man?
8. In 1990, the USSR declared a state of Emergency in Nagorno-Karabakh. In which Soviet Republic is this region located?
9. This power accepted The Nuclear Non-Proliferation Treaty in 1991. What was the name of this power?
10. Who succeeded William H. Webster as head of the CIA?
11. Which organization was founded on December 25th following the break up of the Soviet Union?
12. In which Country did Zviad Gamaskhurdia make headlines?
13. The U.S. suspended aid to this Country after troops seized the President in an uprising on September 30, 1991. Which Country was this?
14. The U.S. indicted two Libyans for the bombing of a Pan Am Flight in 1988 over Lockerbie, Scotland. What was this Flight Number?
15. What did The U.S. Supreme Court limit in 1991?

**Answer to The 1990s (I)**

1. Violetta Chamorro.
2. Czechoslovakia.
3. F.W. de Klerk.
4. Edouard Shevardnadze.
5. Mary Robinson.
6. Michael Heseltine.
7. Brian Keenan.
8. Azerbaijan. It is an Armenian enclave.
9. China
10. Robert H. Gates.
11. The Commonwealth of Independent States.
12. Georgia. He was its president.
13. Haiti
14. Pan Am 103.
15. Death row appeals.

# 295. The 1990s (II)

1. This Eastern European Federation broke up in 1992. What was it?
2. This former Secretary of Defense was indicted in The Iran-Contra Affair in 1992. Who was this man?
3. Who won the 1992 Israeli Presidential Election?
4. Who is the odd one out: Tom Harkin, Paul Tsongas, Jerry Brown, Dick Gephardt?
5. Which important Security Agreement was ratified by the senate on October 1st 1992?
6. This Japanese Political Power Broker resigned in 1992 after a scandal. Who was this man?
7. This Country split up into two nations in 1992. Which Country was this?
8. U.S. Forces left this country in 1992 after nearly one century of presence. Which Country was this?
9. This Treaty went into effect in 1993 creating the European Union. Which Treaty was this?
10. This Sri Lankan President was killed at a May Day Rally in 1993. Who was this man?
11. Fill in the number to replace the question mark: Jean Chretien was the ? Prime Minister of Canada. He was sworn in, in 1993.
12. This Elected President man declared Bosnia and Herzegovina to be independent. Who was this man?
13. This Bosnian Serb an Arch-Nationalist was both a Poet and a Psychiatrist. Who was this man?
14. Collor de Mello was impeached in December 1992. Which Country was he President of?
15. This individual replaced Edward Perkins as U.S. Representative to the UN. Who is being described here?

### Answers to The 1990s (II)

1. The Yugoslav Federation.

2. Casper Weinberger.
3. Yitzhak Rabin.
4. Dick Gephardt. All of the others contested the 1992 race for the Democrat Presidential Nomination.
5. The Second Strategic Arms Limitation Treaty.
6. Shin Kanemaru.
7. Czechoslovakia. It split into the Czech Republic and Slovakia.
8. The Philippines.
9. The Maastricht Treaty.
10. President Ranasinghe Premadasa.
11. The $20^{th}$.
12. President Alija Izetbegovic.
13. Radovan Karadzic.
14. Brazil
15. Madeleine Albright.

## 296. The 1990s (III)

1. The U.S. ended a trade embargo on this Country in 1994. Which Country was this?
2. This international terrorist was captured on August 15, 1994. Who was this man?
3. Where did John Salvi kill two people on December 30, 1994?
4. This man resigned as Treasury Secretary in 1994. Who was he?
5. In which Country did Ernesto Samper win an election in June 1994?
6. To the closest 100,000, how many Tutsi civilians and moderate Hutus were slaughtered by Hutu extremists in The 1994 Massacre?
7. This agreement outlined a five-year plan to provide self-government for the Palestinians in the West Bank and Gaza. What was the Agreement?
8. The North and South portions of this Middle Eastern Country fought a civil war in 1994. Which Country was this?
9. The Appeals Court upheld a woman's plea to enter this Military Academy in 1995. Which Academy was this?

10. This Cult was responsible for a nerve gas attack on the Tokyo Subway. Which Cult was this?
11. How much money did the U.S. provide to rescue the Mexican Economy in 1995?
12. Which two entities were created in Bosnia-Herzegovina as a result of The Dayton Accords?
13. This writer was hanged in Nigeria in 1995 along with eight other minority rights advocates. Who was this man?
14. This world-renowned Paleontologist helped set up a Party in 1995 to oppose the government policies of Daniel Arap Moi. Who was this man?
15. In 1995, Crown Prince Hamad bin Khalifa deposed his father in which Persian Gulf Country?

**Answers to The 1990s (III)**

1. Vietnam
2. Carlos the Jackal.
3. At a Massachusetts Planned Parenthood Clinic.
4. Lloyd Bentsen.
5. Colombia
6. 800,000
7. The Oslo Agreement.
8. Yemen
9. The Citadel.
10. The Aum Shinrikyo ("Supreme Truth").
11. $20 billion
12. A Muslim-Croat Federation and a Serb entity.
13. Ken Saro-Wiwa.
14. Richard Leakey.
15. Qatar

## 297. The 1990s (IV)

1. This went into its fourth month by January 1996. What was it?

2. This Commerce Secretary was killed in a plane crash on April 3, 1996. Who was this man?
3. From which Country is UN Secretary General Kofi Annan?
4. The City of Kabul fell to this group in 1996. Who were they?
5. In a cemetery in which Country did a bomb kill 13 people on November 10, 1996?
6. He was elected as Israeli Prime Minister on May 31, 1996. Who was this man?
7. A mid-air collision killed 342 people in which Country on November 12, 1996?
8. This Country announced an end to nuclear testing on January 29, 1996. Which Country was this?
9. On January 16, 1997, Israel agreed to give up a large portion of this West Bank City. Which City was this?
10. What did the U.S., UK, and France agree to freeze on February 3, 1997?
11. How old was the Chinese Leader Deng Xiaoping at his death? To the nearest 2 years.
12. Where in Egypt were 62 people killed at a tourist site on November 17, 1997?
13. This Country fell into a state of anarchy after many in the population lost life savings as a result of a failed pyramid scheme. Which Country was this?
14. What US economic indicator was reported to be 4.8 % in June 1997?
15. This American Politician was found guilty of ethics violations on January 17, 1997. Who was this man?

**Answers to the 1990s (IV)**

1. The U.S. Budget Crisis.
2. Ronald Brown.
3. Ghana
4. The Taliban.
5. In Russia.

6. Benjamin Netanyahu.
7. India
8. France
9. Hebron
10. Nazi Gold Loot.
11. 92
12. In Luxor.
13. Albania
14. The U.S. Jobless Rate. It was the lowest since 1973.
15. Newt Gingrich. The man who had masterminded the Republican Revolution in The House of Representatives since 1994.

## 298. The 1990s (V)

1. This man was sentenced to life on January 9th for the bombing of the World Trade Center. Who was he?
2. Between January 21-25th, 1998, the Pope visited this Country. Which Country was it?
3. This Peace Settlement was reached in Northern Ireland on April 10, 1998. Which Peace Settlement was it?
4. To how many life terms was the Unabomber sentenced to on May 4, 1998?
5. In which Region did fighting begin between the Serbs and the ethnic Albanians?
6. What was thrown out of court on April 1, 1998?
7. For which two charges was President Clinton impeached?
8. This gay Wyoming student was beaten to death in a hate crime. Who was this man?
9. Which Capital City of Chechnya was in the news in 1999?
10. Who was the Iranian President in 1999?
11. The Coalition Government in this Southeast Asian Country was defeated by a vote of 229 to 125 when accused of mismanaging the economy. Which Country was this?
12. What change occurred in German Politics in September 1999?
13. Which Country led the International Forces into East Timor?

14. This Indian Prime Minister lost a confidence vote on April 17, 1999 following the testing by the country of nuclear-capable missiles. Who was this man?
15. This Mexican Party broke with an old tradition of a handpicked successor and opted for a candidate chosen through a primary type selection process. Which Party was this?

**Answer to The 1990s (V)**

1. Ramzi Ahmed Yousef.
2. Cuba
3. The Good Friday Accord.
4. Four Life Terms.
5. Kosovo
6. The Paula Jones Case.
7. Perjury and obstruction of justice.
8. Matthew Shepard.
9. Grozny
10. Mohammad Khatami.
11. Thailand
12. The Parliament returned to its traditional seat in Berlin.
13. Australia
14. Atal Bihari Vajpayee.
15. The PRI

## 299. Successions

Fill in the missing individual/entity (indicated by a ?) in the sequences shown below:

1. Rocard, Cresson, ?, Balladur
2. Ortoli, Jenkins, Thorn, ?
3. de Valera, Griffiths, Cosgrave, ?
4. Sharett, Ben—Gurion, Eshkol, ?
5. Jefferson, Burr, ?, Gerry, Tompkins

6. Tilden, Hancock, ?, Blaine, ?, Harrison
7. Johnson, Mansfield, Byrd, ?, Daschle
8. Lewis, Irons, ?, Pacino, Hanks
9. Masefield, Lewis, Betjeman, ?
10. Byatt, ?, Unsworth, Ondaatjie, Doyle
11. Giyatso, Gorbachev, ?, Menchú
12. Costner, Demme, ?, Spielberg
13. Lange, Russell, Moore, ?
14. ?, Rosebery, Salisbury, Balfour
15. Oklahoma, ?, Arizona, Alaska, Hawaii

**Answers to Successions**

1. Pierre Bérégovoy—(French Prime Ministers).
2. Jacques Delors—(EU Commision Presidents).
3. Éamon de Valera—(Irish Prime Ministers).
4. Golda Meir—(Israeli Prime Ministers).
5. George Clinton—(U.S. Vice-Presidents).
6. Grover Cleveland—(losing Presidential candidates).
7. George Mitchell—(Democratic Senate leaders).
8. Anthony Hopkins—(Best Actor Oscar Winners).
9. Ted Hughes—(Poets Laureate).
10. Ben Okri—(Brooker Prize Winners).
11. Aung San Suu Kyi—(Nobel Peace Prize Winners).
12. Clint Eastwood—(Best Director Oscar Winners).
13. Jim Bolger—(New Zealand Prime Ministers).
14. William Gladstone—(British Prime Ministers)
15. New Mexico—(order in which states gained entry into the Union).

## 300. What-Ifs

These questions have no exact answers. They have been offered as an exercise in divergent thinking. Try and see what scenarios you would come up with, if the 'ifs' themselves held true:

1. What if Alexander the Great had had an heir? What form would his Empire have taken?
2. What if Hitler had died from a Gas attack in World War I? Would Communism spread much quicker? Would the State of Israel been born?
3. What if the American Revolution had failed? Would the U.S. be part of the Commonwealth today or would it have gained independence later? Would it still be a Superpower today?
4. What if Japan had defeated the U.S. in the Second World War's Pacific Theatre? Would communism still have taken hold in China? Would the Soviet Union have emerged as a Superpower? Would the Cold War involve three parties instead of two?
5. What if Alaska had never been sold to the U.S. by the Russians? How would this have affected Canada and the U.S.? What type of Cold War situations could have arisen in such a universe?
6. What if paganism had succeeded in halting the advance of Christianity in Europe? Would the Jews still have been persecuted? Would Europe been saved the ravages of religious war? How would Islam have spread with no large scale counter-balancing force?
7. What if the English had not defeated the French in Canada? Would a significantly larger portion of North America have become Francophone? How would this have changed the complexion of the U.S.?
8. What if Britain had been connected to Europe by an isthmus? Would the country have developed the Great Empire it once held? Would English been so universal a language? How dominant would the Royal Navy have been in power politics? Would Napoleon and Hitler have successfully invaded and conquered Britain?
9. What if the Ancient super-continent of Pangaea had not split apart? How would this have changed Power Politics assuming the development of modern countries?
10. What if males and females had equal physical strength? Would so many societies have been male—dominated? Would there be more or less strife? Would the population have increased by the large number that it has?

11. What if the Arabs had accepted the 1947 Palestine Partition Plan? Would an Arab state have existed in peaceful harmony with a Jewish state? Would the region be wealthier for it? Would the Arab-Israeli Wars that followed still have taken place?
12. What if the American political and economic experiment was copied in South America after many countries on that continent gained independence in the 19th Century? Would South America be a center of power today? Would the U.S. role in Western Hemisphere politics have been diminished? Would the South American countries eventually have united to form a Federation?
13. What if Genghis Khan's hordes had reached Paris? How would this have affected European History?
14. What if the Magna Carta had never been signed? Would British Liberalism still have evolved? Would the country have been cursed by a greater degree of reactionary tendencies?
15. What if the Roman Empire never existed? Would Western Civilization have been so pervasive?